A FAIR TRADE CAMPAIG

Not in my Lifetime

Bruce Crowther

Published in 2021
by Bruce Crowther

© Copyright Bruce Crowther

Edited by Graham Brown

Photos (unless credited) by
Bruce Crowther, Tom Bamber and Robin Graham

ISBN: 978-1-913898-20-5

Cover and Book interior Design by Russell Holden
www.pixeltweakspublications.com

Pixel Tweaks Publications
SELF PUBLISHING MADE SIMPLE

Acknowledgements

First and foremost, I would like to thank my wife Jane, for putting up with me in those 'difficult moments', providing comfort during the low times, sharing the highs and most of all making it all possible.

I also thank the rest of my family. Tom for realising that there is a point to it all, for taking photos when it really mattered, for providing his support and commitment for the Garstang campaign, the link with New Koforidua and for Fair Trade and the anti-poverty campaign in general. His wife, Ruth, for helping with chocolate production at The FIG Tree and Jack for enjoying his first taste of FIG Tree chocolate. Ben for his time working in the café, surviving the stresses of our Ghana Exchange in 2011 and sharing with me the highs and lows of being a football fan. Anna, again for her work in the café and her support as FIG Tree secretary along with Matthew for his IT support.

FIG Tree patron Joanne Harris and directors past and present: Graham Hulme, Danny Callery, Rita Verity and David Marle.

Christina Longden for her constant encouragement and support in writing and publishing this book and in setting up The FIG Tree.

All FIG Tree members, staff, supporters and volunteers, including Christine for managing the FIG Tree, and historian Melinda Elder and other team members for our two Heritage Lottery Fund projects.

People named in the book, including Robin for his excellent poems, helping out with workshops and making me laugh; Rita for her never ending belief in me and for being able to read this book; Nicola for her wise words of encouragement and all she does for the children of SALVE; Richard for his work on the Cooperative House, Joe Human and Nick Maurice for all their guidance on all matters to do with public speaking, institutionalised campaigning and forming and maintaining North-South links; and so many more.

The Garstang Fair Trade pioneers Peter, Gail, Betty, Avis, Rachel and Dorothy for their support when we needed it most: in the beginning. Sadly, Betty, Avis and Rachel have now passed away and are deeply missed but well remembered.

Catja Kaloudis

Members of the International Fair Trade Towns Steering Committee and UK Fairtrade Town Campaigns officers, past and present. Other Fairtrade Foundation staff, Oxfam staff and those working on Fair Trade Towns for other organisations across the world, especially in memory of Catja Kaloudis, a former Fairtrade Towns Coordinator for Sweden and member of the International Steering Committee, who sadly passed away while this book was being edited.

The members of the Garstang Oxfam Group, the Garstang and New Koforidua Linking Association and the Garstang Fairtrade Group for all their local support.

Rachel Ward for her initial encouragement and inspiration to write this book.

David Greenwood-Haigh and Tom Steele for teaching me how to make bean-to-bar chocolate.

Andy, Cliff, Dave, Pete and Steve for being the Chester crew.

Last, but by no means least, the people of New Koforidua for their warm welcomes, generosity, friendship and producing the very best cocoa in the world; pa pa paa!

Dedication

I would like to dedicate this book to the anti-poverty campaigners and fair trade producers who work tirelessly and endlessly alongside each other because, like me, they believe it to be unacceptable to live in a world in which a small child dies every three seconds from poverty-related causes. You know who you are, and I sincerely hope you enjoy reading this book.

Foreword

There aren't too many people who wake up one day and decide 'I know! I'll set up a global system of connecting people together whilst combatting poverty, fighting injustice and educating people about economic inequality. All with no funding whatsoever!' And although Bruce Crowther didn't exactly do this, either, he certainly achieved it.

I first met Bruce through my work with the Lorna Young Foundation. The Foundation was supporting Oromo refugees to create the world's first Fairtrade coffee social enterprise in Manchester, as well as setting up our first 'Not Just Us' young ethical entrepreneur groups. After returning from living in Namibia with the Kalahari bushmen, I had heard Bruce's name bandied about in fair trade circles and, although I've always been inherently suspicious of famous (or infamous!) folk, I was assured by others that he was a 'good egg' and so I got in touch. Bruce agreed to come and meet the Oromos and to give a speech at the world's first ever Fair Trade Eid party that we were holding in Huddersfield.

One of our aims at the Lorna Young Foundation has always been to go 'beyond Fair Trade', to ensure a better deal for producers by building future solidarity with them through educating disadvantaged people in the UK about trade injustice. As Bruce mentions in *Not in My Lifetime*, the fair trade movement in the UK to date has been criticised as being a preoccupation of mainly middle class people; it therefore came as a pleasant surprise to see that Bruce was every bit as fired up as we were to blast through class barriers and make ethical trading something that we all place at the centre of our lives.

It was even more of a surprise to discover that Bruce and I had something else in common: our Quaker beliefs. It was partly this – and our meandering chats and respective rants at governments and institutions – that led to me calling him one day and throwing an idea at him: a Fair Trade Visitor Centre, where people who were not necessarily part of a Fair Trade Town or group could visit and grow their awareness of the history of enslavement and trade injustice. I remember Bruce being taken slightly aback by my approach. Perhaps I was still on a high from the creation of the Oromo Coffee Company and Not Just Us initiatives but, whatever the reason, it didn't take more than a minute for him to catch the bug. In fact, I'm pretty sure that he had been thinking about this all along and it just needed a fellow Northern crackpot to voice the idea out loud. But it was Bruce who created the organisation, found the funding and volunteers, brought in the punters, developed the business plan, fought the floods, reviewed and re-evaluated the initiative and committed his life to this additional branch of his fair trade work.

I'm very aware that my experience of work and of friendship with Bruce represents just one tiny corner of what is contained in this remarkable memoir. He has been remarkably candid about the ups and the downs throughout his fair trade life and, as always, wonderfully generous and humble in acknowledging the roles that others have played alongside him.

I hope that you enjoy reading this book as much as I did. In fact, I have only one complaint about *Not In My Lifetime*, which is that you can't hear Bruce's chuckle emanating from the pages. Bruce has a terrific, infectious laugh and I think that his capacity for mirth and for seeing the humour in serious situations has probably done as much to spread the Fair Trade Town movement across the world as his drive and passion for justice has.

Christina Longden, The Lorna Young Foundation

Contents

CHAPTER 1

Diesels and Steam Trains

"Is it a diesel or a steam train?" I demanded to know. But as I started to see the smoke belching out of the rapidly approaching engine, I knew it was the latter. Immediately I ran for the exit, but it was too late, the steaming monster was already screaming past with its whistle blowing, its enormous wheels clanking, smoke belching from its funnel and high-pressure steam intermittently and unpredictably released from various small outlets.

Bruce & the Flying Scotsman

I would have been five or six at the time, not old enough to know better. My fear of steam was a fear of something I did not understand. The beauty and majesty of steam was not apparent to me in those early years. But it was with joy and enthusiasm that I showed my own children the steam engines at York National Railway Museum, albeit these docile monsters stripped of their power and pride were a long way from the sight, sound and singeing heat of steam that I once feared at Wendover station. As I was to find throughout my life, people often feared what they did not understand and in turn this could lead to anger, hatred and even war.

Until the age of seven I lived in the village of Wendover in Buckinghamshire. The back of our house faced the station, which lay on the Chiltern line between the better-known Great Missenden, of Roald Dahl fame, and the renowned hospital at Stoke Mandeville. My father worked for the RAF as an instructor at nearby Halton camp. Despite the fact he was not enlisted in the RAF and worked as a civilian, my early life was to be under the auspices of the air force. I was born in the RAF hospital in Halton on 19th October 1959. I was the youngest of four: Graham was the oldest, being 12 years older than I, with my only sister Lynda and then Ian being three years and two years older, respectively. I had another brother called David who died many years before I was born at just six months of age.

Bruce with Lynda and Ian

My full name is David Bruce Crowther. I was given the name David in memory of the brother I never knew, but my mother did not want to use the name and so I always went by Bruce. This was a complication that was not only also inflicted on my wife, Nancy Jane, but for some strange reason one we also bestowed on our son Ben, who was christened Daniel Ben Crowther.

Bruce was never a name I particularly liked, even before Monty Python made it a subject of ridicule. Having a slight lisp, I even had minor problems in pronouncing it correctly. Mum had chosen the name solely to please the midwife who assisted my birth. She had told my mother that despite delivering hundreds of babies she had never known one called Bruce, a name she liked. So, my mum being the woman she was made her day and I had to live with it.

I attended the RAF school in Halton sited opposite the hospital. I have many fond memories of this time, particularly the excellent firework displays at Halton camp. There was the humorous and most popular Mr. Bangey, the lollipop man outside the school who used to put his transistor radio in the tree and tell the children that the tree was singing. Although my older and wiser brother and sister knew his game, I was never sure.

Despite the fond memories, I do not think that my early school years were necessarily a good time. My father was a civilian lecturer in computing and most of the children at the school had fathers who were actually in the RAF. I can faintly recall children not wanting to be with me and being told by my 'best friend' Gerald that I was not invited to his party because all the invitations went to children of officers. With hindsight, the expression that I learnt from a Jewish friend many years later comes to mind: my life was "like a pork pie at a Jewish wedding". Perhaps it is this recollection that has led me to feel this way many times in my life, or perhaps it was simply because I was someone that would always struggle to fit in anywhere?

Right from day one I found it difficult to understand 'the system'. Unlike my later years, when I would find myself fighting against the injustices of a system for which I didn't approve, at this time it was simply that the 'rules' seemed to go over my head. I remember that fifteen minutes or so before the end of the last primary school class before lunch we were all let out in groups of four or five for a toilet break. Only I seemed to have a problem with this, never being sure of what I was supposed to do when let out of the class and, on one occasion, perhaps at the delight of being let out, or perhaps because I did not want to follow the crowd, I proceeded to walk off in the direction of home. I must have looked a little like Eric Morecambe during the Morecambe and Wise Christmas specials when he walked off the stage dressed in his coat and holding his carrier bag, occasionally taking a lonely look back to see if anyone was to follow. After watching all the other children go and return from the toilets, I eventually thought it best to return to the class and distinctly remember standing quietly outside the door, too afraid to go in and too afraid to go home. Luckily, on that occasion I think my action was only noted by the children and therefore I escaped any sort of reprimand.

I do, however, remember standing outside the headmaster's office on several occasions, although I can rarely recall why. One of the teachers always parked their little blue mini in the school grounds but we were forbidden to go anywhere near it, let alone use it as a tactical barrier in a game of tag. That was the crime for at least one of the occasions I stood outside the headmaster's office.

Halton camp was exactly one mile from Wendover village and our home. We were supposed to get the bus to school but sometimes Lynda and Ian persuaded me to walk and then we could spend the bus fare on sweets. What we called the 'white house' stood at the halfway mark and was usually accompanied by an ice cream van. It is amazing how certain things stick in your mind when other far more important events do not. All I can remember from the epic year of '66 when England won the world cup is the distinct pleasant smell of that ice cream van and my joy at getting a free World Cup Willie badge, which somehow came with an ice lolly.

A few years later my mum took Ian and I to see Manchester United play at home to Crystal Palace. Watching the great George Best perform was enough to make Ian a lifelong United fan. They say that once you'd seen Best play you never forgot it, but when I laid my tribute down at Old Trafford after his death in 2005, all I could remember of the one and only time I witnessed the genius live was the great big wooden rattle that I swung above my head, much to the annoyance of the surrounding fans.

My dad was never a football fan; being a Yorkshireman, cricket was his game. He used to captain Wendover cricket club, which perhaps is not as great as it sounds or, indeed, as great as we thought it was. It did get us into the clubhouse during matches and occasionally we were even allowed to change the numbers on the scoreboard.

Despite his great love for cricket my dad rarely ever played the game with his children. In fact, I can only recall one time and that was not when he played for Wendover. So, I never really enjoyed playing any sports and certainly never learnt how to play any of them well, or even learn the rules properly. Ian did do his best to get me to play football with his friends in later years and I can recall some

Bruce with Dad

long summer evenings playing football as a self-given reward for many hard hours of revision during my 'O' level exams.

At the age of seven we were apparently living through the 'summer of love': 1967 - sunshine, Sergeant Pepper, hippies and miniskirts, but I remember it as the year we moved to Chester. We were so excited to be going to this Roman walled city in the north of England; a city unknown to us all, although I was in fact the only Southerner. Both my parents and Graham came from Yorkshire and Ian and Lynda were Lancashire born; again the 'pork pie' but this time between white and red roses.

We couldn't wait to see our new house but had to stay a few days in the Deva Hotel before we could move in. The hotel was on the north side of the city, a long way from our home, which was near the Welsh border towards the southwest. Little did I know it at the time but, in one of those amazing coincidences, Jane, my wife-to-be, was living just a couple of hundred yards away from where we stayed. As it happened, she was to move away from Chester just as we moved in.

Things were going to be different in Chester, as I suddenly found myself at the 'better' end of the hierarchical chain. I attended Lache Primary school, which was not one of the best thought-of schools in this affluent city and was certainly no RAF school. I found myself top of the class and easily became the teacher's pet, although it was never my intention to be so. I was the posh boy from the South who wrote good stories and poems. I often took things in to show the class, such as my model working steam traction engine. Sometimes this was at the request of the teacher and other times because my mum genuinely thought the other children might like to see them. Maybe they did, but this was before the days of 'show and tell' and on reflection perhaps I came over as a little precocious.

Keith lived a few doors from me. He was my first proper friend. His dad took me to my first football match: Chester City vs. Crewe at Sealand Road. I must confess that did little for me, but I did start going more regularly to watch Chester play when Ian became an even greater fan of Chester than he was of Manchester United.

It was at this time that I met my oldest friend, Steve Williams, who I still know today. Steve, like me, loved the Beatles, but then who didn't in those days? But even after 'Let It Be' and the parting of the ways, Steve and I spent many hours in the front room listening to their music and analysing every word and record sleeve. We did all the usual stuff of playing the record backwards to uncover hidden messages and, even better, taping the record on our reel-to-reel tape recorder and experimenting with the sound. My brother Graham used to have all the Beatle records and I fondly remember him playing us our favourite tracks such as 'Little Piggies' and 'Maxwell's Silver Hammer' while Ian and I lay in our bunk beds; me on top and Ian below.

Graham had stayed behind to study and live in Bletchley when we moved to Chester, but I always loved it when he came to visit. He encouraged me to build a model railway in the garage. He was a very keen railway modeller and had his own layout in the attic when we lived in Wendover, but I was too small to make it from the last step of a step ladder and through the square door. There was no floor in the attic so once in there you had to step between the wooden supports. Despite everyone's efforts to help me I never did get to see Graham's layout. Perhaps that is why I was so keen to have my own when in Chester. Graham, of course, loved it too. He had his very own sense of humour and always told me that the BR on the side of the models stood for 'Bruce's Railway' instead of 'British Railways'.

My mum used to occasionally treat me to a trip to Liverpool on the bus and then cross the Mersey on the famous ferry. I loved Liverpool and my mum used to really spoil me. Sometimes she'd take me to China Town where I'd try strange dishes such as birds nest soup and attempt to use chop sticks. I can only remember there being the two of us, although I'm not sure why. I do recall my mum and dad having terrible rows, which I believe affected us all more than we ever realised at the time. I used to go to my room and try to block out the shouting. That was the first time I experienced that dreadful feeling of emptiness in my stomach which in later years I knew to be depression. This may have been the reason my mum used to take me away: perhaps to escape or because she felt sorry for me having to listen to the constant arguments.

Several times my mum left home. Each time I thought it was for real and tried to work out what life would be like from that point onwards, but to my great joy and relief she always came back. On at least one occasion she took me with her. We spent the night in a small hotel not far from the one where we spent our first day in Chester, although this was much cheaper and off the main road. We went for dinner in a nearby café where I ate the most delicious lemon sponge pudding and had my first taste of pineapple juice that left me with a headache. Again, why is it we remember the most unusual things? Perhaps because we don't wish to recall our emotions.

Soon I was sitting my 11+ exams, not that I knew it at the time. That is one of the reasons I am so much against selection at such a young age, or any age for that matter. It seemed so unfair. I'm sure in some schools the pupils were pre-warned and prepared for the great day of judgement, but we were not.

For the very bright pupils, or those with rich parents, there was the Kings school. I sat the entrance exams for this public school but failed miserably. I'll never forget pondering over the question asking to calculate a third of one hundred. I got it down to thirty-three, but just could not work out what to do with the remaining one. Perhaps I was not so bright after all, but who knows how I would have turned out if I'd got that question right. For better or for worse, I'll never know.

I did pass my 11+, however, and was one of only three children from Lache Primary to make it to Grammar school. Not that it made much difference, because after the first year there was a merger with Overleigh secondary school to form Queen's Park High Comprehensive. That is where I met my five good friends we call the 'Chester Crew': Cliff, Dave, Andy, Pete and Steve. We still meet up today for annual 'Chester Crew' reunions. Between us we make up another strong case against the 11+ system. Half of us were from the Grammar school and the other half from Overleigh, but I would defy anyone to tell us which were which today. I often wonder how the three from Overleigh would have got on if it was not for the merger. Overleigh was not a good school and there is no doubt that the lower standard of education experienced there would have prevented one half of us from reaching their full potential. So much for selection I say!

The Chester Crew: Pete, Bruce, Dave, Andy, Steve and Cliff

At the age of twelve I won an essay competition with the children's TV programme Magpie in conjunction with the World Wildlife Fund, as it was called in those days. The content of the essay had to explain why I wanted to win a wildlife and skiing holiday in Aviemore, Scotland. I wrote that I wanted to see the wildlife and experience nature before it was too late and left destitute by man.

It was at this time that I got my first taste of twisted journalism. I've never had a problem with journalists, they just want to sell papers, and throughout my life I've only ever been approached for a good news story. Nobody has ever tried to dig up dirt on me, at least not so far. But the way they alter the truth and put words into your mouth never ceases to amaze me.

You can imagine the delight of the headmaster when the local newspaper came to the school to cover the story before I set out on my Scottish adventure. But there wasn't much of a story until I mentioned that one element of the holiday was a trip on Loch Ness. "Would you like to see the Loch Ness monster if it existed" asked the journalist? "Of course," was my reply, "but I think it extremely unlikely". Somehow that was interpreted into the headline "Bruce hopes to see Loch Ness monster" with a rather embarrassing photo to match. I can understand the need for journalists to embellish a story, and in my later years I learnt to feed it, but still always wished they could tell things just as it is.

My parents drove me all the way up to Aviemore and then left me there with a rather mixed bunch of kids. I shared a room with an overweight boy from Yorkshire who never stopped complaining about his problem with his armpits, a Scottish National Party potential 'terrorist' and a boy who loved horse riding. The 'terrorist' hated all Sassenachs but for some reason took an even greater dislike to me. He seemed to be very popular with the girls, which perhaps explained why I was not. One day all three of my roommates had run off without me and I eventually found them in another room with some girls. The 'terrorist' made sure I was unwelcome and somehow even the guy with the armpits had a better attraction rating than I.

At least the other boy tried to be friendly, but that might have been because he wanted me to go horse riding with him. He didn't want to go alone, so despite the fact I'd never been on a horse before I took up his offer. Was I that desperate to make friends or did I fancy the adventure?

Of course, I could not handle my horse and it did not take long for my four-legged friend to discover the fact. As we were making our way into a hollow in order to dismount and have lunch, we were asked by the instructor to take the long way around along the gentle decline. But my horse had a different plan and preferred the more direct route down the steep slope. "There's always one who has to be clever" the instructor bellowed at me. Could he not see it was the horse, not I, that was the clever one? The horse was fully controlling me.

A year later I won another Magpie competition but this time the prize was far grander: a safari in Kenya. The subject for the essay was the same as before and believe it or not so was my entry, only this time it was focused on lions, savannah and flamingo lakes, as opposed to foxes, Scottish woodland and lochs.

On arrival in Nairobi, we were divided into four groups; three of them went out to safari in modern, clean buses and attracted the TV crews wherever they went, whereas for some reason the fourth got a dirty old charabanc and was kept well out of sight of the TV cameras.

No guesses which group I was assigned to, but as always, on reflection, it was for me the best option. I'd much rather be slumming it with the 'out crowd' and I'm sure we had the most fun when singing songs in Swahili while waiting for the mechanics to fix the bus.

I often wonder if this first experience of Africa, at just 13 years of age, planted the seed for the many years I volunteered with Oxfam, beginning eleven years later. I am sure that standing on the Greenwich Meridian and the equator within one week of each other ignited the spark that fired my passion for travelling and visiting the Masai village and witnessing the way they lived certainly made me ask probing questions. But all that was for the future; I still had my education and career to think about.

When I went to the careers open day at Queen's Park High School there did not seem to be an awful lot that impressed me. Whether I liked it or not I was a scientist at heart and in no ways creative. I'd always had a liking for animals, so I went to listen to the local veterinary surgeon promote his profession. It appealed to me a little. I have to say not a lot, but a little. I went to a couple of other sessions, but they did nothing at all. So, I was set on becoming a vet. Not because I had any great conviction, but simply because nothing else was remotely attractive.

This meant I had to take the three sciences at 'A' level, and taking Physics without Maths was not a recommended option, making it difficult for me. I managed three B grades, but this was not enough to get me in to vet school.

I had put veterinary schools down for my first three choices on the university admissions form and zoology for fourth and fifth. I went for a very disheartening interview at the Royal Veterinary College in London. Nervously I sat in the queue alongside other students who all had at least one A grade at 'A' level. When I entered the interview room, I could feel the damp sweat against my shirt. There was a very large table with five men in suits behind and a much smaller chair in front, which just had to be mine. I sat down to face their questions. They knew I was a member of the World Wildlife Fund, so they put forward an intellectual argument on why we should allow animals to become extinct. "Isn't it just a part of the evolutionary process?" they exclaimed. I realised that they may well have been playing devil's advocate, but I failed to impress them, and then I was asked the unanswerable question: "Do you like animals?" To this day I am not sure what the 'correct' answer to this question is for a prospective vet, but I know my affirmative answer was not well accepted.

They did not consider me vetting material and advised that I should give up any further attempts to get on the course. I kept the letter. I was offered places on both zoology courses but turned them down. On reflection I would have been better leaving these places blank in the first place. This was a valuable lesson that was to serve me well in future achievements. If you really want something and are not prepared to settle for second best then go for it, make your commitment known and don't let anyone else tell you otherwise.

So, I decided to resit my 'A' levels. The school was not prepared to let me stay on in the sixth form because they felt I'd overachieved, so I had to pay to take evening classes at the local college. My friends were now all at university, except Pete who had stayed on in Chester for a short while, and my girlfriend, who was a year below me, was now entering the upper sixth at Queen's Park High.

I volunteered to work at the RSPCA home, partially to fill the many empty days, but I also thought it might stand me in good stead in my continuing attempts to get onto the veterinary course. I developed a far greater interest in Physics that year. It was 1979, which was the 100th anniversary of Albert Einstein's birth. I found the many documentaries about his life and his work on nuclear physics and the universe fascinating. There is no doubt that studying is far easier when you have an interest in the subject, so I thought this time I was bound to get an A grade in Physics.

I managed an A and two B grades. Strangely the A grade was in Chemistry and not my new-found love of physics after all. This time I put just two places on the admissions form: Liverpool and Bristol. Despite being previously advised not to go to a university close to home, I felt Liverpool was my best chance and I was going for it. Both my choices turned me down, so I decided to go to Liverpool and see the admissions officer in person in an attempt to prove to them my determination. It worked, and they offered me an unconditional place for the following year if I was prepared to wait. That meant adding an extra two years to my education and then a five-year vet course after that, but I was not going to give up and accepted their offer.

It was one week before the start of the university year. My parents had gone out for the day and left me alone in the house when the phone rang. It was the Liverpool admissions officer and I'll never forget his words. "I was looking outside my window today and saw a pink pig fly past". A student had dropped out and he was offering me a place for that year. I was overjoyed and as soon as I'd put the phone down I picked up and kissed our very aggressive miniature poodle. It bit me, but ironically, I was going to vet school.

CHAPTER 2

All Creatures Great and Small

From the first day on the five-year veterinary course we were told that we were the 'crème de la crème'. It was emphasised how difficult it was to obtain a place on the course and therefore we were the 'elite'. I'm sure that all medical students are told the same, which may go some way to explain why so many doctors and vets are full of confidence, close to the point of arrogance, and are more than happy to play God when required.

But I believe everyone is equal. We all have our strengths and weaknesses and the important thing in life is to learn those strengths and weaknesses at the earliest possible stage, then play to them. The education system in the ideal society would enable students to do exactly that, instead of selecting the 'brighter' or richer pupils and dumping the others.

Veterinary students were encouraged to stick together: to 'work hard and play hard' together. We were placed in pairs within the student accommodation blocks so that we could travel to university together and support each other with our studies. This did make some sense, as life as a veterinary student was not your everyday, run-of-the-mill student life. We had lectures from 9am to 5pm five days a week and were expected to work and study throughout lunch breaks and much of the holiday period. I tried to mix and socialise with other students as much as possible, but this was not easy, as you were alien to most people outside the veterinary faculty.

As you may imagine, I found myself the 'pork pie' yet again. I grew my hair way past my shoulders so that my appearance reflected what I felt inside. I was different from everyone else. The head of the Physiology department used to compare the course to a fishing net that would take out those people who were not suited, those that were not 'vetting material'. Would I slip through the net? Did I want to?

Perhaps the net was closing in, as I failed my first year. I still took time out in the summer to visit the French village of Soustons in the Southwest of France. I had been there the previous summer working on a maize farm with the 'Chester Crew', and Soustons was to become a place of annual pilgrimage for many years to come. I came back refreshed and passed my exams on the second attempt that September.

For the second year I shared a house (with veterinary students, of course) in Allerton, South Liverpool, just around the corner from the famous Penny Lane. On 9th December 1980 I woke up to the sound of endless Beatle music being played on the local radio. I was an adamant fan and my first thought was to question why there was a tribute on a day that did not feature in the Beatle calendar? Then I heard the tragic news: that John Lennon had been shot the previous evening, during the night according to British time.

We were due to take a mock animal husbandry exam at the field station on the Wirral. I sat there quietly on the journey through the Mersey tunnel as others talked about the exam and this new world event. After the exam I decided to put some flowers on Matthew Street where the Cavern once stood. There were very few

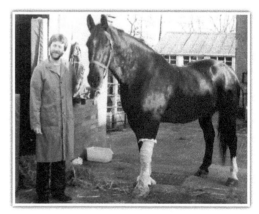

sites dedicated to the Beatles at that time, so this would have to suffice. For some strange reason I thought that I would be alone in making a tribute at this site and felt a little embarrassed as I bought the flowers off a street seller. How wrong I was; a mountain of flowers and messages awaited at this famous Beatle landmark.

In one of his last interviews, John Lennon said "Mahatma Gandhi and Martin Luther King are great examples of fantastic non-violents who died violently. I can never work that out. We're pacifists, but I'm not sure what it means when you're such a pacifist that you get shot. I can never understand that." I find this quote uncanny and remarkably poignant; reality is always far stranger than fiction.

Another coincidence was finding myself in the same pub as Julian Lennon (John's son from his first marriage to Cynthia) just four months later. It was Easter and I had to get work experience for animal husbandry, so I had gone with my friend Gary to a sheep and poultry farm just outside Ruthin in North Wales.

We had very little free time, not that we minded, but being students, we did make it to the pub in Ruthin on a few occasions. I knew that Julian Lennon lived in Ruthin but never expected to see him in the pub with friends. The juke box had the usual collection of John Lennon and Beatle hits but, unusually, nobody was playing them. They must have been hard times for Julian, so as much as I would have liked to go over and buy him a drink I thought it best to leave him be with his friends.

I should perhaps explain that Gary's real name was, in fact, Mike. I have never been good with names and, after spending the first term sitting beside him during dissection classes, I was too embarrassed to ask him his name. There were only fifty students in our year. I really should have known. He looked like a Gary, so I took my chance. He accepted it and it was several weeks later before I learned it was not his real name. I have called him Gary ever since.

Gary and I had gone to the farm of Edgar Lloyd for two weeks' lambing experience. Edgar was a remarkable shepherd, one of the best. The local vets used to say that if they were called in after Edgar had tried to lamb a ewe then they knew it was going to be a caesarean. There were over 1,700 ewes on his farm, not to mention the poultry, and Edgar was responsible for them all. His brother, who would normally be available to help, was unfortunately ill. We were there to help, but Edgar was a proud man and he didn't ask us to be there. He treated us well and got on with his job. There is no doubt that our time there was of far greater value to us than it was to him.

He was a great teacher and because he had so many ewes to look over he didn't have time to watch and wait for a ewe to lamb. If it showed the right signs then we were advised to restrain the ewe and pull the lamb. This provided both of us with invaluable experience.

We had to learn how to imitate the ewe when calling the lambs. This led to a fun game we played to pass the time. One of us had to impersonate

a ewe and if the other noticed it was an impression they had to acknowledge it by putting up their thumb. I don't know what Edgar must have thought as we followed behind him while mimicking sheep, but he never said anything.

Much to Gary's annoyance Edgar said I was a natural shepherd with "lambing hands". I thoroughly enjoyed my two weeks in Ruthin and when I decided to work only with small animals, just three

years after qualifying, lambing was the only large animal work that I missed.

* * *

I passed my second-year exams on the first attempt and, having completed the necessary six weeks of work experience, I was looking forward to a free summer. I'd hitched several times from Liverpool, to see my girlfriend at Newcastle University, and across France to Soustons. Now we had become engaged and decided to hitch across Europe together.

It was the summer of 1981 and we set off with just £200 between us, intending to travel for as long as the money would last. Apart from the first crossing of the English Channel nothing was spent on transport or on accommodation. Lack of money forced us to hitch a lift for the return crossing and at night we either slept rough or in the homes of hospitable people. One homeless person that we met on our travels exclaimed, "Why pay for a bed? When you are asleep you do not know where you are." Our journey lasted eight weeks and took in eleven countries.

I had bought a rucksack from a specialist shop in London that was recommended to me by a travelling friend of mine. I went for the largest size. The plan was to travel light but you know how it is: I didn't pack the kitchen sink but I did have a cooking stove and a tent.

We had barely left English soil when I had my bag stolen while taking a nap in Versailles near the Palace grounds. My girlfriend carried a much smaller bag which contained most of her clothes, so she was okay, but I had lost everything, including the cooking stove. It turned out to be a blessing in disguise; there was very little of value in the bag and it was all insured, anyway, but most importantly I could now travel light, as originally intended. It was literally a great weight off my shoulders, because carrying the bag in those first three days, not to mention having to find the space in the cars of our hosts, was becoming a great strain. It is no coincidence that the Latin for baggage is *impedimenta*.

Soustons was our first destination and I had called my mum to tell her the news of our loss so that she could send on a 'Red Cross' parcel ahead of us. It contained a few essential items such as clean underwear, some toiletries and, well, not much else, really. I had learned a valuable lesson and was now a 'real traveller'; sleeping rough and travelling light; the world, or at least Europe, was our oyster.

Now, I say sleeping rough, but we still had our tent. That was, until early one morning when someone had decided to put a knife through the outer layer. I had been putting up the tent anywhere we could find, once even in the middle of a roundabout. On another occasion, I thought I had found a nice quiet spot by a lake but, on awakening next morning, we were surrounded by day trippers, playing children and picnic baskets. Nobody seemed to bother as we packed up the tent and walked away, dodging the children's footballs and Frisbees as we went.

On the day that the tent was attacked we had camped on some quiet waste land. As the sun rose, I thought I could hear someone outside but thought it best to keep quiet and let them make the first move. Little did I know that the first move was going to be the slashing of the outer layer of our tent, followed by nothing. I waited awhile before finally deciding to go outside and take a look.

To this day I am not sure what happened. Was it just some vandals who perhaps threw a stone that tore the taught outer lining? Or was it an opportunist who thought the tent might have been left empty, but then took fright on the realisation that someone was inside, but they did not know who or what?

It was not the only time I was to encounter knives. While sleeping in a busy subway in Nuremberg, a schizophrenic drug addict persistently waved a knife at me. One minute he was engaged in friendly travelling banter, the next he accused me of being "Polizei" followed by the words "kill Polizei". Occasionally he would grab my arm while singing the words to the Beatles' classic 'Hey Jude'. In this scenario, however, the words "the minute you let her under your skin" took on a distinctly different and disturbing interpretation.

In Amsterdam I was 'mugged' no less than three times in one night. I had taken the advice from the traveller's guide to Europe and chose to sleep in Vondelpark on the outskirts of the city. I selected what I thought would be a secure spot hidden amongst some shrubs next to the lake, but close to the main road. I should have realised, however, that it is not just travellers who read these books and that when a good sleeping spot is so well publicised it ceases to become safe.

After checking the area to ensure that we could not be seen and nobody was around to see us bedding down, I lay down looking up at the stars, as I had done many times before. I loved sleeping under the stars and still do, but on this occasion something unsettled me.

The next thing I remember was waking up with a knife against my throat. I kept what little money and valuables I had in a money belt that was strapped below the rim of my trousers and fortunately the two muggers were not that good at their vocation. Despite one of them putting their hand down my trousers they obviously and understandably felt uncomfortable, so didn't discover the belt with everything in it. They believed my tale that we had no money and left.

On the assumption that lightning doesn't strike twice, I thought it best to stay put. How wrong I was; in no time at all two more people came through the shrubbery, again carrying knives. They were North Africans and for some reason became quite pleasant when they found out we were British. This was long before the days of anti-US and British terrorism. Having just escaped one mugging I was not happy to be facing another. I told them we had just been mugged, which was true, and that all our money had been stolen, which was not. I must have sounded suitably stressed, and probably was, because they started to feel sorry for us. When my girlfriend started sniffling because of her cold they assumed she was crying, which further fuelled their sympathy. They talked a little about their relatives in the UK and then, remarkably, left us in peace.

We started to pack our things. I needed no more persuading to leave the area but got it none the less. Someone else came through the shrubbery; he was alone, well dressed and carried a plastic bag folded around something solid. He said we should move on. Wasn't it obvious that we were doing so? Despite confirming that fact, he didn't seem to believe me and, in an attempt to convince me, he said that several people had been stabbed on this exact spot in the last month alone. It turned out that he was some kind of plain clothes officer and the solid object in the bag was a handgun.

After leaving the park I thought it best to head for the busy streets well in sight of Amsterdam's night life and made camp in a bus shelter not far from the Van Gogh Museum. This was very close to the sinister Holocaust memorial that stood there at the time. It emitted its macabre beats through the night and repeated its perpetual sequence of lighting again and again. This was going to be a sleepless night but at least I would survive to feel tired the next day.

I had just about managed to fall into a semi slumber when a police car drove onto the pavement and shone both its headlights right at us. I explained about our nightmare of events and the suggestion from their plain clothes colleague to leave the park. They asked if we had any money (déjà vu, I thought), then they informed me that it was illegal to enter Holland without available funds and told me we had to leave the country. "Right now?" I asked. They accepted that was not possible and again we were left alone.

There is no doubt we experienced some bad times on our travels but, on the whole, we met more good people and shared good moments than bad. But as one traveller put it, "The bad people do you more harm". Perhaps he was right, but the good memories stay with you and have an impact on your life just as much as the bad, such as the time we spent a day or two in a small village in the middle of the Pyrenees.

This was the first time I had visited most of the countries we passed through and I was keen to experience the culture and traditional food and drink at every opportunity. We had just enjoyed 'huevos con fritos', which rather disappointingly turned out to be egg and chips. A traditional dish none the less and, with bread rolls and a glass of dry white wine, was a meal that I came to love and have enjoyed as one of my favourite dishes ever since.

Despite not being able to speak a word of Spanish, and very few locals being able to speak English, somehow we still found ourselves in a crowded room of locals until the early hours of the morning. On awakening, the house was empty and the village was extremely quiet. There was no one and nothing about and I was beginning to wonder how on earth we would get a lift out of the village. Then I heard noises from what must have been a bar. We boldly went in to find a large crowd of local people watching a television screen. It was the day of the royal wedding between Charles and Diana. To be honest the event had escaped us, but we were British and therefore very welcome guests at this Spanish gathering. We were renamed 'Carlos y Diana' and bought drinks by just about everyone in the bar.

So often, it is those people that have so little who offer so much more, but there was one moment of kindness from a very wealthy person that stays in my mind. Hitching was slow on that particular day, with little distance covered, but we had just received a lift in a hearse, which was worth a few points on the novelty front. It took us to Monte Carlo, which was no place for paupers like us, so we continued on our way. On walking out of the principality, more novelty points were to be gained by getting a lift in a Rolls Royce. It was only a short lift but it took us to the main road. Our generous driver told us that in Monte Carlo you can hire a Rolls as a taxi and even though we had only travelled a few miles the cost of our journey, had we been paying for it, would have been greater than our weekly budget. "When I am older and richer, I'll pay you back," I replied. "No," he said, "when you are rich you buy your own Rolls Royce and give someone else a lift". I have given many people lifts since then but I am still waiting to buy that Rolls.

We had met with many wonderful and kind people on our trip; some fed us and others even gave up their own beds. Some became good friends, others just passing acquaintances. Sometimes the kindness came from expected sources, such as a lovely lady in a soup kitchen who gave me a pullover when she discovered I had a cold. Sometimes it came from the least expected sources, such as the police in Zurich railway station who gently woke us up in the morning to tell us we should be on our way. But in every case their kindness has stayed with me. It has had an impact on my life and provided me with at least some faith in humanity. My George Orwell 'down and out in Paris and London' experience was a roller coaster ride, but the highs more than made up for the lows.

* * *

Back at university, the third year was always set to be the highest hurdle, so it was no surprise to me when I failed to jump it. Once again, I had planned a trip to Soustons for after the exams and after discussions with my tutor I took his advice and went anyway, as I had done after failing the first-year exams. The theory was again to get some much-needed time out and then knuckle down to work on my return. This time it didn't work; I failed the resits and my future lay in the hands of the dreaded Progress Committee.

As I stood outside the interview room awaiting my fate, memories of the admissions interview for the Royal Veterinary College four years earlier came flooding back to me. Once more, the sweat on my shirt caused it to cling to my back as I faced their probing questions. "Did you think it a good idea to take a holiday before your resits?" they asked. My tutor was on the panel, so I had no choice but to look to him and point out that I had taken his advice. "Yes, that is correct," he confirmed.

21

I was permitted to stay on the course and repeat my third year.

I was delighted. This was the point when I knew that I would make it as a vet; with a little effort, I should get through my repeat year; after that, it was highly unlikely that anyone would be turned away in the final two years. As it happened, I passed my exams on the first attempt in each of the final three years, including the final year, which came as something of surprise.

During my fourth year I was living in a flat in the student area just off Lark Lane in Aigburth and still in South Liverpool, and attended a workshop held above an Oxfam shop. I had no idea what to expect, thinking that a workshop must mean that we would be using tools to produce something concrete. I certainly did not think that this workshop would transform the rest of my life and eventually take me well away from the vetting world that I had worked so hard to enter.

It was 1984, the year of the Ethiopian famine that gave rise to the famous Band Aid record 'Do They Know it's Christmas?'. I had started my final year, which was spent at the field station at Leahurst on the Wirral, and for now had to focus on the career I had chosen. I did, however, manage to take part in my first Oxfam 24 hour fast, though I failed to get the catering department to donate the money from the meals that I and the other fasters saved from missing their three meals at the field station. I kept on repeating that I was genuinely interested and wanted to be more involved, but first I had to finish my final year. It sounded like an excuse, but I knew differently.

In the New Year my relationship, which had survived throughout the university years, came to an end. It meant six lonely months at Leahurst, but this also meant I could focus on my studies.

After I passed my final year, I took the opportunity to travel to Pamplona in the Basque region of Spain for the week-long festival and the famous Bull Run. I went with my friend, Pete, and we hitched, of course. Strangely enough we found ourselves in the same small village in the Pyrenees that I'd visited four years previously when hitching across Europe the first time. This time, our evening's entertainment was provided by the 'John Lennon Club', which must have been built since my last visit as I couldn't have failed to miss the place on that first occasion. The locals were still very friendly, but Pete managed to get his luggage stolen.

Everyone was very helpful, but apart from searching the village to see if any remaining contents had been abandoned after looting, there was very little that anyone could do. Pete decided to stay on in the hope of retrieving something whilst I went on ahead, with the plan to meet up again in Pamplona.

It was early morning in Pamplona. I was sat on the wooden barriers that kept the bulls on track as they are driven from their pen in the lower part of the city to the bull ring higher up. A cannon fires to alert people when the bulls are released and then again as they enter the bull ring, so everyone knows it is safe to walk the streets once more. Just minutes before the sound of the first cannon shot, I saw Pete walking across the street. I ran to greet him and then as we were talking the cannon boomed. The bulls were coming, so we decided to run with the crowd. As soon as the bulls were in sight, I ran under the barrier well out of the path of the bulls, but, for a reason I still don't understand, Pete chose to continue running.

To prevent the bulls making a U-turn and running against the unsuspecting public behind them, enormous solid wooden barriers are brought down as the bulls pass into streets that are enclosed by buildings on either side. The barrier came down ahead of me. I was on one side of it and Pete on the other, along with the bulls. At this point the bulls are more enclosed and therefore become more aggressive. I could hear the screams and looked through a knot in the wood. To my horror I saw a man being flipped by a bull's horns but just there, close by in a shop doorway, was a very pale-faced Pete. Fortunately, he had escaped unscathed!

I had to return to Liverpool in time for my graduation ceremony and hitching is never as much fun when you have a deadline to meet. I was therefore delighted when we got a very long lift from a lorry driver in France. He stopped off overnight at a 'Les Routiers' restaurant, the French equivalent of a transport café. Pete and I were going to sleep under the lorry but went inside for something to eat first. Paul McCartney was on the TV screen singing 'Let it Be' when suddenly his mike stopped working.

Although we didn't know it at the time, we were watching the finale of Bob Geldof's Live Aid, one of the largest-scale satellite link-ups and television broadcasts of all time and the very first of its kind. I didn't even know it was planned when I left home for Pamplona, but when we returned to the UK it was on everyone's lips. It has been estimated that almost 40% of the world's population watched the live broadcast, but I was not one of them. No matter; my mother had taped every second of it for me to watch at my leisure.

The Oxfam flame had been ignited when I first attended that workshop in Aigburth, but there is no doubt that Band Aid, Live Aid and the focus on the Ethiopian famine of 1984 had a huge impact on my life and motivated me to become more involved in the fight against poverty. It poured fuel on flames until they became a great fire that still burns deep inside me today, and I know that I was not the only one affected in this way. At an Oxfam Assembly more than ten years later a facilitator asked everyone to gather in a line, placing themselves at the point that corresponded to the year when they first became involved with Oxfam. It was interesting to note the large swelling around the years 1984/85. I have always said that Bob Geldof achieved so much more than just raising £150 million for famine relief, as important as that was. He inspired many, myself included, and who knows how my life would have turned out without this influence?

I made it back to Chester late in the evening just one day before my graduation ceremony in Liverpool. The next day my father drove me to the university and, as you can imagine, I was feeling exhausted. There were the usual obligatory speeches, which did go on a bit, and in the heat of the stuffy lecture theatre I inevitably fell asleep. I woke just in time to hear the last words from the final speaker. Much to my amusement he finished with the ironic line, "So the moral of the story is don't mess with bulls." Unfortunately, the advice was given too late for me to take it.

CHAPTER 3

The Leaving of Liverpool

I stood on the deck of the Belfast Ferry watching Liverpool's famous Three Graces fade into the distance behind me. I had never been to Ireland; I was going to a strange place where I knew nobody. As I thought of the friends and relatives I was leaving behind, the words of the Irish sea shanty 'The Leaving of Liverpool' came to mind: "It's not the leaving of Liverpool that grieves me / but my darling when I think of thee." However, the Irish Sea is not a great divide and I would only be away for a few months.

I was going to work as a deputy veterinary officer, a new temporary post developed by the Ministry for Agriculture, Fisheries and Food to entice vets to work for the Ministry in Northern Ireland. It was still the time of 'the Troubles' in Northern Ireland and working for the Ministry there was perhaps not the desire of every newly-qualified veterinary surgeon. The job paid well, and I had debts to clear, but more than that the adventurer in me wanted to see Northern Ireland and learn a little more of what lay behind the conflict there.

Upon arrival, I drove my blue Mini Clubman estate car, which I'd named 'Bluebird', off the ferry and then had to negotiate the streets of Belfast to find the road to Dungannon, where I'd be based. 'Bluebird' was my first car; I'd just bought it in Chester at a cost of £300. It was a wreck and close to the end of its life, but I needed a car for this job and 'Bluebird' should suffice.

It was late in the day and, therefore, despite being summer it was getting dark. As I drove through Dungannon, I inadvertently went through an army check point without stopping. I saw a soldier come out of the pillbox in my rear-view mirror, but all seemed well. Later, I was told that if my car had not been carrying a British number plate then things may well have been quite different.

The guesthouse I was to be staying in was off the main road that led from Dungannon to Cookstown, famous for its Cookstown sausages once advertised by George Best. Cookstown was also the best example of a linear settlement that I'd ever come across. Basically, it consisted of two rows of houses on either side of Church Street, the longest street in Northern Ireland.

I was soon to learn that most places in the country were not going to be easy to find and the guesthouse was no exception. However, eventually I was driving down a small country lane and finally reached the place that was to be my home for the next five months.

The guesthouse was run by a middle-aged couple who were both Ulster Unionists. As well as the guesthouse they owned a bakery and every evening we were treated to a supper with sandwiches and plenty of cream cakes, which had not sold in the shop that day. My teacup was never empty, with regular 'scoots' added whenever I wanted it, and often when I didn't. It reminded me of the high teas I had as a child when visiting relatives in Yorkshire, only in this case the slap-up offering was served as well as, and not instead of, dinner. If that wasn't enough, you knew that before work the next day you'd be served a huge Ulster fry-up for breakfast. One thing was certain: I was not going to starve.

Other guests in the house included an Irish republican sympathiser and a friendly, jovial guy from Dublin who, like me, took up the middle ground where politics and religion were concerned. Before leaving England, I had been advised to avoid talking about politics and religion when in Northern Ireland, but I soon learned that here people spoke about nothing else. Everything and every place were designated either Protestant or Catholic, but never both. My naivety and lack of knowledge ensured that I remained impartial. I would unknowingly and unwittingly walk from a Catholic pub into a Protestant pub and suffered no ill effects.

The people, however, were amongst the friendliest I'd ever met. On my first visit to the local pub with my new Dublin friend a local at the end of the bar bought me a drink just because he noticed I was a stranger. There were no strings attached; he didn't even come over for a chat, he just wanted to make me welcome.

On my first working day I was sent out to visit a farm and inevitably had to stop to ask for directions. I wound down 'Bluebird's' window and asked a local farmer. He slowly walked over to me, poked his head through the open window while leaning on the closed door, and proceeded to chat at considerable length. I could not possibly drive away, so by the time he had finished I was delayed by a good hour or so. On returning to the office, I explained to my manager why I was so late. "I hope you spent time talking to him," she replied, "it is very important that we remain friendly with local farmers on every occasion." I was going to enjoy this job, I thought. Ironically, despite 'the Troubles', the atmosphere was far more friendly and relaxed than it ever was on the 'peaceful' but stressful side of the water.

People were always so willing to help, which was a good thing since 'Bluebird' often let me down. Some of the luck of the Irish rubbed off on me, at least where the car was concerned. My landlord had run Minis all his life and did not believe in leaving anything to waste. He ran the cars to the ground and then stripped them of every nut, bolt and working part, selling the remaining carcase to Gypsies as scrap. I soon discovered the huge hoard of Mini parts he stored in his garage. When I needed a new windscreen wiper, he would pull out a drawer full of them; in another drawer he had three alternators. Of course, the parts weren't a gift; he sold them to me, but at a good price, and as he was such a good mechanic he often repaired the car as part of the deal.

I had also joined the AA and got far more than my money's worth. The fuel gauge did not work so I had to measure the amount of petrol in the tank using a wooden cane as a dipstick. This meant that I often ran out of petrol, usually at the worst times. Once I ran empty late one night while driving back from Belfast on the M1. The man from the AA was not only remarkably pleasant but even put enough petrol in my tank to get me home, at no extra charge.

On average, I must have called the AA every month. Usually, they got me home, where my landlord would take over armed with his stock of Mini parts and excellent mechanical skills. The car was not worth any great expense, however, and most of the time we just made do with what we had. By the time I drove it back to England even the petrol tank was tied up with pieces of rope.

The broken fuel gauge, combined with the fact that, at that time in Northern Ireland, it was illegal to carry petrol in a can, did lead to some very difficult situations. Once I was overtaking a lorry on a dual carriageway when fuel starvation hit me. I managed to pull into the side of the road but found myself opposite an army check point stopping cars coming in the opposite direction. There was a petrol station ahead, but as I got out of the car, I noticed at a distance several soldiers had trained their guns in my direction. It occurred to me that I must have looked very suspicious, and 'Bluebird' was a likely candidate for a car bomb. What was I to do? I pointed at the car, pointed at the petrol station, and slowly walked towards it. I wondered if the soldiers would simply blow up the car, but it was still in one piece on my return. I filled up the tank, keeping everything well in view of the soldiers, slowly got into the car and drove away. Perhaps that was another incident where I was saved only by the British registration on 'Bluebird's' number plate?

I had plenty of free time working for the Ministry. The other lodgers often went home at weekends, and I was never on-call and knew nobody. This was the time to take up my promise to become more involved with Oxfam. I contacted the Oxfam campaigns office in Belfast and set up what proved to be the only Oxfam campaigns group in Northern Ireland: the Dungannon Oxfam Group, which rather appropriately for a vet abbreviated to DOG.

Oxfam had decided to put more emphasis onto campaigning against the causes of poverty and was in the process of setting up 'Hungry for Change' groups across the UK, including the workshop I had attended in Liverpool the year before. I had gone to Ireland armed with my 'Hungry for Change' materials branded with the large yellow 'H' but was soon told that they were not to be used here. It was just four years since the Republican prisoner Bobby Sands had died from hunger strike in the

H-block wing of HM Prison Maze . 'Hungry for Change' and the large yellow 'H' had quite different connotations in Ireland.

To set up DOG I placed posters around town and arranged a public meeting at the library in Dungannon, which drew quite a crowd. This was the first time I was to give a public presentation and I was feeling nervous. Before speaking I showed a film about small-holders who were driven off their land by powerful coffee barons. The injustice of it enraged me, which overcame any fear I had. The meeting was a success and DOG was born. We were a small group, primarily made up of members from the local Protestant girl's school, but incredibly we had many achievements in the short time I was in Dungannon.

We sold over 50 copies of the excellent Oxfam publication 'The Hunger Crop', which was not available from the local Oxfam shop; shops and campaigning were quite separate entities in those days. A few years later Oxfam published 'The Oxfam Report – It's time for a Fairer World' in which I heard for the first time that "A small child dies every 2.4 seconds from poverty." Unfortunately, although the frequency of deaths has slightly decreased, this terrible statistic has shown little change. The tragedy is entirely preventable, which in my view makes it totally unacceptable. That is a fact that continues to motivate me to this very day. Whenever I am asked why I do what I do, I always turn the question around and ask; "How can you not take some sort of action when this shocking statistic still remains true?"

DOG also managed to get frequent articles in the Dungannon press, albeit our press releases were often just printed word for word. When they did need to edit a piece, they simply removed two or three middle paragraphs.

We had some success lobbying our Ulster Unionist MP, whose daughter was one of the members in our group and his wife and son were both active with the Irish development charity Concern. So, despite the fact that he obviously had other fish to fry, he did at least agree to meet with us and offer us a sympathetic ear now and again. On one occasion I joined a car full of people to make up the Northern Irish contingent for the mass lobby of Parliament on the issues of DATA: Debt, Aid, Trade and Arms control. Unfortunately, these are also issues that have changed little in all my years of campaigning.

A few weeks into the job I was joined by another deputy veterinary officer called Eileen, who became a strong ally and a very active member of DOG. Eileen soon decided to give up her career as a vet and follow her true calling, a decision I was also to make 26 years later. Eileen became a nun working in South America and we still keep in touch today.

Just before I left Ireland, we organised a very successful 'Rich Man Poor Man' Christmas dinner, in which the diners drew lots to decide whether they got a full three course meal with wine and all the trimmings, or a bowl of soup and dried bread. The proportions for each mirrored the proportions between the rich and poor people that made up the world.

By far our most memorable event, however, took place in support of the annual Oxfam 24 hour fast. We had enrolled the support of the local Catholic Boy Scout Troupe to build a shanty house in Dungannon's main square. A large group of us then spent the night in the Scout hut so we could all fast together. Just before I settled down to sleep, I realised what we had done. Most of our members, and therefore fasters, were Protestant young girls from the local high school and here they were sleeping overnight in a Scout hut full of Catholic Boy Scouts. We attracted a reasonable amount of press coverage, but no-one picked up on this remarkable achievement, which with hindsight I am sure would not have taken place if we had deliberately planned it.

Dungannon Oxfam Group with shanty house

My time with the Ministry eventually came to an end and I returned to Chester to spend a family Christmas at home. In the New Year I had to find a new job and I had lined up a couple of interviews in Birmingham. 'Bluebird' was deteriorating fast, and I suspected that this could be its last journey; I was right. Water was leaking into the engine making the oil a light grey colour and regular stops every ten miles to take on water were essential. I made it to Birmingham, drove back to Liverpool and parked on a side street off Lark Lane while I visited a friend nearby. This was to be 'Bluebird's' final resting place.

The next day I decided to take the train back to Chester and await the outcome of the interviews. I was offered, and accepted, a 100% small animal job at a practice in Handsworth Wood in Northwest Birmingham, close to the M6 and M5 junction. The job included the use of a car so all that remained was to return to Liverpool and pay someone to take 'Bluebird' away for scrap.

My heart dropped as I turned the corner to see the burnt out wreck that was formerly my beloved car, but then the realisation hit me that I had been going to scrap the car and someone had done it for me at no charge. I had to report it to the police so caught a bus to the nearest police station in Garston. This turned out to be the wrong police station. as Lark Lane came under the jurisdiction of the police in Toxteth. I was told to return to the car where a policeman would meet me and take my report. Once again I was to be hit by surprise: on this occasion the car had gone.

I took another bus, this time to Toxteth police station. I had assumed the police had towed the car away without waiting for me; astonishingly, someone had stolen the burnt-out wreck while I was reporting the original incident. This could only happen in Liverpool.

The final outcome was very lucrative. 'Bluebird' was insured and, now there was not even a wreck to value, I was able to claim back the full £300 that I had paid for the car, all perfectly legal and above board. I often wonder why the police officer at Toxteth station was not even a little suspicious when I was able to pull out all the relevant papers, which I happened to have with me.

I had by now well and truly caught the Oxfam bug, so as soon I settled into my new job in Birmingham I contacted the nearest Oxfam group, which was in Erdington, just north of Spaghetti Junction. This group was well established, well supported and already active and now that I was working in a veterinary practice there were night duties and weekends on-call to contend with, which meant less free time to devote to my newly found passion. I did attend meetings when I could, however, and did what I was able.

It was while working in Birmingham that I got my first and only dog: a three-year-old crossbreed called Sandy, or a 'Heinz 57' as we called it in the trade. He had been brought in to be destroyed, with permission given to rehouse him if possible. Although I was not planning on having a dog at that time, the nurses managed to persuade me to take him on. I have no regrets; Sandy became a very loyal and friendly companion to me for the next nine years.

Much to the disappointment of my employers I only stayed in Birmingham for a few months. I was tempted back to Liverpool, and in August 1986 I started work at Adams Veterinary Surgery in Allerton. I was once again next to Penny Lane and just a stone's throw from the house I had lived in for three years as a veterinary student.

CHAPTER 4

My Lost Weekend

John Lennon referred to his 18 months parted from Yoko Ono in 1974 and 1975 as his "lost weekend". Perhaps we all have a 'lost weekend' of one sort or another somewhere in our lives. Mine lasted four years from 1987 to 1991.

It was good to be back in Liverpool; in fact, it was as if I'd never been away. Even the lady in the nearby Chinese takeaway greeted me in the usual way, as if I'd only been away for a summer vacation. I had a good boss in John Adams, a great night life and when I started going out with one of the nurses in the practice it seemed as if things couldn't be better. I was gravely mistaken.

In the summer of 1987, I went to Turkey for three weeks with the nurse and that was when things started to go wrong. Even the weather was against us. Three weeks in Turkey and yet only two days of sunshine; every other day it rained. When the sun finally shone, we made the most of it by sitting on the beach all day and I ended up with sunstroke. If that wasn't bad enough, on returning home I discovered that the UK had experienced a three week-long heat wave.

Our relationship was not working out and shortly after the holiday it came to an end. She began seeing my colleague, another veterinary assistant and an old student acquaintance, who occupied the flat above me. This, perhaps combined with the stresses of life as a young, recently qualified vet in a busy practice, drove me to do something I thought I would never do.

During my final year at the Leahurst field station, I distinctly remember telling my good friend Mark, who occupied the room next to mine, that I could never understand why anyone would commit suicide. "Surely when things are that bad you can just walk away; they are bound to get better at some stage in your life," I remarked. Now, I was actually in that position and things no longer looked that simple.

There was a large tub of Paracetamol tablets in the practice stock room and I took a handful. I'm not sure how many I swallowed, or what my intention was. Perhaps I was just seeking attention, or had I genuinely sunk that low? It all just seems a blur, now, and all I remember is that the day before my 28th birthday I was admitted to hospital, having attempted suicide. I spent my one and only night in a hospital bed, or was it two? I can't quite remember.

The next day, 19th October 1987, was named 'Black Monday' because of the stock market crash. It was certainly the darkest day in my life. The nurses on the ward didn't want to know me. Did they take a dislike to me for taking up a much-needed hospital bed with a self-inflicted injury? Were they too busy? Or was it all in my own paranoid mind?

I had a session with the psychiatrist before being discharged and he arranged for me to be referred for further therapy, which didn't start until three months later. He told me that I should never have allowed things to get that far and if I ever felt that way again I should seek help either through my doctor or through A&E if necessary.

I had been to my GP just a week or two before taking the pills, but I hadn't demonstrated the 'right symptoms' that would have led to a diagnosis of depression. I slept too well through the night, it seemed.

A few weeks after the 'incident' I took the advice of the psychiatrist and was taken to A&E by my boss's wife following a particularly low spell. After a very long wait I was told in no uncertain terms that I was wasting the doctor's time. With the benefit of hindsight, I can now see the flaws in a National Health Service that simply did not cater for depression as an illness, but at the time I was in no position whatsoever to consider making any form of complaint.

I can't remember telling anyone what had happened, but word had got around somehow, and my family and friends were there for me. My mum was great; she didn't panic or overreact but did what she could. She felt a little guilty because my parents had moved from Chester to Knott End, near Blackpool, just months before and she mistakenly thought that might have partially contributed to my problem. I remembered one time as a child being present when my mum tried to take an overdose, but I managed to stop her. Perhaps that is why she now understood that there is no place for logic in a depressed mind, just the need for someone to be there to talk to?

Sometimes I felt guilty; I knew I had no genuine reason to be depressed, but I was. It reminded me of what a lecturer at university had advised us: "A problem is not a problem unless it causes a problem." Likewise, it is true to say that a problem, even if it has no real foundation, becomes a genuine problem if it causes a problem. I woke up feeling depressed and therefore I was, logical or not.

You learn who your real friends are at times like those. Don't get me wrong; everyone meant well and tried to do what they could, but some friends come out of the woodwork and surprise you with how much they are willing to give. Mark and Dave particularly spring to mind and I'll never forget what my ex-girlfriend did for me at that time.

Dave's father was learning the science of hypnosis and offered me regular therapeutic sessions in Chester. He was using me as a guinea pig, which was fine by me, and it was kind of him to offer his help. I was willing to try anything and the consultations were free. Towards the end of the course, he tried out a questionnaire on me which revealed, amongst other things, that I was immature. I think that not only I but also his son Dave knew that already. Tragically, Dave's dad died suddenly two years later at the age of 56, never realising his dream of helping people through hypnotherapy, although he had helped me.

I'd been given a self-help book to read; I said I would try anything. One piece of advice for when things felt bad was to look around you, as there would always be something to make you smile. I remember driving back from Chester to Liverpool after a session with Dave's dad. It was dark, pouring with rain and I felt quite miserable. As I drove over the River Dee on Grosvenor Bridge, I looked around to find something to make me smile. There was nothing apparent but, somehow, I found that quite amusing so I laughed quietly to myself.

It was only a matter of time before I felt strong and brave enough to leave the practice. I knew I had to. Each day I was hanging on a thread and, if I didn't get out soon, that thread would break for a second time. My employers John and Rita Adams were very understanding and supportive. They let me go without warning and paid me until the end of the week. They even allowed me to use the practice car until I no longer needed it.

I went to stay with my good friend Mark, and his wife Trish, to recuperate. Mark was my neighbour at Leahurst and now he and Trish were both vets working in nearby Warrington. They cleared out their spare room and said I could stay there as long as I wanted. Time dragged by, ever so slowly. It was simply a matter of getting through each day as it came and went.

In February 1988 I took a week's holiday in Lanzarote with one of the nurses I'd met while working at the practice in Birmingham. We were just friends, and I think the trip away provided a much-needed break for both of us.

I knew I had to get back to work and went for an interview for a job in the same practice Trish worked in. It involved running the branch surgery in Newton-le-willows, which was quite a challenge for me at that time. I got the job and with it came a house and car, so I thanked Mark and Trish for the use of their room and moved in a few doors away into the practice house on the same road as theirs.

Eventually, I started the psychiatric therapy sessions that I was promised when in the hospital. This meant regular visits to Liverpool, which brought back memories that I had to face up to. On one occasion I found myself behind the new assistant and my replacement driving the practice car from my old workplace: a remarkable coincidence. I was never sure if the psychiatry did me much good, but perhaps the most important lesson to learn was that no-one was going to provide any magic solutions; that had to come from me alone.

Some normality was coming back into my life. Monday was my day off, so I used it to prepare a dinner party that I held each week. Mark and Trish were excellent cooks, so this was my way to repay them for their kindness and the many meals they had cooked for me when I stayed in their home. I would invite them and two or three other guests, giving me the opportunity to meet with people again and make new friends.

I even ventured back into Liverpool for the occasional night out and met with old friends from the Oxfam group there. Then, by some miracle, I met up with a girl that I'd known from my teenage days in Chester. I had gone to see a band playing in a pub on Lark Lane and there she was. We started seeing each other, but not for long. This chance meeting did, however, lead to a relationship with her flatmate Judy. Judy and I were together, on and off, for the next three years. Despite the ups and downs, my time with Judy brought me much happiness during a low period in my life and for that I was grateful.

I'd always wanted to travel around the world but was waiting for a travelling companion. My job in Warrington was not going too well and then Judy and I split up for what was to be the first of many times. I decided that if I didn't travel now I never would. The world seemed too big to travel alone so I packed in my job and after Christmas set off for Central America instead.

My journey gave me the opportunity to find myself in my 'lost weekend'. It provided a breath of fresh air in a stuffy room and, as such, does not belong in this chapter, so it shall be dealt with in full in the next.

My 'lost weekend' was not over, although at times things were definitely brighter. Judy met me at the airport when I returned from my Central American travels. I had no luggage to collect so came straight off the plane into the arrivals area. I was rugged, wearing my Guatemalan fleece with my Nicaraguan bag slung over my shoulder. I had credibility to match that of the traveller returning to his lost love 'Isis' in the Bob Dylan song of the same name. It obviously had a positive impact on Judy, as we drifted back together once more.

What few belongings I owned at that time were at my parent's house in Knott End, which I now used as a base as I decided to do veterinary locum work. I would go anywhere in the country, but it had to be working with small animals only.

In the summer, Judy and I went to Spain. It was not your usual package holiday but a voyage on the ferry to Santander. We then toured Northern Spain with no pre-booked accommodation, just going wherever felt best whenever we wanted. We had a wonderful time, and it was clear that Judy enjoyed my way of travelling but it wasn't to last; as soon as the school year started and she was back at work, we split up again.

Life was lonely again and I spent my 30th birthday in a bed and breakfast in Scarborough while doing locum work there. The landlady had seen the couple of birthday cards that found their way to the guesthouse and gave me a glass of wine with dinner that evening, on the house. It was a kind gesture and she meant well, but it just emphasised how lonely I was.

I felt a need to settle down and then, for some strange reason, I bought a house in Morecambe. It made no sense at all; property prices had peaked and I was still doing locum work countrywide. The house was not a necessity and in fact became more of a burden, somewhere that I had to keep visiting to ensure the property was safe and to keep the insurance company happy.

I moved in just before Christmas and while visiting friends in nearby Garstang I met Jane, my future wife. Jane was a single parent with a two-year-old son called Tom. She worked as a nurse in Preston and had her own house in Garstang. Jane had, and still has, compassion in abundance, wanting to help anyone whenever she could. I've never quite understood why she cares for me in the way she does, but thankfully she continues to do so and has stood by me through the most difficult of times of my life.

It would be another 18 months before I settled down with Jane and Tom. Before that was to happen, I was to go back out with Judy and then, as if I was a real glutton for punishment, I returned to work in Liverpool and started going out with the nurse again. I was lost in my 'lost weekend' and made some bad choices.

It was not until the late summer of 1991 when, with a feeling of déjà vu, I left the practice in Liverpool and went to live with Jane in Garstang. We had been to Cyprus together and become engaged. My long 'lost weekend' was finally over.

CHAPTER 5

Threat of a Good Example

One of the first Oxfam publications that I read was the book *Nicaragua – The Threat of a Good Example?* by Dianna Melrose. Oxfam was running country themes and Nicaragua was the first to be explored. During my time in Ireland, I was thrilled to see Dianna Melrose give a presentation about Nicaragua in Belfast, and then even more so to be able to have a chat with her in a pub after the meeting.

The Sandinistas had been in power in Nicaragua since the overthrow of the Somoza dynasty in 1979. The book suggested that Nicaragua was not a military threat to the United States for having a communist regime but was, instead, a threat to the Western world in general in other ways. It was a working model that demonstrated what a developing country could achieve in health and education, despite Western boycotts and constant attacks from the US-backed Contra, hence the title 'Nicaragua – The Threat of a Good Example?'.

I couldn't believe what I had read. The book explained how illiteracy rates had fallen since the revolution and that healthcare was improving. Instead of suppressing democracy, the Sandinistas had introduced arguably the fairest elections in Nicaragua's long, violent and tyrannical history and certainly the first elections in over forty years of rule under the Somoza family. The death penalty was abolished the day after the Sandinistas took power. This was all so different to what I saw on the news or read in the papers and yet these words were approved by a respectable charity; it was not ultra left-wing propaganda. I had to go to Nicaragua to see for myself, but that would be over three years later.

When I left my job in Warrington in 1988, I was again bitten by the travelling bug and Nicaragua was to be my destination. It was not possible to fly directly to Nicaragua, so I planned a round trip taking in Jamaica and trekking up through Central America from Panama to Belize, before meeting my return flight from Miami. I left Heathrow airport on Monday 9th January 1989 and returned on Wednesday 29th March: almost three months away, including almost seven weeks in Nicaragua.

I had bought a new bag, the exact same type as the one I took when I first hitched across Europe, but two sizes smaller. I had learned to travel lighter and this one seemed just right, but once again I was to lose the bag and all its contents when it was stolen within the first two weeks of my travels.

It was the first time I'd set foot in the United States and my first impression was not good. I hated Miami airport. Only the 'normal' rich fitted in here. I decided to take a short walk away from the airport in the hope of getting a better taste of the 'American dream', but I should have known that walkers were not catered for in Miami. As I walked out of the air-conditioned complex and into the glorious natural sunshine, I could find only taxis and large cars; there were no footpaths. I walked down the edge of the road to the sound of car horns and abuse. Obviously, walking was not the done thing in Miami.

I touched down in Kingston, Jamaica at 8.30pm local time. It was dark and I had nowhere to stay. Outside the airport everything looked and felt threatening. I began to wonder what I'd done and why I'd done it. A taxi driver said he could take me to a cheap hotel, so I got in the car. Did I have any choice? Buses, I was told, were "not safe for whites after dark". I was taken to a seedy but safe hotel. It cost me over the odds, but I'd survived and now had a bed. I finally hit the sack at midnight local time; I'd been awake and travelling for over 22 hours.

During my six days in Jamaica, I managed to travel right across the island and tried my best to keep away from the tourist areas. I wanted to know the 'real' Jamaica, but I was white and in Montego Bay the locals spat on the pavement as I walked by. I was beginning to experience racism from the other side, only here I understood their bigotry.

Their history was full of white supremacy and even now I was told there were beaches that only white people frequented. Any resentment was more than understandable.

Rose Hall had been a sugar plantation run by a cruel 'white witch' called Annie Palmer who tortured her slaves for fun and murdered three husbands. They had been killed in all but one of the four bedrooms. She was buried next to the house and supposedly haunted the grounds every night from 6pm to 4am. On completing a tour of the house, the guide said that anybody was welcome to stay overnight in the one remaining bedroom that had not witnessed a murder. I had nowhere to stay and was tempted until I found out that the offer was not genuine. Perhaps that was a good thing, as I realised that I would have awoken the next morning on Friday the 13th.

A friend of mine in the UK had suggested I contact someone they knew in Ochos Rio called Dee. Dee lived in a very upmarket apartment with a private beach and swimming pool. Understandably, she was a little suspicious of me at first, but after a long evening talking mainly about her Baha'i faith, she agreed to let me sleep on her balcony, albeit behind a locked door. I was grateful none-the-less and despite an evening of thunder and lightning, unaccompanied by rain, I had a magnificent night sleeping under the stars to the sound of the roaring sea and crickets.

Dee gave me a Jamaican-style English breakfast the next morning: boiled egg, toast, cereal and pawpaw. Dee was most proud to have what she believed was the only toast rack in Jamaica; perhaps symbolic of the last bastion of British colonialism that was now giving way to modern-day American imperialism, which had an altogether different format.

On Sunday 15th January I took a walk though 'downtown Kingston' before taking a flight to Panama City. The date was significant as it was election day in Jamaica. Once on the plane I was told that to be a white person walking through 'downtown Kingston' on election day was akin to attempted suicide.

Panama, like much of Central America in the 1980s, was under the influence of the United States and certainly appeared so. The land on either side of the famous and strategically important Panama Canal was controlled by the US, though that would change. Just eleven months later saw the American invasion of Panama and President Manuel Noriega deposed. Ten years after that the control of the canal was transferred to Panamanian rule.

I travelled north into Costa Rica and to the capital San Jose, where I foolishly fell for an obvious con trick and lost my entire luggage. My valuables were safely down my trousers as always, but with my luggage I lost the gifts that I'd bought in Jamaica and, most importantly, my camera and the photos that I'd taken while in Jamaica and beside the Panama Canal.

Some say it is better to experience the world on your own, but I never wanted to travel alone and missed having a companion. Even though I still fell victim to thefts and attacks when travelling as a couple, at least any trauma was shared and decisions could be made jointly, not to mention sharing the joys when taking in a view, visiting a landmark or enjoying a good meal. But I was alone and getting a little used to it.

Nicaragua was three days away and I thought it best to wait until I was in the country before replacing my clothing, on the assumption that things would be much cheaper there. It turned out this was a mistake; clothing was cheap, the only problem was that there was so little of it, or anything else for that matter, available to buy. I often regret not spending more time in beautiful Costa Rica, as it had so much to offer, but regret or not I was now approaching the Nicaraguan border.

I started to feel apprehensive; what if all I'd read in the Oxfam publication was misguided and I really was about to enter a communist-controlled country that was at war with the greatest power on earth? My fear was unfounded. The border guards were all very pleasant young girls who could barely write. In examining my passport photo, they remarked "bonito y simpático". My Spanish was not good, but I knew they were being complimentary. I later discovered that the men who had not been killed in the revolution and Contra war were taken up by more important military duties, leaving the young women to take on many of the administrative roles.

10,000 was printed over the 10 Cordoba note due to the rapid inflation rate

At the border you were obliged to exchange $60 into Nicaraguan córdobas before you could enter the country, but when it came to my turn there were no more córdobas left in the safe. The man before me had taken a huge bundle of them, which is hardly surprising when you consider that at the time $60 was equivalent to 270,000 córdobas. The economic stranglehold that the West had on Nicaragua had resulted in a rocketing inflation rate. I can recall drinking a bottle of coke in a beach café. The radio announced a change in the inflation rate and by the time I finished my drink it had increased in price by 33%. That was one occasion where I preferred the British system of paying for your food and drink before you consume it.

The friendly border guards told me to pass through even without my córdobas and I walked out into the Nicaraguan sunshine. A small boy came running up to me shouting "gringo, gringo". I was still a little apprehensive so reached for my passport to prove I was not American.

He walked away in dismay. When I asked him why, he replied, "I thought that you were American, and I wanted to talk to someone about baseball."

As I stepped off the bus at Rivas the level of poverty shocked me, yet everyone was so friendly. I was glad that I'd lost my expensive rucksack; this was a place where I didn't want to stand out any more than I had to. I eventually found a bus to the beautiful beach resort of San Juan del Sur. Perhaps I should say ex-beach resort; nobody visited now, at least not for a holiday anyway. The luxury beach apartments were all boarded up; the rich elite of Nicaragua had fled to the USA after the ousting of Somoza. But in many ways, this made the beach even more attractive; it was all the more natural and certainly much quieter.

Despite the lack of tourists Nicaragua was not short of foreign travellers. I soon met up with some 'Brigadistas'. These were volunteers who went to Nicaragua to help pick coffee. I think it is fair to say that they were of limited help where coffee picking was concerned; the local farmers did not need foreigners to help them do their job, but this act of solidarity was of great importance in a country that had been isolated by so much of the world. I learned from these volunteers what was going on in the country and how to get by. I was to spend most of my time teamed up with 'Brigadistas' for the remainder of my travels, not just in Nicaragua but throughout the whole of Central America.

A small group of 'Brigadistas' accompanied me on my long, epic and exhausting journey to Bluefields on the Atlantic coast, which had been hit by Hurricane Joan just three months earlier. I arrived in the capital, Managua, and set off for Bluefields the next day. The convoy of three buses left Managua at 3am and arrived in Rama eight hours later. Nicaragua was at war, and we were entering the conflict zone. The soldiers on the roadside were much older and war weary than we'd seen previously. We passed close to minefields and took diversions around bridges that had either been blown up by the Contra or blown down by the hurricane.

There were no roads into Bluefields; access was by boat or plane only, so from Rama we had to wait for the one existing boat. Everyone from the three buses clambered onto the crowded vessel, which carried everything from large cheeses to small goats and chickens. There was one toilet, which was basically a hole over the water at the end of a wooden plank, surrounded by makeshift panels. Six 'soldiers', including one child, sat on the roof armed with a heavy machine gun. We asked if we could also sit on the roof where there was more room and cooler air to breathe. They said that we could, but pointed out that if the Contra should attack, they would shoot at the people on the roof first. We chose to stay on deck amongst the livestock and sweaty cheeses.

The sun was setting behind what had been a luscious, green, tropical rainforest. For mile after mile, the bare trees had been stripped of their leaves in a scene reminiscent of the film *Apocalypse Now*. Wrecked, barren boats lay on the riverbank; some casualties of war, others swept onto the land by the sheer strength of Hurricane Joan.

After fifteen hours of travel by road and river we finally arrived at the hurricane-damaged port and were shocked by the sight that greeted us. Bluefields had taken the full force of the hurricane. Almost every one of the 7,500 structures in the city had been demolished or had their roofs blown off and, apart from the hundreds of corrugated iron roof tops donated by Oxfam, there was little sign of repair. This was in stark contrast to the scene in Kingston, Jamaica, which had been hit by Hurricane Gilbert just one month before Joan destroyed Bluefields. In Kingston, everyone spoke about Gilbert and there were even souvenirs such as the "I survived Gilbert" T-shirts, but the closure of the zoo was the only tangible evidence that the hurricane had ever passed through.

Jamaica had received foreign aid, especially from the UK, but Nicaragua hadn't received a penny from any overseas governments.

Hurricane Joan lifts a ship onto the riverbank.

The then UK prime minister, Margaret Thatcher, had said that the UK favoured Jamaica over Nicaragua because of our strong historical and colonial links. She had implied there had been no links with Nicaragua, but this was simply not true. The Atlantic coast of Nicaragua had twice become a British protectorate in the 18th and 19th centuries. Supposedly this was in order to protect the indigenous Miskito Indians from the tyrannical Spanish, but cynics might argue it was a strategic move to secure the supply of valuable hardwoods in the area. Likewise, the denial of aid to Bluefields had nothing to do with greater needs or past links; it was purely based on politics and the democratic Sandinista government did not qualify. Apart from the Oxfam roofs, however, there was one other small charitable gift from the UK. This was three dustbin wagons given to Bluefields in an act of solidarity from their twin town council in the London Borough of Lambeth.

We stepped off the boat, tired and weary after our long journey, when an anxious young soldier came running towards us. He needed to check our passports and started with mine. His English obviously was not that good because it took him a considerable amount of time to record all the necessary information. When he had finally completed my details, he handed all the paperwork over to me and asked me to complete the same details for everybody else. This typified procedures in Nicaragua, perhaps due to inefficiency or perhaps simply because they trusted travelers like us who had come to visit their country. It was the same in Rama when the guard asked to see our permits. We told him truthfully that we didn't know permits were required. Consequently, he just wrote in his report that "they didn't need permits because they said so."

There was no doubt that the authorities were happy to have us there. We had trouble finding a room for the night in a city so badly damaged and there were times when we felt we were a burden on already strained services. But even the mayor of Bluefields gave up some of his precious time to meet with us; as another Sandinista official had said, "We are fighting the greatest propaganda machine in the world and all we have to tell our version of events are travellers like you." They wanted us to see things for ourselves and then go out and tell the world what was really happening in Nicaragua.

It was important, back then, to bring some balance to the propaganda war between Nicaragua and the US but, if anything, the task of seeking out the truth is of even greater importance today. In a world of 'fake news', where mass media really does control the stories and therefore people's mindsets, it is crucial that people travel and find out for themselves. That is why Fair Trade is so important, as it not only addresses trade injustices directly but also tells the producers' stories so that consumers can make the right choice when deciding what products they should buy.

Few places had running water in Bluefields, and I soon got used to taking a shower armed only with a bucket of water. This was a technique that was to serve me well many years later, when I was to make regular visits to Ghana and, to this day, I still refer to it as taking a 'Bluefield's shower'.

Despite the poverty and deprivation, Bluefields had still maintained its fabulous joy for life. The black Caribbean slave influence had mixed with the British tradition of May Pole dancing to produce a unique style of music that they called 'Palo de Mayo'. The night life in Bluefields, like the Nicaraguan Flor de Caña rum, was second to none.

After five days in Bluefields, including one false getaway when the propeller broke on a boat, we finally left for Managua. I had acquired some form of 'Bluefields belly', making for a terrible return journey. I was almost sick on the boat and had diarrhoea when in Rama. One of the buses got a puncture on the last leg of the voyage, so we ended up on the roof of one of the remaining two buses. Now we understood why they only travelled in a convoy of three. Normally, I would have enjoyed travelling on top of the bus with such wonderful views and then watching the stars light up the sky, but on this occasion I felt very ill and by the time we arrived in the capital I was shivering like a jelly.

Hospediaje Chepitos was the first choice for cheap accommodation in Managua, but there were no rooms available on our return, so I had to settle for another hostel nearby. I couldn't complain. I was just happy to have a room with a bed, running water and a flushing toilet. I managed to get a room in Chepitos the following day and that was to serve as my base for the next four weeks as I chilled out in Managua.

As is so often the case in developing countries, you had to take life slowly in Managua, or go insane. The capital had been hit by an earthquake in 1972 that destroyed most of the centre. The only three buildings to fully survive the earthquake were the cathedral, Somoza's palace and the Bank of America, which said a lot about the makeup of Nicaraguan society at that time. Foreign aid was ploughed into Managua, but very little rebuilding was done, as in one of Somoza's many callous acts the money ended up filling his pockets. Consequently, Managua was left with a very small centre surrounded by acres of wasteland and the rest of the city on the outskirts.

The post office was at the city's heart, with the main administration housed in the former palace. Chepitos lay in the outskirts with all the other buildings, so the daily routine often consisted of walking into the centre just to collect my post. If you allowed it, this became a very relaxing and enjoyable pastime, meeting people on the way and finding other pleasurable distractions and diversions.

Everything was very open in Nicaragua, totally contrary to the Western view that the country was run by a tyrannical military regime. It was the only place in Central America where a guard would apologise for inadvertently pointing his gun in your direction. On one occasion I accidently wandered onto a military base and was well inside the main building before someone finally came running up to me and apologetically told me I should leave. Although I never managed to visit the Oxfam project that I'd hoped to see (I lost my contact details along with my luggage in Costa Rica), I was able to visit a general hospital, a malaria research centre, a psychiatric hospital and even join in a march for women's rights, where men were made welcome. I also made trips to Masaya, Granada, Chinandega and Liverpool's twin town, Corinto, each time returning to my base in Managua.

Exactly two months after I left the UK it was time to leave Managua for the last time and head north towards the Honduran border, but not before attending a mass rally at the US embassy early in the morning. The US embassy had to be the most secure and fortified structure in the whole of Nicaragua. Of course, we could not get past the main gate, so the protest took place outside on Nicaraguan soil.

This meant, rather ironically, that the embassy was protected from the protesters by Nicaraguan troops. Again, they were very pleasant young guards, but in this case perhaps their smiles reflected the irony.

The next day I went to the Salvador Cooperative near Estelí to 'help' on a farm. Whether I was of any help is doubtful and, like so many things in Nicaragua, the experience was of far more use to me than any assistance I could offer them; but again, the act of solidarity had to mean something.

Our accommodation on the farm was very basic but was all they had, and they gave it to us freely. The farmers even gave up their hammocks for us; "You can't possibly sleep on the floor because there are rats and other creatures that come out in the night," they insisted, but now they'd given up their own beds they had exposed themselves to those very same threats. That evening, while lying in my hammock, I heard a loud blast followed by the sound of light debris falling on the corrugated iron roof. It was a mine detonated by some animal but that could so easily have been detonated by one of the farmers while searching for food. This was another reminder of the hardships and dangers faced by these already poor farmers due to the Contra war financed by the US government.

Next morning at breakfast (our hosts had already done a couple of hours work in the fields since sunrise) I saw a possum's head staring at me from a pan of simmering stew. It was the quarry from the previous night and was to be our lunch later that day.

I only worked one and a half days on the cooperative and even that was only by the Western definition of a full day's work. I weeded with machetes and picked and planted tomatoes. I'd never known such hard, back-breaking work and the bigoted words of a Protestant I'd confronted in Northern Ireland came rushing back to me: "The reason they are so poor is because they do not work hard. They are all Catholics and do not follow the Protestant work ethic." In my lifetime I have heard many bigoted and misguided myths attempt to explain why people are poor, but this one surely has to be the worst of them all.

My journey then continued onto the border with Honduras but not before seeing a news report about a Contra attack on a school. The images included the bodies of two children, yet the six Contra arrested would be given 'forced amnesty'. The injustice enraged me, and the world needed to know the truth.

Leaving Nicaragua was very different to entering the country. The border was manned by large, heavily armed, well-uniformed guards. There was a sense of fear as I studied the pile of Nicaraguan passports that lay on the side. Who did they belong to? Why had they been confiscated?

I had been warned about the difficulties of leaving Nicaragua and the danger of being labelled a 'Sandinista sympathiser', so I had put a copy of the right-wing newspaper 'La Prensa' at the top of my luggage and had given such souvenirs as my red-and-black Sandinista salt and pepper set to my friends to take home, as they were flying out of the country. But still, the right-wing guards felt the need to confiscate my book entitled 'Eye of the Storm', which was about the effects of Hurricane Joan hitting Nicaragua. They must have considered it Sandinista propaganda, because there may have been a mention of the evacuation of Bluefields and the relatively successful handling of the Hurricane. The words of the mayor of Bluefields were true; we were fighting the greatest propaganda machine in the world and they were going to do all they could to prevent us from telling our story. I was angry, but at that moment there was nothing I could do and at least I had not met with any physical violence.

Soon I was in a bus riding through the Honduran capital of Tegucigalpa. I witnessed the rows upon rows of shanty houses built precariously on the steep slopes overlooking the city. How vulnerable they looked and, indeed, just weeks after my return to the UK I saw and heard on the news how a landslide had caused the houses to collapse, with the loss of many lives. But what struck me was the fact that every single home had a TV aerial. Poverty cannot be measured by possessions or even income. As I was to learn at the Oxfam Assembly just five years later, when Stan Thekaekara spoke about the poverty he saw in Easterhouse, Glasgow and compared it to that in Southern India, when you look beyond the TV, car, and washing machine, the impact of poverty was the same, leading to fear, poor self image and the feeling of being caught in a trap. Poverty is a disease that is about a lack of empowerment and not the amount of material wealth.

I spent just three days travelling through the so called 'free state' of Honduras and was stopped by police on many occasions, with a body search occurring at least twice. I had been in the equally fictitious 'communist dictatorship' of Nicaragua for more than six weeks but only had my passport checked twice, and was never searched. It seemed the words in the Oxfam publication were true, but how different it all was to the perceptions of people back home in the UK.

The remainder of my journey took me through Guatemala and Belize before flying to Florida to meet my return flight home. I saw the amazing ruins at Copan and Tikal and visited a village in Guatemala where almost every house had its own loom donated by Oxfam. In the warehouse I learnt where the colourful cloth was exported to but there was no mention of the UK. "This cloth is far too brightly coloured for the UK market," I was told.

Like the country and its people, Guatemalan cloth was beautiful, but behind this beauty there was a terror and a fear. Whole villages could be destroyed overnight and removed from the map the very next day and yet few, if any, would speak of this horror for fear of retribution. It was easier to learn the truth about Guatemala by listening to news reports outside the country than actually visiting the place for yourself. That was true in many cases; for example South Africa under apartheid - and yet so often I'd heard from white South Africans that I could not understand a country that I had never visited.

I arrived back in the UK just in time for Central America Week in Liverpool. I was asked to make an appeal for the Nicaragua Solidarity Campaign during the interval for a performance at the Bluecoat Theatre. I was far from comfortable with public speaking and did not believe I was up to it, but then I remembered the anger I felt at the Honduran border and the words of the Sandinista official who spoke of the importance of telling the world the truth about Nicaragua and the Contra war.

I stood trembling on the stage and decided to tell it just as it was. I acknowledged my nervousness and told them that the only reason I was able to overcome my fear was because I needed to tell them the story of the guard and my experiences at the Honduran border. Following my speech, the money just piled into the collecting buckets. One should never underestimate the power of the spoken word from a passionate and dedicated individual. This was a lesson to serve me well when working on Fairtrade Towns over a decade later.

CHAPTER 6

GOG is Born, and the Family Grows

Garstang is a small, traditional Lancashire market town less than forty miles from the large cosmopolitan city of Liverpool, but a long way from it in every other sense. A two-up, two-down end-of-terrace house on Croston Weind, in the centre of Garstang, was to be my new home and where I was to start married life with Jane, her son Tom, who was now four, and Sandy, rescued from the vets in Birmingham six years earlier. It was time to settle down and exchange my campaigning life for a family one; or at least, that was my intention.

Tom went to the local community primary school and soon after I arrived in Garstang I attended their harvest festival assembly. I was pleasantly surprised as the Methodist preacher, the Reverend Peter Haywood, turned away from the apples and pears to talk about poverty in the developing world. He had just set up a fair trade shop called the Mustard Seed that was sited next to the Methodist church. Coincidentally, many years later I discovered that Jane had been their very first customer. His surprisingly unconventional presentation at the assembly reignited a flame that was still sputtering and sparking inside me.

At that moment I decided to form an Oxfam campaigns group in Garstang and I approached Peter Haywood for his support, which he gave freely. I was a newcomer to Garstang, so the backing of a well-respected, popular local figure was crucial if the group was to succeed.

The Garstang Oxfam Group (GOG) had been born. GOG did not have the same ring to it as its Irish counterpart in Dungannon, but its formation was to be an important step in the history of Fair Trade Towns that eventually were to spread across the world.

Peter had said that we could use the Methodist church hall for meetings and GOG's first meeting took place on 23rd April 1992, almost eight years to the day before the declaration of Garstang as the world's first Fair Trade Town. This landmark inaugural meeting was attended by myself, Jane, our babysitter and the Oxfam campaigns officer from Manchester.

Jane and Tom at an early Garstang Oxfam stall.

The first GOG event, however, took place before that first meeting. Just before leaving Liverpool, I had taken part in another 'Rich Man Poor Man' meal like the one we organised in Dungannon. It had been a huge success, with some people from the rich tables giving their food to those on the 'poor' tables and, where that didn't take place, groups of people from the 'poor' tables went on raids to steal the food from the 'rich', providing an interesting reflection on the state of the world.

Garstang Oxfam campaigners Graham and Belinda with Hilton Dawson MP

I still had all the necessary materials so it was very simple to repeat the meal in Garstang, just before Christmas. We managed to sell all the tickets with relative ease, but when it came to holding the event only my mum and one or two others turned up. They all meant well, but because the event had Oxfam's name to it, they just saw it as a fundraiser, for which only their money and not their presence was of importance. Campaigning was going to be very different in Garstang.

After that disappointment things could only get better, but this was not the first time I'd been involved with an event that fell flat on its face. Back in Liverpool we had organised a public meeting at the newly-restored Albert Dock, which is now a busy, bustling tourist centre with an equally hectic night life but back then was full of empty premises waiting to be utilised. We had been given use of one of the larger rooms on the north side of the dock and had arranged for the Radio One DJ Simon Bates to give a talk about his recent around-the-world trip with Oxfam. The site is now occupied by the Maritime Museum and, on the third floor, the excellent International Slavery Museum that was built in 2007 for the 200th anniversary of the abolition of the British slave trade.

With just one minute to go before the start, not one person was in the audience. I was sent out to try and rally up some support, but it was not possible. I stood helplessly gazing across the water at the hordes of people on Liverpool's waterfront, but they were too far away to engage. Simon Bates had started talking so I went in and sat on the back row to watch. At the end of his presentation, he immediately came towards me, shook my hand and said, "Thank you so much for coming. I was beginning to think that no-one would turn up." I didn't have the heart to tell him that I was also one of the organisers. After that humiliation anything would be acceptable and, by comparison, the let-down in Garstang didn't seem half so bad.

* * *

Jane and I were married at Sts. Mary and Michael Catholic church on 30th May 1992. Jane had attended the adjacent Catholic primary school as a child, but although I had always had some belief in a 'God' I was uncomfortable with any religion. Perhaps Father Murphy would not agree to marry us? I consulted Eileen, my former veterinary colleague from Ireland who was now a nun living in Brazil. "It is God that marries you and not the priest," she replied. This went some way to ease my anxiety when Jane and I had our first meeting with Father Murphy.

"You believe in Jesus, don't you?" Father Murphy asked. "Well yes, I believe he existed," I replied and that was good enough for him. Father Murphy was a caring, compassionate man who had all the time for those who needed him the most. Although he wasn't able to devote much time to our Oxfam campaign, he always responded positively to my messages and we knew we had his blessing and full support. Tragically, he died just months after our marriage and was buried in his hometown of Charlesville in Ireland. We took time out of our Irish touring holiday just one year after our wedding to visit his grave.

It amazes me how much money some people will spend on a wedding. I would not consider myself miserly, but we could not justify spending so much money on one celebration, no matter how important the occasion. So instead of champagne we drank Spanish Cava 'Freixenet' sparkling wine (this was always a favourite of mine from my travelling days to Soustons and northern Spain, so it was a preferred option) and we used my beloved MG Midget to whisk us away from the church.

The MG was the other love in my life and was rather appropriately purchased on Valentine's Day earlier that year. It took eight family members a total of five hours to get it ready for the big day. I had tried to combine my three passions for Oxfam, the MG and wine by organising an MG Rally to collect the Beaujolais Nouveau for Oxfam's 50th anniversary celebrations that same year. But this turned out to be one vision that sadly never materialised.

* * *

16th December 1993 saw the birth of our son, Daniel Ben Crowther. Like Jane and I, his middle name was the one to be commonly used. We wanted to call him Ben and liked the name Daniel; this also happened to be the name of Nicaragua's revolutionary Sandinista leader and president, Daniel Ortega. But Ben Daniel Crowther did not work, so Daniel Ben it was. To make matters worse, we had inadvertently given him the same initials as me, which caused confusion as soon as he was old enough to receive mail.

I have always been vulnerable to fainting attacks, usually following intense pain or witnessing it in someone close to me. It struck me that passing out was not a particularly good survival response in the face of a threat, but I was troubled with it none-the-less. Ben was born at around 1.15am, less than an hour after we arrived at the hospital. So far all was well, but Jane required stitches, the sight of which was not a problem for me. Watching Jane in such extreme pain, however, was enough to trigger my unfortunate response.

They had placed Ben in a cot, but I stayed with Jane in an attempt to offer her some support. I could feel the familiar sickness that always came before I collapsed. I knew the pattern well and at this point would normally find somewhere dark and quiet to lie down, but I didn't want to leave Jane until I had to. I had meant to hold onto Jane's hand for as long as I could and then move away at the last minute, but I held it just a little too long. I fell off the back of my stool onto the floor with what must have been a large crash, causing mayhem in the maternity room. The next thing I knew, it was me who was receiving the stitches, in the upper left corner of my forehead.

With two sons and a dog, our two-up, two-down on Croston Weind was becoming crowded; we had to move but loved the location. Thankfully, our dream house was less than fifty yards up the road. It was a Victorian semi-detached house on a slight rise and fronted with a beech hedge, hence the name Beech Mount. Both Jane and I had independently admired it, so we couldn't believe our luck when we heard through the grapevine that it was to be put on the market.

On inspection, the house was even better than we'd imagined. Jane adored old houses and much of the character in this house had been restored. I loved the cellar; it was ideal for storing wine and the lean-to greenhouse outside even had its own grapevine. We made an offer before the owners had approached the estate agents, but it was not accepted. Then we heard the devastating news that the house had been sold. We could not believe it. This was meant to be our home; we both knew it.

The owners were to move to Australia and the day before they left, we received a phone call telling us that the offer on the house had fallen through. After a roller coaster of a ride with many joyous uplifts but shattered hopes, culminating in an undisclosed bid, the house was finally ours. Ironically, we eventually bought it for the same price we originally offered before it went on the market.

Jane continued the restoration work started by the previous owners in her own special, creative and exquisite way. We opened up the fireplaces, removed most of the carpets to expose the beauty of the underlying floorboards and bought an old, working Bakelite, wall-mounted phone. I fitted a traditional sprung bell for the front door, using the original pulley system that still lay embedded in the wall, and connected it to a plastic knitting needle attached to a brass knob that ran through the original door mounting. We loved our new family home and at the time believed it was to be our house for the rest of our lives.

On 15th August 1995, just twenty months after Ben was born, Jane gave birth to our third child: Anna Naomi Crowther. Apartheid had ended in South Africa the year before, so giving Anna the same initials as the victorious African National Congress seemed to me appropriate recognition of this momentous event. Anna's birth was much longer and more complicated than Ben's, but with her golden curly locks she was beautiful and well worth waiting for.

* * *

As well as the end of Apartheid, 1994 was the year that saw the introduction of the FAIRTRADE mark in the UK. The very first Fairtrade label, however, had appeared in Holland in 1987. This was applied to Max Havelaar coffee sourced from Mexico, but now the Fairtrade label had reached the UK and the first products to be licensed here were Maya Gold chocolate, Cafedirect coffee and Clipper tea.

GOG had been campaigning on the FAIRTRADE mark two years previously; in fact, almost from the first day of the group's inception in 1992. Oxfam wanted to 'test the water' to see whether people in the UK would buy Fairtrade products if they became available, so they ran a survey, which I conducted on Garstang High Street on behalf of GOG. A total of 200 people were surveyed in the four months from July to October 1992. Our results correlated perfectly with the national survey, showing that 81% of people would buy products that were identified as giving a better deal to Third World producers if they became available. In Garstang the figure was 82%.

The stage was set for the launch of the FAIRTRADE mark and the formation of the Fairtrade Foundation as the body responsible for licensing, monitoring and promoting awareness of the certification label in the UK. These were very exciting times. There was nothing new about the concept of fair trade in Britain; fair trade handicrafts, coffee, chocolate and other items had been sold in alternative specialised shops like the Mustard Seed in Garstang and through outlets such as Traidcraft and Oxfam since the late 1950s. However, now there was an independent certification label, which meant that fair trade, or Fairtrade products as these new labelled products were called, could be sold anywhere. Fairtrade could enter the mainstream. Perhaps eventually it could even become the norm rather than the alternative? An independent certification label was essential if this was to happen.

There was no need for a FAIRTRADE mark on products in an Oxfam shop or other alternative outlet. You could trust the ethical sourcing of the product because that was the whole purpose behind the people running it, but when you bought an 'ethical' product in a supermarket, could you trust the manufacturer when *they* told you it was ethical? Probably not, unless it had an independent label that verified their claim.

In my view, this was the problem with some products that claimed to help protect the environment. Green issues were originally only supported by the 'beard and sandal' brigade and environmentally friendly products were only sold in alternative shops. When the movement became popular, any company could dress a product up in nice green wrapping with pictures of squirrels and trees on it and claim it was saving the planet. In those early days, there was no independent label to look out for. The fair trade movement, however, would not repeat that mistake.

GOG was an Oxfam campaigns group that campaigned on many development issues such as Third World debt, increasing aid and preventing conflict through the control of small arms sales. However, as the group grew larger, promoting Fairtrade became a campaign that we just kept coming back to again and again throughout the 1990s.

Fairtrade was far easier to understand than the other, more complex, issues. It was simply about giving people a 'fair day's pay for a fair day's work'. This was a message very close to the hearts of people in the Northwest of England, where not so long ago people had sacrificed their lives fighting for the same rights for British workers. Perhaps more importantly, once people understood the Fairtrade message, they knew what they could do about it. They were not being asked to sign a petition or go on a march or even give a donation. They only had to

Garstang Oxfam campaigners dressed as Fairtrade products.

switch their brand of tea, coffee or chocolate. What could be simpler? Indeed, what action could be more enjoyable?

Despite these two strengths, our campaign was a struggle and there were two main obstacles to overcome. Earlier 'campaign coffee' and fair trade chocolate had left a lot to be desired where the taste and even the texture were concerned. I had drunk the Nicaraguan Solidarity coffee as a student, which may have been one of the reasons why my room was so rarely one of those full of coffee-drinking students and I may have unknowingly lost quite a few friends because of it. If that was not bad enough, fair trade also had the reputation of having to pay more for the poorer quality.

The way I saw it, with the advent of Cafedirect, things had changed. I was convinced that the taste would be acceptable to most coffee-drinking palates and their dislike for fair trade was only because of its past reputation. Pepsi Cola had run an advertising campaign called the Pepsi Challenge, where people were asked to blind taste Pepsi Cola alongside its more popular rival, Coca Cola, the idea being that when people were not aware of what they were drinking, they would prefer the Pepsi taste. Based on this concept, I devised the Cafedirect Challenge.

I set up a stall, usually outside supermarkets and shops but once at an indoor event in Preston, and asked people to blind taste Cafedirect instant coffee alongside Brand X. The unknown brand changed throughout the tastings but was always of a comparable price to Cafedirect and looked similar in colour and texture. People were asked to make their own drink, adding milk and sugar to their own taste so the two coffees could be compared equally.

Six tastings were carried out from July 1995 until May 1997 and the total sample size, like the previously conducted Oxfam survey, was 200 people. I was expecting, and hoped, for an approximate 50% split in preference, because I believed there was little difference in taste and, generally, people's dislike for fair trade coffee was all in the mind. To my pleasant surprise, I found that 49% of people preferred the Cafedirect coffee and 20% had no preference at all. I was later informed by the staff at Cafedirect that this was the first reported taste trial for the coffee ever performed in the UK.

We had exploded the myths against Fairtrade so now we just needed to provide a good, positive reason to make the switch. That should, in theory, have been easy: it tasted as good, didn't cost any extra and it had the advantage of helping people in developing countries escape poverty. This was a message to take to the churches; if they didn't use Fairtrade products, what chance did we have of convincing anyone else?

Using our own funds, we decided to donate a large catering pack of Cafedirect instant coffee to each of the five churches in Garstang. "You should not leave out the Quaker Meeting House," Jane informed me. I knew nothing about Quakers; in fact, I thought they were something confined to our history books, but we wanted to treat everybody equally and fairly, so we bought six catering packs and included the Quaker Meeting.

Both Jane and I went to the Quaker Open Day on the outskirts of Garstang at what was then the Calder Bridge Meeting; Jane had an interest in the Meeting House from a local history perspective and I had the job of presenting the Fairtrade coffee. Quakers don't have a hierarchical priesthood, so I presented the Cafedirect catering pack to Rachel Rogers, the clerk of the Meeting. Rachel was to become a strong supporter and a major player in Garstang's declaration as a Fairtrade Town four years later. "You're knocking on an open door," was Rachel's response to my gift, but since they were not already using Fairtrade tea and coffee it was obvious to me that the door may have been open, but someone still had to go through it.

None-the-less, the reception was warm and the more I learnt about Quakers the more I felt at home. This was a place that was not trying to 'convert me'. My views and admiration and respect for the non-Christian Mahatma Ghandi were accepted here without question. I decided to attend the following Quaker Meeting. I had gone to the Open Day to introduce Fairtrade to the Quakers and in the process had found my spiritual home.

I was also given the task of presenting the Cafedirect coffee to the Methodist church. This should have been a done deal; after all, the Reverend Peter Haywood had set up the Mustard Seed and had been my inspiration in starting up the Garstang Oxfam campaign. You can imagine my surprise, therefore, when he told me that the church was not yet using Fairtrade products, but he did promise that they would do so from that day on and, indeed, they have done so ever since.

Only three out of the six faith groups that were presented with the coffee made a commitment to switch to Fairtrade. We were disappointed, but now realised what a difficult task this was going to be. We decided to persevere none-the-less.

On the positive side, three faith groups in Garstang were now using Fairtrade coffee as a consequence of our campaign, so we went on to our next target. We wrote to Garstang Town Council asking if they would agree to use Fairtrade tea and coffee at their meetings. Their response was that they never drank enough tea and coffee at meetings to make any switch to Fairtrade worthwhile. Clearly, they were missing the point. This was a matter of principle that should be backed by action, no matter how small or how easy that action may be.

We also tried to get the local press interested and one Christmas donated a small hamper of Fairtrade goodies (again using our own funds) with the message that this was a gift from the South to the North at Christmas time. The idea was to emphasise the truth that we in the rich North take more money from the poor South than we give in aid. We didn't even get a mention in the paper that week. Instead, on the front page was a story about a duck that had a plastic beer can holder stuck around its neck.

Moreover, our Oxfam group, despite having grown in membership, was now facing a crisis and needed new blood urgently. We called in Oxfam's Campaigns Officer for an emergency meeting and developed a strategy aimed at recruiting new members. We were successful, but in one of those strange ironies none of the recruits came as a direct consequence of our new strategy.

GOG was active and healthy in number and was now meeting in the Royal Oak Pub at the end of Garstang High Street. The Royal Oak was one of the first places in Garstang to sell Fairtrade coffee, but for reasons we never quite understood they later reversed the decision. When it became difficult to compete with the regular jazz nights, we eventually moved down the road to the Crown Hotel, where we were given a quiet back room to hold our meetings.

Before making the move, however, in October 1998 we were honoured by a visit to the Royal Oak by David Bryer, the then director of Oxfam. As well as David and the Northwest campaigns officer, we had no fewer than nine GOG members attending this meeting.

Despite all our hard work in those early days, as the Millennium approached we had little to show for all our time and effort. What perhaps we did not realise at the time was that we had laid strong foundations for what was to come. With the turn of the new Millennium, our efforts were to be more than rewarded as Garstang became a world icon as the world's first Fairtrade Town.

CHAPTER 7

The Lord God Made Us All

Throughout the 1990s I still worked full time as a self-employed locum vet, although now I was permanently stationed in Garstang and went to and from the veterinary surgeries each day. At one point, I was travelling to five different local vets in Garstang, Longridge, Preston, Blackburn and Blackpool every week. On picking up the phone it took me some time to remember where I was working that day before stating the name of the surgery.

As I became more involved with Oxfam campaigning work, I became more disillusioned with my career as a vet. Vetting should be a vocation, but for me it was slowly becoming just a means of paying the bills.

The more I learned from Oxfam, the harder I found life in our rich and privileged world. I still took part in the Oxfam 24 hour fast each year and on two occasions extended it to three days in order to try to understand what hunger really felt like. The first time I did the fast, in my final year at university, it made me realise that very few people in countries like ours ever went 24 hours without food, whereas in developing countries this was a common occurrence. I recall several times when my advice to starve a pet for 24 hours when treating a dog with dietary diarrhoea was greeted with looks of horror and dismay. Once, I was even called a "murderer" by a client when speaking to the nurse after a consultation and, when you consider it is normal for a dog to eat just once a day, I was only asking that their pet should miss dinner.

As a locum I had worked for many different vets, some in deprived areas and others surrounded by affluence. I therefore understood when a client rejected vaccinating their pet due to the price, although obviously it was my duty to recommend it on health grounds. But I found it difficult to accept the logic of one client who did not want their puppy vaccinating against the killer Parvovirus because "God did not intend it." Did God intend them to have a pet in the first place or, indeed, drive around in their large four wheel drive car?

When I thought of the many children dying each day due to diarrhoea, dehydration, starvation and disease, all for the want of a simple sachet of salt or a relatively cheap vaccine, I just wanted to scream. But, if only to keep me sane, I tried to understand and, when possible, see the funny side.

Let me take you through an imaginary but very possible scenario: a worried owner carries a dog into the consulting room because it reportedly has collapsed and can't walk.

Worried owner: "He's in a terrible state, he can't walk, there's horrible stuff coming out at both ends and he's not eaten for a week."

Me: "So he has diarrhoea; is there any blood in it?"

Worried owner: "Well, I wouldn't say it was diarrhoea; just a bit soft but no blood in it."

Me: "When did he last eat?"

Worried owner: "He had a couple of biscuits this morning, but he isn't keeping anything down."

Me: "So how often is he vomiting?"

Worried owner: "Oh, he isn't being sick!"

On completing the consultation, it turns out the dog is eating, is not vomiting, has no diarrhoea and when you put him on the floor runs out of the surgery wagging his tail behind him.

Less worried owner: "Oh, that's marvellous, thank you. He certainly wasn't like that when he went for a sleep in the kitchen corner."

It seems all the dog wanted was to sleep and get some peace and quiet, but instead it was dragged off to the vets. It is clear in this example to see there was nothing wrong with the dog, but one must be careful not to be caught out. For every hundred false alarms like this, there may be one hiding a mysterious, covert illness, making the thorough examination absolutely essential.

Through all my years at university I always said that I would stick to my Yorkshire roots and tell it as it is, but out there in the real world I was finding this difficult. If you try to tell the truth, and in cases like this one do not give any form of treatment, not only will the client often be reluctant to pay for your time and consultation, but at worst may take their custom elsewhere and may even write a letter of complaint to the Royal College as part of the bargain.

I understand that many owners really love their pets, often as much as if they were their own children, and when undergoing great stress it is clear how this type of communication breakdown can arise. Although my example is not factual, it is by no means an exaggeration and the more I came across incidents like this, the greater became my resolve to promote awareness of what was actually going on in the world; that is, quite simply, that every three seconds a small child dies unnecessarily.

Another matter of concern was the expectation for vets to make difficult decisions on behalf of pet owners. When deciding whether to elect for treatment or have an animal destroyed, for example, vets, like doctors, should not, in my view, play God. Of course, clients need professional guidance so they can make an informed choice. It is also the duty of the vet to protect the animal from any unnecessary suffering, so in some cases euthanasia may be the only humane option available, even if it means going against the wishes of the owner. This type of decision, however, is rarely black or white. As difficult as it may be, in most cases the final decision should rest with the owner, albeit following understanding and compassionate guidelines from the veterinary surgeon concerned.

In our modern times, almost anything can be cured if there is enough money available. There are some terminal cases where an animal may be in such pain that putting an end to that suffering is undoubtedly the best option. In most situations, however, the question is not whether there is a need to put the animal out of its misery but whether the owner has the available funds or is willing to spend it on their pet, and this judgement can only be made by the owner.

It is wrong for the vet to make assumptions. From my experience, I can recall many occasions when a judgement made on first appearances or past history would have led to the wrong conclusion. The owner needs to be fully informed as to what options are available, but this needs to be done with sensitivity. One cannot truthfully but harshly say: "Well, Fido could be cured if you could find the necessary £5,000 to do so." A fine balance must be found, and the vet needs to provide all the information required. This can take a considerable amount of time and that is not always easily available in a busy surgery.

As with human health care, people expect too much from our medical professionals and value the wrong things. Pet owners often enter the consulting room thinking that the vet will have an injection for whatever illness confronts them and this is all-too-often reinforced by a level of arrogance on behalf of the practitioner. Humility is a virtue too often lacking in the medical professions. I often remind myself of something that one of the older, more experienced lecturers told us during my time at Liverpool University: "You should always bear in mind that 50% of animals will get better without your treatment and 50% of the remainder will get better despite your treatment." Yet it is so often the treatment, the contents of the syringe or the 'magic pill', that people value instead of the expert advice. I'll never forget the words of one client who, after I'd spent a considerable amount of time giving nutritional advice and rightly avoiding reaching for the syringe or the pill box for a case of dietary diarrhoea, remarked that, "I don't come to the vets to be told how to feed my dog."

Sometimes there may be nothing wrong with the patient, any problem being incorrectly perceived by the owner. Having given a thorough clinical examination this then needs to be explained. Again, I recall the words of a wise lecturer: "A problem is only a problem when it causes a problem," but this may not be what the owner wishes to hear and, even if they do accept your explanation, they surely will not wish to pay for the examination and advice when no treatment has been given.

Even though the treatment may be valued it is also true that clients often underestimate the cost of that treatment. In the veterinary field the cost of surgery is substantially less than in human healthcare; sterilisation procedures do not have to be so rigorous, there is rarely a specialised anaesthetist and far fewer nursing assistants. Yet on presenting the bill for surgery clients are all too often shocked at the level of cost. I blame this on our excellent National Health Service, which is greatly undervalued primarily because it is free. Generally, people don't appreciate the cost involved in treating even a minor ailment such as a tendon strain and how just a small fraction of this cost could save the life of a child in a much poorer country. The situation could be substantially improved if patients were presented with the actual cost of their treatment when discharged from hospital. They would, of course, not be expected to pay for it, but this at least may make people more appreciative of our healthcare system and the relatively small cost of saving the lives of the world's poorest people.

Despite all my good intentions, as my veterinary career progressed I was finding it harder and harder to hide my frustrations and feel understood. Even when dispensing drugs, I would take a considerable amount of time to explain the dosage and ensure that a follow-up consultation was always timed to coincide with the point the treatment needed reviewing. But simple instructions such as "give one tablet twice a day" were so easily misinterpreted as "give two tablets once a day", even when a full explanation was given and clear directions were written on the bottle.

Feeling misunderstood was not anything new to me, but something I'd experienced throughout the whole of my life. I have always felt isolated, as if I am on a completely different planet to everyone else, viewing the world so differently.

This led to great insecurity on my part, but just because I didn't fit in and was in the minority did not make my views and opinions any less worthy than anyone else's. Perhaps it was even possible that on some issues I might have been right while the majority was wrong? I was 36 years old before I found my spiritual home with the Quakers and that helped strengthen this belief, although even with Quakers I often felt different to them, and by no means was I a typical Quaker - if there was such a thing.

* * *

There is no clear definition of what makes a Quaker; therefore, it can be difficult for a Quaker to speak about what they do or do not believe. I will endeavour to speak about what Quaker beliefs mean for me personally, but I do want to emphasise that this may be very different to the views of another Quaker, even within the same Meeting.

After presenting the Fairtrade coffee at the Quaker Open Day on the outskirts of Garstang, I had become attracted to the Quaker faith and decided to attend their next Meeting. I soon learned that many of the things I'd admired and respected throughout history had their roots with Quakers; the abolition of the British Atlantic slave trade, the formation and development of Oxfam and even Gandhi's visit to the cotton mills of Lancashire. I later discovered it was the Quaker millowner, Corder Catchpool, who invited and encouraged Gandhi to visit Darwen in 1931. Despite the detrimental effects of India's cotton boycott, the mill workers greeted him with great affection even when they were out of work. They understood it was not the Indian people but greedy and irresponsible mill owners who were to blame for their situation.

Quakers, or the Religious Society of Friends as they are correctly known, was a faith that appealed to me. "But Quakers don't drink, do they?" I worriedly asked my wife. I had a lot to learn. My very poor understanding of Quakers at that time was that they wore strange clothes, like the smiling man on the front of the porridge oats packet, and categorically did not drink anything remotely alcoholic. I was pleased to learn, however, that Quakers did not have hard and fast rules to live by and, unlike some religions, they *did* move with the times.

Quakers do use the Bible and are rooted in Christianity, but the scriptures can be, and are, so often misinterpreted. Whether it be the Bible or the Quran, it is not enough to read the words and take their literal meaning. Instead, I believe they should be interpreted in the light of the Spirit. By practising silent worship, Quakers wait for the word of God to come to them and, if they feel moved to do so, will give spoken ministry. There is no hierarchical clergy; George Fox, who founded the Quakers, believed that everyone was equal in the eyes of God and therefore God spoke to us all on equal terms. There was no need for a middleman to communicate the message. The only condition was that one had to be prepared to listen, hence the silent worship.

As well as the Bible, Quakers refer to a book called 'Quaker Faith and Practice', which includes the 'Advices and Queries'. Like the scriptures, these words should not be taken as rules but as words of guidance. The postscript included in the introduction of 'Advices and Queries' explains this in the eloquent way that only Quakers can: "Dearly beloved Friends, these things we do not lay upon you as a rule or form to walk by, but that all, with the measure of light which is pure and holy, may be guided; and so in the light walking and abiding, these may be fulfilled in the Spirit, not from the letter, for the letter killeth, but the Spirit giveth life."

It could be said that it is easy to follow a faith that has no rules, but I would beg to differ. Nobody needs rules to know they have done something morally wrong and, in any case, rules are so easily broken. Take the Sixth Commandment, for example; how often is the rule "Thou Shalt Not Kill" disobeyed and supposedly justified by faiths that claim to follow the leadings of the Old Testament? How much clearer can the words "Thou Shalt Not Kill" be?

The scriptures say "Ask and it will be given." Obviously, this does not refer to material desires, but perhaps it does mean if one asks for guidance that it will always be provided. Accepting guidance, however, does involve first listening to the message and then, most importantly, obeying it, even if it is not what one wants to hear. To disobey that guidance is, in my view, the true meaning of what constitutes a sin. No other person can tell you this, only the receiver of the message will know what it entails and if it has been conveniently ignored.

As with the Ten Commandments, these messages are clear and simple, yet so often they appear to be either misinterpreted or disregarded. For example, President George Bush claimed that he was told by God to invade Iraq, but how could that be? Is this a case of misunderstanding or just a convenient lie? Only he can know the truth.

In my early campaigning days, I wrote to my MP about increasing the aid budget. "Charity begins at home," was the response, followed by a reference to the parable of the Good Samaritan. Surely the message within the parable was that the converse was true. The Samaritans were a foreign race, if anything, disliked by the Jews and yet it was a

Samaritan that chose to offer charity when the priest and the Hebrew Levite passed by.

From an early age I never understood how there could be so many different religions in the world with each one being so certain that only they were the true faith, that only they worship the one and only God. They can't all be right, or can they?

I do not think that God is too concerned with the detail that religions offer. It is the 'detail' that usually lies at the root of conflict between religions and keeps them apart. For me, God's message, be it through Christ, Mohamed, Buddha or whoever, is simple: 'Love thy neighbour as you would love thy self.' If all religions focused on this one simple, central message that is common to them all, then perhaps we could all come together, whatever our beliefs.

'God works in mysterious ways' as they say and perhaps it is possible that when it comes to the 'details' that God has a different plan and different messages for us all, and does not care what religious banner we march under. The 'detail' is perhaps unnecessary trivia. An Oxfam friend once described life as a mountain, on which we are all walking to the peak. We may take different paths to the top of the mountain and occasionally the paths may cross. When they do, we meet, we talk and may even walk together for a while, but eventually we can all reach our destination in different ways. We can accept each other's beliefs and even learn from them. Why on earth should we fight each other or attempt to convert everybody to believe in the same thing? Why do we all have to take the same path?

There are a total of 42 Advices and Queries but the one that speaks the loudest to me is number 17, which reads: "Do you respect that of God in everyone though it may be expressed in unfamiliar ways or be difficult to discern? Each of us has a particular experience of God and each must find the way to be true to it. When words are strange or disturbing to you, try to sense where they come from and what has nourished the lives of others. Listen patiently and seek the truth which other people's opinions may contain for you. Avoid hurtful criticism and provocative language. Do not allow the strength of your convictions to betray you into making statements or allegations that are unfair or untrue. Think it possible that you may be mistaken."

I particularly like the last line: "Think it possible that you may be mistaken." I am a scientist. I question everything, but it is God that made me that way. For me, there is no conflict between God and science. It was Albert Einstein who asked if God had ever intended him to discover all the things that he did. The more one explores science, whether it be at a microscopic or universal level, the more one discovers the true beauty and wonder of God.

As a university student I once attended a 'born again' Christian meeting. I don't know what made me go; perhaps I had nothing better to do that evening or I just felt like a bit of constructive debate. If I thought I was going to get an open discussion, however, I was wrong. I was alone in a room full of people who were all well and truly set in their ways. It struck me how certain they were. I could never be that certain about something for which there was no concrete evidence. They clearly pitied me and offered to pray for my soul. But why was it so wrong to doubt? It was not my fault that God made me question everything. I pointed out that doubting Thomas had to put his finger through the holes in Christ's hands before he believed and he had the living, resurrected body of Jesus standing there before him. There was hope for him so surely that demonstrated that there was hope for me, no matter how often I doubted. If there was a God, then he (or she) would one day make it known to me. I was not doing anything wrong by just waiting.

This meeting took place early in 1981, the same year that I spent the summer hitching across Europe. While in Zurich, I had a strange experience. Many would call it a spiritual experience, but of course I wasn't so sure. It was no extraordinary setting. We were just about to eat our lunch on a bench in the city centre when suddenly, in broad daylight, a series of images went through my head. They were all of moments in my life for which I felt regret, shame and sorrow. One image that I remember so well was of shopping in Liverpool with my mum. She had bad arthritis and on that day was having great difficulty in walking. I must have been about twelve or thirteen years old and very impatiently I kept telling my mum to walk faster. The images were over in a matter of seconds and I was left with a deep sense of remorse. Is this what is meant by repentance?

My first taste of religion was with the Mormons, or the Church of Latter Day Saints as it is correctly known. I was baptised as a Mormon when a teenager. My mother had invited some Elders into our home and joined up. Everyone in the family, apart from my older brother Graham and my father, followed. My sister Lynda and her children are still members, but the rest of us strayed away.

Mormons practice baptism by full immersion and I clearly remember having a warm feeling deep inside following my baptism. The Elders told me it was due to the Holy Spirit that had now entered my body, but I wondered, was this not the warm feeling one always felt once dressed following a swim? Even then I had my doubts.

Before being baptised I had to spend some time with the Elders and demonstrate to them that I had fully repented. At that age there was no way that I could fully understand what repentance meant. With hindsight, I don't think that this was something I could learn no matter how many hours I spent with the Elders. It took my experience in Zurich several years later to understand the meaning of repentance and even later still, as a Quaker, to understand contrition.

The concept of heaven and hell was something that I struggled to accept. How could punishment follow judgement from an all- forgiving God? A close friend had once told me that their idea of heaven was at the end of one's life being able to look back on it with satisfaction, in the knowledge that you had lived it well. During an interview just before his tragic death from skin cancer, the comedy actor Paul Eddington was asked how he wanted to be remembered. He referred back to his Quaker schooling and answered that he hoped he would be thought of as someone who went through life without doing any harm.

A feeling of strong uneasiness swept through my body whenever I felt moved to give ministry in a Quaker Meeting for worship. It was like a volcano deep inside that could not be relieved until I spoke. That was how I felt when I suddenly understood how it was possible to have 'punishment' following forgiveness. The answer came to me during a Meeting when I remembered the pain of remorse that I had felt following my experience in Zurich. What made it painful was the sense that despite my misdeeds I was forgiven. On facing an all-loving, all-forgiving God, the level of contrition and thus pain that one felt would be directly proportional to the number of misdeeds committed. The pain in fact would be self-inflicted, as when faced with the overwhelming supreme love of God only the perpetrator would know the true level of their crimes.

After all those years of waiting, God had finally come to me through Quakers; or was it I that I had gone to God? I gave my first Ministry at only my second Quaker Meeting. I was still unsure as to what was acceptable or not acceptable in Meeting, but all the same I felt moved to tell the following joke.

A god-fearing man was sitting in his home when heavy rain started to fall. As he leaned out of his ground-floor window, a small boat went past and offered to take him to safety. "It is going to flood. Climb aboard," said the boatman. "It is okay, save your place for someone else. I am a good man. God will save me." The rain continued and the man went upstairs and again leaned out of the window to see a bigger boat go past. Again came the offer to take the man to safety away from the flood, and again the man refused, claiming that God would save him. The waters continued to rise, and the man was forced onto the roof of the house. A passing helicopter dropped a line down to the man. "Grab hold of the rope," shouted the pilot. "This is your last chance. Soon the flood will rise above your house." "God will save me," came the reply and the helicopter flew away. Sure enough, the waters rose above the house and the man drowned.

At the gates of heaven the man said to Saint Peter, "All my life I have been a good man and have done everything that God has asked of me. Why was I not saved?" Saint Peter replied, "Well, we sent two boats and a helicopter, what more do you want?"

All my life I had been waiting for God to come to me and now that time had come it was important that I should recognise it and accept it. Although I still had my occasional doubts (how could I not?) God was now there for me and I was able to find that guidance whenever I needed it. A year later I became a member of the Religious Society of Friends.

For the first time in my life I was a member of a faith group and willingly and regularly attended their Meetings. Before that, I used to jokingly say that Oxfam was my religion. Oxfam did provide me with a sense of morality and when I attended the three-day-long Oxfam Assemblies, I felt the same warmth, love and friendship that I now also get from a Quaker Meeting. Undoubtedly, through Oxfam, I was listening to God's message and doing God's work and since I believe that is what is of importance to God, then perhaps it was true to say that Oxfam was my religion in those post-student years up to finding the Quakers in 1996. I was just not fully aware of it at the time.

I am reluctant to refer to Quakers as my religion because I do not think of it as a religion in the way that most people perceive a religion to be. On learning that I had become a Quaker, my old school friends seemed to think that I would have less to do with them now that I'd "found God." Dave had another friend that he'd "lost to Jesus" and thought I was going the same way. At our next reunion I told them, "All I believe is that there is something out there, or within us, that is superior to everyone and everything and this power or force can guide us for good." "I can accept that," Andy replied. "Well, I call it God, what do you call it?" was my response.

I detest the hypocrisy that I see far too often amongst people for whom God is just for Sundays and Christmases. It is far better to have no belief at all, in my view, than to pray in Church on a Sunday, but act immorally for the rest of the week. Most Quakers that I know do as they say throughout the week and all year long; "God is for life not just for Christmas."

Quakers do not just tolerate other beliefs and faiths but accept them. Everyone is welcome into a Quaker Meeting regardless of their own beliefs, without the fear that attempts will be made to convert them. I have taken my Ghanaian Christian and Muslim friends to Quaker Meetings in the past and have heard of some people combining their religion with Quakers and calling themselves a Catholic or Methodist Quaker, for example.

Gandhi attended a Quaker Meeting in Yorkshire following his visit to the cotton mills in the neighbouring county across the Pennines. He reportedly said it was one of the most spiritual experiences in his life. It is a great irony that the man I consider to have lived the words of Christ better than anyone was himself not a Christian; perhaps this is evidence that God has a sense of humour?

Gandhi asked, "Why should I be denied Jesus's teaching just because I do not believe that he was the son of God?" I was once told that Gandhi would be condemned to hell just because he held this belief, but there would be none of this nonsense with Quakers. One of the many things that endeared me to Quakers was that Gandhi was admired and respected for the devout man that he was and not condemned for his beliefs.

Quakers believe there is "that of God in everyone". It was this acceptance of everyone and that all were equal regardless of race, colour, creed, wealth, power or, most importantly, their belief that made me feel at home with Quakers.

After watching Manchester United win their historic treble in 1999, I gave ministry at a Meeting on the following Sunday. I spoke about the joy I felt while being amongst swearing, drinking fans during the Champions League final, yet a part of me felt that this was not the way a Quaker should behave. My ministry was followed by another who spoke about the importance of living life amongst all types of people. It was not good to live in a cocoon, disconnected from the real world. Quakers are actively encouraged to be a part of it, to travel while living a life of truth, integrity and practising what one believes.

The final word from George Fox in 'Advices and Queries' again puts this in a way that only 'Quaker Speak' can: "Be patterns, be examples in all countries, places, islands, nations, wherever you come, that your carriage and life may preach among all sorts of people, and to them; then you will come to walk cheerfully over the world, answering that of God in every one."

Becoming a Quaker confirmed my beliefs and strengthened my resolve to see an end to poverty as we know it, once and for all. Although I had no wish to convert people to my faith, I did want them to follow a journey similar to the one I had taken, to be made aware that poverty is the greatest injustice in the world today and that its eradication is possible. So, when the opportunity came for me to give up some of my days working as a vet in order to become the Fairtrade Towns coordinator for the Fairtrade Foundation, I naturally jumped at the chance.

CHAPTER 8

The Difficult Birth in Garstang

The new Millennium had dawned, the first Fairtrade bananas in the UK were on sale in the Co-op and Fairtrade Fortnight 2000 was approaching. Following the 'Give it up for Ghana' theme for the 1999 Oxfam Fast, we had started to focus our campaign on Fairtrade chocolate. One morning while working at the local vets in Garstang all these things came together, as they so often do when new creations are born.

Just before leaving for work I had received an invitation to enter the 'Stir it up' competition from Cafedirect. The group that created the greatest awareness for Fairtrade during Fairtrade Fortnight would win the competition and be invited to have lunch in the House of Commons with George Foulkes, the then Under Secretary of State for the Department for International Development (DfID). I must confess it was not the prize that attracted me, but our campaign needed the boost and recognition that winning this competition would provide.

I was thinking of doing something around bananas and chocolate and, low and behold, when I arrived at work one of the nurses handed me a recipe for a banana and chocolate pancake. Shrove Tuesday that year would lie within Fairtrade Fortnight, so I decided to invite all the people we were failing to reach in the community (which was just about everyone) to enjoy a Fairtrade banana and chocolate pancake.

The owner of 'The Jacobite' restaurant on Garstang High Street was already using Fairtrade products and agreed to host the event. The restaurant has had several changes of ownership since then and is now called 'Pipers', but Fairtrade hot drinks, wine, sugar and other ingredients are still used on the premises. Our offering soon extended from a pancake to a three-course meal, with the banana and chocolate pancake as the Fairtrade 'piece de resistance'. At that time, it was not possible to have a three-course meal made up entirely of Fairtrade products, so local produce would be used where Fairtrade products could not; right from the start, we wanted to show empathy and support for local farmers who also suffered from not getting a fair price for their produce. The issue was the same and local farmers did suffer, albeit to a far lesser degree than their counterparts in poorer nations.

It was important to have the backing and approval from the other GOG members. I was willing and able to do all the necessary organisation for the event, but I needed other Fairtrade supporters to attend on the night and the whole thing would carry far more weight if it could be part of a GOG campaign. Everyone agreed, so the invitations were sent out to the heads of schools, churches, youth groups, other community organisations, the Chamber of Trade and specific businesses and town councillors, including the mayor. The whole purpose of the event was to persuade all these people to switch to selling and/or using Fairtrade products on their premises.

Even though the meal was not to be a fundraiser, we attracted a great deal of support from local farmers and businesses. The beef for the main course was donated by a local farmer, as were the mushrooms and many other ingredients. The local florists even donated several centre pieces for the tables. As it happened, this was a good thing as we had very little funding and the owner of the restaurant had only agreed to cook the meal and allow us the use of his premises. It would have been too much to expect him to also contribute to the cost of the food. It was crucial that we did not charge the guests, not just to ensure a good turnout, but primarily to help persuade the guests to take the all-important action that we wanted. We did not even have collection boxes at the event or allow donations. Once we had gained the support of the guests, we did not want them to be able to buy off that support by giving a donation. Instead, we asked them to sign a pledge stating that they would sell Fairtrade products if they could and/or use Fairtrade products on the premises, whether it be when organising events or simply having an afternoon tea break.

Several days before the meal, an idea came to me in the middle of the night (the best ideas always seem to come during the night or while taking a shower). In selecting our guests, we had invited a cross-section from the whole community. If the event was a success and we persuaded everyone attending to switch to Fairtrade, we would in fact have created a Fairtrade community or, indeed, a Fairtrade Town. I knew I had to get out of bed and write the idea down immediately or else there was a danger the idea would be lost by morning.

The meal was a success and by the end of the evening we had pledge forms signed by representatives from all four of Garstang's schools, all six faith groups, many businesses and we had attracted interest from the town's mayor. "But does being a Fairtrade Town mean that we could not sell Nescafe in any of the shops?" the mayor asked. Since nobody had any idea exactly what a Fairtrade Town meant at this time, I answered by suggesting that a Fairtrade Town was not about boycotting 'unfavourable' items but about giving people the choice to be able to buy Fairtrade items if they so wished. The mayor invited me to speak at the next council public meeting and warned me that they were usually poorly attended, with only one or two members of the public present. Although nervous of public speaking, I have always considered it worthwhile to talk to any number of people, no matter how few, and still take that view today, so I accepted his offer.

It was the evening of Thursday 27th April 2000 and I had rushed back from working at a veterinary surgery in Blackpool to speak at the meeting held at the United Reformed Church Hall in Garstang. I walked into a room full of between 30 and 40 people. This was going to be a council meeting with a difference.

I spoke for a few minutes, finishing with the proposal that Garstang become the first Fairtrade Town. There was time for questions before a refreshment break using Fairtrade tea and coffee that the mayor had personally supplied. At that point, a fellow Quaker said, "It was all well and good to listen to Bruce speaking about becoming a Fairtrade Town, but what are the council going to do about it?" "We shall take this away and discuss it at our next meeting," was the mayor's reply.

The clerk then intervened to say that it was possible to discuss it now, so the mayor asked the councillors what they thought about the idea. His question was met with silence and heads turned to the floor. The clerk intervened again and, although none of us were aware of it at the time, he came out with a statement that would eventually lead to the creation of the mass movement of people that now lies behind the name of Fairtrade or Fair Trade Towns. He explained that this was a public meeting and councillors did not even have to be present, but it was the members of the public that had the power of the vote. They could use the meeting to vote councillors out of office if they chose to do so. At this point the councillors raised their heads and they appeared to pay far more attention. The clerk went further to state, "If the members of the public wish to make Garstang a Fairtrade Town then again they can vote to do so." Immediately a lady near the back row raised her hand and proposed that Garstang became a Fairtrade Town. I later discovered this lady to be the calligrapher Dorothy Bicknell. Her Quaker friend, Rachel Rogers, seconded the proposal and it was put to the vote. The vote was virtually unanimous, with just one councillor abstaining. The mayor and I left the hall that evening wondering just what we had done.

The day after, I called the Fairtrade Foundation to tell them what had happened. "Bloody hell, what gives you the right to do that?" was the rather surprising response from their campaigns officer. I later understood the reason for the abrupt retort. Our campaign had always been about promoting Fairtrade and the FAIRTRADE mark. When we declared ourselves a 'Fairtrade Town', therefore, it would be written 'Fairtrade': as one word with a capital 'F'. The fact of the matter was, however, that we had no right to use the word 'Fairtrade', as this belonged to the international Fairtrade Labelling Organisation (FLO) of which the Fairtrade Foundation is the UK representative.

Strangely enough, we did not win the 'Stir it up' competition and did not have lunch with George Foulkes in the House of Commons, but George Foulkes decided to come to us instead. He congratulated us and had a Fairtrade and local produce breakfast at the 'Coffee Pot' café in Garstang, which was far more convenient from our point of view. Our declaration had attracted the attention of the media, starting with coverage on North West BBC news. That was when George Foulkes spoke those immortal words "The beacon that has started in Garstang can spread like wildfire through the whole country and beyond."

It was the small Scottish town of Strathaven that was the very first place to show any desire to copy the Garstang model. Just weeks after our self-declaration, I received a phone call from Linda Fabiani, the member of the Scottish Parliament for Strathaven. She was calling from her Edinburgh office and in a most bizarre and stereotypical fashion, I could hear bagpipes playing from outside her window. Strathaven was to become Scotland's first Fairtrade Town, declaring jointly with Aberfeldy in November 2002.

I began to realise that we had started something special. I dared to believe that one day even Edinburgh would become a Fairtrade City, but I never dreamt that Greater London, with a population of seven million people, let alone other international cities such as Paris, Rome, Brussels, Copenhagen, San Francisco and Seoul would all one day follow Garstang's lead.

As the word spread, recognition of our achievement grew. Our MP, Hilton Dawson, passed an Early Day Motion[1] in Parliament congratulating the community, with a specific mention given to the Garstang Oxfam Group. He also told us that when he announced he was returning to Garstang following a speech he gave in London, someone in the audience asked if that was the Garstang known for being the world's first Fairtrade Town.

One evening in the summer, my stepson Tom and I created the Garstang Oxfam Group website, which is now the Garstang Fairtrade website[2]. As well as telling the story of how we became a Fairtrade Town, it also provided information about the Fairtrade campaign and our link with New Koforidua in Ghana. The IT input in those early days was provided by Peter Fenton, the son of Marlene and John, two of our strongest Oxfam supporters. Tom was a great help with the design,

---

1 Early Day Motion No. 694 passed on 10th May 2000.
2 www.garstangfairtrade.org.uk

while I provided the content. We stayed up until the early hours of the morning to ensure there was enough information for the site to go live. I remember getting so excited when we reached our first 100 hits. I could never have imagined how popular or how important that site would become in those early years.

Tom was a tremendous support and has been ever since. He was thirteen in April that year and, unlike the character Kevin created by Harry Enfield, Tom underwent a reverse transformation on his teenage birthday. He changed from a young boy who seemed to care about very little ("What is the point?" was his usual negative response to any campaigning action) to a highly committed, compassionate teenager dedicated to changing the world. To this day I do not know what triggered the transformation but I am glad that it happened none the less.

We had attracted a great deal of interest, but being a Fairtrade Town still meant very little. Garstang had to be worthy of its new status, preferably with visible signs around the town. We had decided to have window stickers made that could be awarded and displayed by supporters who had signed the pledge. The green and white stickers carried the wording "We support Fairtrade and local produce". It had the FAIRTRADE Mark at the centre (at that time the mark consisted of an interlocking 'F', the word 'FAIRTRADE' and the strap-line 'Guarantees a better deal for third world producers') with the Oxfam logo and the 'hamburger style' Wyre Brunch Group logo at either side. We were aware that some people would question Oxfam's involvement in promoting local produce so, with their approval, we decided to include the Wyre Brunch Group in our campaign. This small group was the forerunner of the 'Made in Lancashire' movement and at this stage was little more than a diner's club that met regularly to enjoy meals made up of local produce. They did not have a logo, so we invented one just for the purpose of the sticker.

We needed to show that there was support on the High Street from more than just the handful of businesses who signed up to the pledge at the meal. So, in between consultations at the local vets, I approached almost every business in Garstang to ask if they would sign the pledge and display a window sticker. "We are a Fairtrade Town and will look pretty stupid if we have nothing to show for it," was my line of persuasion. It seemed to work, because out of over 100 businesses, 95% signed up to the pledge and the vast majority of them displayed a window sticker. I still have the original pledge forms.

It wasn't all plain sailing, however; I was astonished at just how unfriendly some of the store owners could be. I began to understand what it must feel like to be a salesperson, only promoting Fairtrade in Garstang was not my job, nor was I doing any of it for personal gain.

The other potential obstacle was the town council. I had never attended a regular council meeting before and I was soon to learn about the slow, grinding wheels of local bureaucracy. The council members were under the false impression that they had already shown their support for Fairtrade and for Garstang becoming a Fairtrade Town, but I pointed out that the decision made at the public meeting had been made by the community and not by the council itself. The council therefore ratified the decision at their meeting in May, but they now needed to pass a resolution declaring their support and back it with positive action: that was agreeing to use Fairtrade tea and coffee whenever hot drinks were served.

When GOG had previously written to the council requesting this action, we had been told that hot drinks were only served at meetings once a year, that being the annual public meeting. They had missed the point that this was a matter of principle. It was important that a written commitment was made; one that could not be easily overturned. The fact that hot drinks were rarely served at all made the action even easier to undertake, but the principle was just as strong.

In August, I attended another council meeting in the wedding room at the council offices close to my home and sat on the bench that constituted the public gallery. Again, normally these meetings were poorly attended, with often just the local press represented, but on this occasion the public gallery was at least full. Members of the public were allowed to ask questions at the start but had to remain silent once discussions were taking place. How can one ask questions before knowing what there was to question? I thought to myself. Indeed, this was a quandary that I was to experience again and again where council matters were concerned.

The debate seemed to go on forever, much of it futile. "Does being a Fairtrade Town mean we have to gild the mayor's chain with Fairtrade gold?" was one of the points raised. I was reminded of the bizarre committee meetings held on the TV sitcom *The Vicar of Dibley* starring Dawn French. If it wasn't so comical it would have been so frustrating. I couldn't understand it. They were only being asked to commit to using Fairtrade tea and coffee once a year at the public meeting. What could be simpler? Eventually, the all-important resolution was passed. It was resolved that, "The council be a Fair Trade council using Fair Trade goods and promoting Fair Trade products when reasonably practicable." Okay, not as strong as we would have liked and it certainly did not reflect the amount of effort that went into it, but it would suffice.

Only weeks later, in October, I was back in the wedding room again. This time it was to attend the debate on whether road signs should be erected declaring Garstang as the "World's First Fairtrade Town". There were to be four signs in total that would be attached below the Garstang Town boundary signs: two on the A6 Garstang bypass and one at either end of the town. Again, our request was simple. All we needed from the council was their approval and permission to erect the signs, but again it was not going to be that easy.

We approached the town council about the road signs shortly after the declaration was made and were told that we should take it up with Wyre Borough Council. They directed us to Lancashire County Council and their Highways Department, who had no objection to the placement of the signs providing the town council agreed. The request had gone full circle and landed back with the town council. When the resolution to support 'Fair Trade' was passed at the town council meeting in August, they also agreed in principle to erect the signs. The Co-op had kindly offered to pay for them and the designs and wording were in place. So, what was the problem?

There was a feeling of déjà vu as I sat through another long, futile council debate, again unable to say a word. This time I sat behind a supportive councillor and passed him comments written on pieces of paper to resolve each of their queries. I still had to sit in silence as they discussed whether 'Fairtrade' was two words or one. "I saw a shop in

Manchester the other day and the sign clearly said Fair Trade as two words", one councillor remarked. Apparently, we were only allowed to put four additional words below the Garstang sign, and some councillors thought we were trying to pull the wool over their eyes by using Fairtrade as one word in the wording 'World's first Fairtrade town'. This would make the sign acceptable, whereas the five words 'World's first Fair Trade town' would not. "It seemed once again common sense had fallen victim to red tape.

Eventually, permission was granted to erect the signs, but then we discovered that we were to be charged a fee to put them up. The cost of this relatively small task was going to be more than the cost of the signs themselves. We could not possibly ask the Co-op to pay for that as well and we had no funds of our own to speak of. The contractors who usually made the signs for the County Council stepped in to save the day. They offered to include the cost of erecting the signs as part of the manufacturing cost and the four road signs were finally on display in March 2001.

Despite the difficulties with the local authorities, I felt very proud of my hometown, especially when I passed the signs on my way back following a long day at the vets in Blackpool. Some people claimed the signs were useless because nobody knew what they meant. To some degree that was the point. Passers-by would see the words 'Fairtrade Town' and if they didn't know what it meant it would leave them with the thought. The next time they saw the word 'Fairtrade' or the FAIRTRADE mark it just might trigger something inside them. That was good marketing in my view, rather like the old cigarette adverts that you have to look at again and again before you discover what they are actually advertising. Just weeks later I learnt about a boy from Lancaster Grammar School whose story confirmed my theory. He had passed the sign on the A6 while on his way home to Lancaster and wanted to know what a Fairtrade Town was. This caused him to research Fairtrade Towns and write an essay about the subject at his school. My case rests.

The road signs led to even further publicity and some controversy as to whether we were the 'world's first'. This had occurred to me when we made the claim almost a year before, but despite all the international publicity and putting it on our new website no one had approached us to dispute the claim, so it looked like the title was ours to keep.

The *Garstang Courier* had printed a photograph of the road sign accompanied by Duncan Rees, the regional member services officer for the Co-op, Betty Whittam, the manager of the local Co-op store, and myself. This photograph was to be used to promote Fairtrade Towns again and again across the world. To my knowledge the *Garstang Courier* were rarely, if ever, credited.

In the same month that we saw the road signs erected we celebrated our first Fairtrade Town status with an event at Garstang High School. We were lucky to be joined by three VIP guests: Phil Wells, director of the Fairtrade Foundation, John Whitaker, deputy director for Oxfam and Kingsley Ofei-Nkansah, the deputy general secretary of the General Agricultural Workers Union of Ghana. I had been lobbying John persistently since our declaration to try and get Oxfam involved in taking the Fairtrade Towns initiative forward. Oxfam was a founder member

Bruce with Duncan and Betty at the Garstang road sign. Photo by *The Garstang Courier*.

of the Fairtrade Foundation and John was on the board. I nagged him at every opportunity, "If this is a bad idea tell me so and I'll go away and say no more, but if it's a good idea do something about it." What was not acceptable in my opinion was to be told that this was a great idea, but then nothing being done about it. I made that view known to as many people as possible.

The Co-op had shown a lot of interest in running Fairtrade Towns and they seemed willing and able to give it the financial backing that it deserved. I had said to John Whitaker, "If Nestle had an idea like this they would put thousands of pounds into it." "No, Bruce, they would invest millions," was his reply. But Fairtrade Towns had to be all-inclusive and if it was to be run by a commercial enterprise, no matter how ethical, it would be bound to exclude other rival businesses. Active interest from other mainstream supermarket chains would be difficult if Fairtrade Towns was run by the Co-op, for example.

We had full support from George Foulkes, and I used that contact to approach DfID for funding. Even though years later they were to provide valuable financial support for Fairtrade Towns, I had no success at this time. In fact, I was told that DfID could not fund something that did not directly contribute to the alleviation of poverty. This seemed a strange response, but I was in no position to argue.

There was no doubt about it; the Fairtrade Foundation was the first and perhaps only choice to oversee this new initiative. Back in 2001, the Fairtrade Foundation was a far smaller organisation than it is today and had a severely restricted capacity. Their priority was to focus on licensing the FAIRTRADE mark and at this time they had just one person working on campaigns. Fairtrade Towns, however, had huge potential and if they chose to invest some of their limited resources, the resultant increase in Fairtrade sales might help the Fairtrade Foundation to build on their capacity.

Our survey conducted that summer came at just the right time. It showed that 71% of local people in Garstang recognised the FAIRTRADE mark. It was interesting to note that in the same survey there was only 23% recognition for people outside Garstang and this closely matched the national average at 20%. Fairtrade Foundation staff were discussing whether a 50% recognition of the mark was a realistic target to aim for when these results came in. This was perhaps the trigger required to encourage them to grasp the opportunity of Fairtrade Towns with both hands.

Based on the achievements in Garstang, and following further consultation with other campaigners, Simeon Mitchell, the campaigns officer, developed the five goals [3] required to become a Fairtrade town, city, village, island, borough, county or zone. The Fairtrade Towns Action Guide was published in September 2001 and the stage was set to officially recognise Garstang as the first Fairtrade Town.

We had spent the last year or more securing agreement from the comedy actor Tony Robinson, of *Blackadder* and *Time Team* fame, to attend our official declaration, on the assumption that it would one day take place. Tony was and still is a strong supporter of Oxfam and he was precisely the popular, jovial person that we wanted. Harriet Lamb had just been appointed as the new director for the Fairtrade Foundation and the presentation of our certificate was to be one of her first engagements.

The Co-op again sponsored the event and presented GOG with a commemorative brass plaque that Tony Robinson would unveil. GOG never had much in the way of funding so the financial support from the Co-op in paying for the road signs and the plaque was vital in helping to get Fairtrade Towns off the ground. GOG was a campaign group and, although entitled to claim a small annual budget from Oxfam to cover campaigning expenses, we had so far managed to avoid doing so.

-----

3 The five goals to achieve Fairtrade Town status in the UK are:

   1. The local council passes a resolution supporting Fairtrade and agrees to serve Fairtrade coffee and tea at its meetings and in its offices and canteen.

   2. A range of Fairtrade products is readily available in the area's shops and catering establishments.

   3. Fairtrade products are used by a number of local workplaces and community organisations (churches, schools, etc.).

   4. Popular support is encouraged for the campaign.

   5.A local Fairtrade Steering Group is convened to ensure commitment to Fairtrade Town status.

That was until we used Oxfam funding to pay for the window stickers that were on display throughout Garstang. We produced a Fairtrade directory for 2001 that would be launched at the declaration. Some of the costs were covered through advertising and I paid for the rest. The intention was to recover this expense from local sponsorship and/or support from the local authorities, but even though the front cover included a close-up photograph of the road sign, with the words Wyre Borough Council clearly displayed, we received no council support. A year later I was again forced to recover the cost from Oxfam.

There was no doubt that the money spent by Oxfam and the Co-op was money well spent on such a successful campaign, but with no public expenditure and such obvious benefits for Garstang, the local authorities had made substantial gains. Over the years to come we remained very proud of this fact that should have been to the shame of the town and Wyre Borough councils. At this point I should make it very clear that any criticism of the local authorities is not aimed at all councillors; some showed us great support and they will know who they are, but likewise so will those councillors that continually chose to oppose us for reasons that I will never quite understand.

Our declaration was arranged to be at the Discovery Centre (Garstang Tourist Information Office) on a Saturday afternoon in November, but Tony Robinson had to cancel with very short notice, so it was postponed until the following Thursday on 22nd November 2001. Unfortunately, this meant the ceremony took place during school time, making it impossible for the children (including my own) to attend. Tony agreed to visit the community primary school and high school, however, which more than compensated for any inconvenience.

He drove up from London in the morning and had to be back in the capital to support an Oxfam event the same evening. He was in Garstang for less than five hours, but we made the most of every minute.

Tony was excellent at the unveiling of the plaque, well worth the 18 months and the last-minute hitches it took to get him there. He spoke about how Fairtrade had changed since those days of 'campaign coffee'. I'll never forget his words; "When I asked my son what Fairtrade meant to him, he replied 'crap chocolate wrapped in cardboard". But then, importantly, he talked about the change and how he felt Fairtrade had now reached its "critical mass". I wasn't so sure; we were close, but not quite there yet, but with the advent of Fairtrade Towns we were soon to go way beyond that critical mass.

Tony didn't rest the whole time he was in Garstang; even over lunch he continued to give interviews and pose for photographs. Then we were on our way to the community primary school where my children, Ben and Anna, along with over 200 others anticipated his arrival. The headmaster, Mr McCusker, had his own distinctive brand of Geordie humour that mixed well with the professionalism of Tony Robinson. The two of them performed an impromptu and hilarious 'Dubble act', set around the Fairtrade chocolate Dubble bar made by the Day Chocolate company, later to be renamed Divine. Bob Doherty, the head - and in fact only - sales rep for Day, was one of the few adults privileged enough to witness this one-off performance.

Then it was off to the high school, but not until we had made a quick dash back for Tony's coat, which he had left behind much to the delight of the primary school children and Mr McCusker, who threatened to auction it. More photographs and a more formal meeting with the headmaster and deputy head of the high school followed. Garstang High School had been very supportive of Fairtrade and this was a hastily-arranged last-minute visit that few people knew was taking place. There wasn't time to meet the pupils, but a remarkable coincidence did lead Tony to meet with one class in particular. As an aid to understanding the futility and dismay of the First World War, history students were watching the final *Blackadder* episode, *Blackadder Goes Forth*, which featured Tony Robinson as Private Baldrick. The bold and highly poignant final scene, when Blackadder and his men go 'over the top' and charge into No man's land, is widely considered to be one of the greatest moments in British TV comedy. Not even the history teacher leading the class knew that Tony Robinson was in the school, so you can imagine their surprise when he walked into the classroom. It was a lesson to remember.

I'd promised Tony that he could be away by 3pm and that time had now just passed. As I led him out of the school entrance, I noticed Jane sitting in the car. She loved the archaeological programme Time Team; I'd said at the declaration that Tony Robinson was the only person that Jane would allow to dig a trench across her much-loved garden. She had spent the day chauffeuring the party of VIPs around Garstang, but her modesty prevented her from getting more involved. I had to make one last introduction before Tony was to leave. He walked across to the car, said hello and gave Jane a thank you kiss. He had more than fulfilled our high expectations and we could not thank him enough.

Tony Robinson had unveiled the plaque, but it was Harriet Lamb who presented the Fairtrade Town certificate to the town's mayor. Harriet had done her research on Garstang, announcing that previous to this declaration Garstang's only other world claim was being close to the site of the world's first motorway that by-passed Preston. She then went on to light-heartedly question our first Fairtrade Town status when she said: "I don't know about being the world's first, I think the small 'town' of Paris might have something to say about that." I didn't know what she meant and, although intrigued, this wasn't the occasion to find out. Many years later, when a Fairtrade Town initiative based on our five goals developed in France, the mystery was finally solved. Sometime in 2001, the local authority in Paris had signed up to support Fairtrade and many other French Councils went on to follow their good example, but unlike our initiative only the councils were involved.

The five goals are central to the UK campaign and to achieve them it is necessary to obtain action from the whole community. This is one of the greatest strengths of the UK Fairtrade Towns model: each of the five goals is aimed at one aspect of the community. Although we did not realise it at the time, when we invited everyone to that meal during

Fairtrade Fortnight the year before, we had inadvertently defined what made up the community of Garstang. We invited representatives from the council, businesses, schools, faith groups and other community organisations and our following actions were aimed at all these sections of society. The five goals came out of this community campaigning action and each goal is an integral part of the whole; to take any part away would severely weaken the campaign.

You can imagine my horror, therefore, when, during the declaration ceremony, I suddenly realised that Garstang did not meet all five goals! GOG had run the whole campaign, yet Goal 5 stipulated that there had to be an independent Fairtrade Town steering group. This was vital if the campaign was to be all-inclusive. As much as most people respected and supported Oxfam, there would be some who would not want to be part of an Oxfam campaign. The following example explains this more clearly.

Earlier that year I had wanted to pool all the money raised in Garstang for Comic Relief and present it together from the world's first Fairtrade Town. It was not a large amount, but I thought the principle would send a strong message as well as promote the Fairtrade Town initiative. Unfortunately, our donation never made it onto the TV screen; Comic Relief focused only on fundraising and we had not raised enough to warrant that sort of recognition. This was still a good idea that served to unite the community and attract a great deal of local media interest. My main point, however, is that the secretary from one of the churches refused to take part. I was told that this church only supported Christian Aid and not Oxfam. As it happened, the secretary then went on holiday and the congregation made the autonomous decision to raise money and contribute to the community fund on behalf of the church.

I often tell this story when explaining the importance of having an independent steering group to fulfil the requirements for goal five. Yet here we were being awarded first Fairtrade Town status without an independent Fairtrade steering group for Garstang. This had to be rectified, so in the new year I formed the Garstang Fairtrade Steering Group that was chaired by my friend, Alex Briault. To be honest, the group consisted of the same GOG members and just met on a different day and went by a different name; but this was enough to attract new people who may not have shown the same interest for an Oxfam campaign. Another good friend, Graham Hulme, took over as the chair of GOG that same year, exactly ten years since its formation.

* * *

I was watching Manchester United play Aston Villa in the third round of the FA cup when the phone rang. I have never been able to forgive people who call me during an important football match, but this was one exception. I received the news that Chester had become a Fairtrade City the evening before. It was a coincidence that the place where I'd spent most of my childhood happened to be the second Fairtrade 'Town' and first Fairtrade City. Chester officially declared their status on 13th January 2002. By the end of that year there were ten Fairtrade Towns in total. This included Ammanford, the first Fairtrade Town in Wales, and Scotland's joint first Fairtrade Towns of Strathaven and Aberfeldy.

With other Fairtrade Towns declaring and the now-famous road signs in place, the media attention continued and has done ever since. Garstang was featured on NHK (Japan's national TV station) prime time news and at one point I gave two interviews for the Australian Broadcasting Company in just one week. Remarkably, when the interviews finished, I learned that they knew nothing about the FAIRTRADE mark, only that this small town in the Northwest of England was a world first. When I explained about Fairtrade and told them the FAIRTRADE mark would one day be coming to Australia, they said they would look out for it and warmly welcome its arrival. This was typical of the impact Fairtrade Towns and the Garstang story could have.

Garstang was suddenly on the world map and visitors from all over the world flocked to this small, previously insignificant, Lancashire market town. A film crew from Seattle were making a documentary on ethical trade in Europe, but the only place they visited in the UK was Garstang. Many people came to Garstang to hear the Garstang story and discover how they could start Fairtrade Towns in their own countries. I received an email from someone in San Francisco saying that they wanted their iconic city to "follow in Garstang's footsteps". Japanese visitors and, later, South Koreans were the most common, but although they appreciated what had happened in Garstang and the UK, it was a while before they began to see what their own citizens could achieve in South East Asia.

It is important to understand that, as much as I love Garstang - and it does have a wonderfully strong community - there was nothing special about the place when it became a Fairtrade Town. The fact that our achievements were not easy demonstrated that if it could happen in Garstang it could happen anywhere. As my good friend, and fellow campaigner, Joe Human put it, "Garstang has not shown places like Keswick how to run a Fairtrade Town campaign; in fact, Keswick does it far better. But the difficulties that Garstang overcame in those early days have inspired many other places to follow. You could say the difficult birth in Garstang has enabled others to conceive."

CHAPTER 9

Give it Up for Ghana

The theme for the Oxfam Fast in 1999 was "Give it up for Ghana" and focused on Kuapa Kokoo; the cocoa-growing co-operative set up in 1993 in response to the partial liberalisation of the Ghanaian cocoa sector. Kuapa Kokoo means 'good cocoa farmer' in the Twi language predominantly spoken in the central Ashanti region of Ghana. The Kuapa farmers grow the cocoa that is used to make the Fairtrade chocolate Divine and they are also co-owners of the company Divine Chocolate, formerly known as the Day Chocolate company.

Oxfam fasts had evolved and were no longer just about giving up food for 24 hours; it was now possible to "give up" anything for as long or as short a time as you wished. While getting my hair cut by Gail O'Brien (owner of Kwik Kutz hairdressers and the then president of Garstang's Chamber of Trade) I told her how I'd enjoyed the sensation of a cutthroat razor shave while travelling across Central America. "I've always fancied using one of them, but never found anyone willing to let me have a go," Gail replied. I'd already thought of shaving my beard off for the Oxfam sponsored event and this would prove to be a more adventurous, exciting prospect that would be bound to attract more attention and, therefore, hopefully raise more money.

Garstang hosted a Victorian Festival each year before Christmas, when businesses stayed open in the evening and residents dressed up in Victorian costume. This would provide the perfect setting for my "Give it up for Ghana" stunt, albeit a little later in the year than Oxfam had originally intended. The event was a success. I dressed up as a Victorian gentleman, including top hat and cane, and we got excellent coverage in the local press.

With hindsight, I now realise that far more came out of the "Give it up for Ghana" fast than I appreciated at the time. It had introduced both Ghana and chocolate into our campaign and I had found a new strong ally with Gail, who has ever since supported both Fairtrade and, later, our link with New Koforidua.

When the Fairtrade Towns Action Guide was first published it praised the work we had done with the Chamber of Trade, and for many years to come Goal 3 referred to getting support from hairdressers.

Gail was the reason behind both those achievements. TV and radio reporters always went to Kwik Kutz when they visited Garstang. Not only did the staff use Fairtrade drinks on the premises and offer them to customers, but they often spoke about Fairtrade when cutting people's hair. Hairdressers, like shoe shiners in every good gangster film, were a great source of information and gossip; ideal for spreading the message.

It was Gail who introduced me to Avis and Steve Jones, the owners of the 'Coffee Pot' café just around the corner from Kwik Kutz. Avis was, for me, the 'jewel in the crown' of our Fairtrade campaign. She was one of the first in Garstang to sell Fairtrade hot drinks in the café and sent out a strong message by making no increase in the prices when she did so. The Coffee Pot hosted the breakfast we had with George Foulkes following Garstang's declaration and, like Kwik Kutz and the Co-op store, became a regular haunt for media crews from across the world.

Some people fail to realise that Fairtrade Towns are not about preaching to the converted. Although inclusive, they are not focused on alternative fair trade shops, whose customers would gladly pay over the odds for a fair trade product and, in most cases, had gone out of their way to patronise a shop that was neither open six or seven days a week nor located in the centre of town. Fairtrade Towns were about bringing fair trade to the mainstream, to people who didn't necessarily buy the product because it was fair trade but because it tasted good and was reasonably priced. Whatever the reason for making the purchase, all that really mattered was that the farmer at the end of the chain got a fair deal. That is why Gail and Avis were so important. They won't mind me saying that neither knew about, or showed an interest in, fair trade before our Fairtrade Town campaign, yet they became total converts. Like the well-known beer, Fairtrade Towns could reach the parts that other campaigns could not reach.

Full praise must go to those dedicated and committed fair traders and their customers who, like me, drank the campaign coffee and ate the "crap chocolate wrapped in cardboard" long before they became tasty and trendy. Like all pioneers, they were and always will be the lynch pin behind the campaign, but we had to build on that. The point is that in the same way that the world can never be united under one religious belief, neither can we expect everyone to support fair trade simply because it is the right thing to do, yet the vast majority of people need to be buying into the campaign if the world and its trading system is to undergo genuine change.

Fair trade had to move into the mass market and by promoting the FAIRTRADE mark Fairtrade Towns would help it do so, but not without some confusion and misunderstanding. Goal 3 of the Fairtrade Towns criteria stipulates that, in proportion to the population size of the area concerned, a specific number of retail and catering outlets had to sell a 'range (two or more) of Fairtrade products.' That is Fairtrade products with Fairtrade written as one word with a capital 'F', which means products that carry the FAIRTRADE mark. The problem is that Fairtrade labelling standards are not in place for all fairly traded products and therefore not all fairly traded products can carry the FAIRTRADE mark. This is especially true for traditional handicrafts and jewellery. "Can an alternative 100% fair trade shop that doesn't sell any products with the FAIRTRADE mark be listed under Goal 3?" was a question often raised. This was a hypothetical question, since I have yet to find a traditional fair trade shop that does not sell Fairtrade-labelled products, but strictly speaking the unfortunate answer was a negative. It was important to give full recognition to these pioneers in a Fairtrade Town however, and for that reason we strongly urged Fairtrade Town applicants to list these supporters under the 'Extra Achievements' section.

The other point often raised was that fair trade sales in alternative shops were being undercut and threatened by the increased availability of Fairtrade products in the mainstream outlets. The manager of the Mustard Seed in Garstang made this clear when he complained that he could no longer sell Cafedirect instant coffee in the shop because it was far cheaper in the Co-op supermarket. I explained how important it was for fair trade to get into the mainstream. I had always said to Oxfam staff that in aiming to eradicate poverty they were in fact in the business of putting themselves out of work. Likewise, I wanted to see a world where there was no FAIRTRADE mark and no need for alternative fair trade shops, simply because fair trade had become the norm. Surely that's what we were all working towards? Soon after I went into the Mustard Seed to see a sign on the jar of coffee that read "You can buy me cheaper at the Co-op".

The essential role played by the pioneers and alternative fair trade shops was far from over now that fair trade was hitting the mainstream; in fact, one could argue it was more important. Shops like the Mustard Seed had to stay one step ahead, not just to stay in business but in order to keep pushing the boundaries of fair trade. Once the supermarkets started selling Divine milk chocolate, for example, the alternative shops should sell the new mint Divine. When that became a mainstream product then the fair trade shops should sell other types of fair trade chocolate and so on. The important thing was to always stay one step ahead and keep moving on to the next level.

It was the same for the Fair Trade organisations such as Cafedirect and Divine. Many years before Cadbury made the switch to Fairtrade, I asked Bob Doherty, then leading sales of Divine chocolate, what would happen to Divine when the confectionary giants started selling Fairtrade chocolate. Like me, he felt it important that they stay one step ahead. Divine was not just a company that sold Fairtrade chocolate; it was a Fairtrade pioneer that was also co-owned by the producers themselves. Most Fairtrade supporters would remember this and therefore continue to buy Divine even if every chocolate bar in the world was Fairtrade.

* * *

Before "Give it up for Ghana" was launched I am almost ashamed to admit that I could not even point to Ghana on a map, let alone know anything about the Ashanti region or how cocoa was grown. Oxfam, Fairtrade and then our community link with New Koforidua led me through a journey of enlightenment, and I wanted others to follow. I have never had a problem with ignorance - we are all ignorant about some things - but what I cannot bear is ignorance combined with a lack of desire to learn; even worse, to have the arrogance to think you know everything already.

"Give it up for Ghana" was the start of my wonderful journey built around Ghana and chocolate. Chocolate is a great campaigning tool because everyone loves it. As the American artist and cartoonist John G. Tullius said, "Nine out of ten people like chocolate. The tenth person always lies." These were the days before 'healthy eating' was introduced into schools and the children loved to learn about Fairtrade through the vehicle of chocolate. Harvest festivals were my favourite, watching the children's faces light up when I told them that chocolate grows on trees.

My daughter Anna was a fan of the writer Roald Dahl. He had clearly had a difficult school life and at one time worked in a chocolate factory, providing inspiration for his novel *Charlie and the Chocolate Factory*. His love for chocolate and dislike for the way history was taught in schools were clearly reflected in the following quote:

> "Never mind about 1066 William the Conqueror, 1087 William the second. Such things are not going to affect one's life. But 1932 the Mars Bar and 1936 Maltesers and 1937 the Kit Kat – these dates are milestones in history and should be seared into the memory of every child in the country."

As for history teachers, he went on to say,

> "If I were a headmaster, I would get rid of the history
> teacher and get a chocolate teacher instead and my pupils
> would study a subject that affected all of them."

We were very proud of the fact that with the help of Bob Doherty at
Divine we succeeded in getting a small food shop called 'The Arncote'
to be the first to sell Divine chocolate in Garstang. Our MP, Hilton
Dawson, attended the launch, which again received good coverage from
the local press. Considering Bob was the only salesperson for Divine
chocolate in those early days, his support was remarkable. I have always
felt that if Fairtrade was to be the norm, then we needed to give the same
level of support to the small independent stores and petrol stations etc.
as we gave to the supermarkets. Getting 'The Arncote' to sell Divine
chocolate in Garstang may not have done a great deal to boost sales
of Fairtrade chocolate, but to me it was an important milestone in the
Garstang Fairtrade campaign.

The dawn of the new Millennium not only saw the birth of Fairtrade
Towns, but also the foundations laid for our link between Garstang and
New Koforidua in Ghana. Although these were two separate campaigns,
they both ran alongside and highly complimented each other.

In conjunction with television's Channel 4, Oxfam launched the
Millennium 'On-the-line' award scheme. The idea to award grants for
projects that linked countries that lay upon the Greenwich Meridian
came from the Channel 4 presenter Jon Snow. All these countries were in
the same time zone and therefore would celebrate the new Millennium
at the same time.

We already had a link with Ghana through the Fairtrade chocolate
Divine, but there was also a darker, more insidious link. Nearby Lancaster
was the fourth biggest slave trade port in the UK. It was a long way
behind the big three of Liverpool, Bristol and London, but the fourth
biggest slave trading port none-the-less. Like Liverpool, Lancaster
owed its prosperity to trading with the West Indies, which included
the infamous triangular slave trade. Many of Lancaster's buildings were
built as a consequence of this wealth. Charles Dickens wrote:

"Mr. Goodchild concedes Lancaster to be a pleasant place. A place dropped in the midst of a charming landscape, a place with a fine ancient fragment of castle, a place of lovely walks, a place possessing staid old houses richly fitted with old Honduras mahogany, which has grown so dark with time that it seems to have got something of a retrospective mirror-quality into itself, and to show the visitor, in the depth of its grain, through all its polish, the hue of the wretched slaves who groaned long ago under old Lancaster merchants. And Mr. Goodchild adds that the stones of Lancaster do sometimes whisper, even yet, of rich men passed away upon whose great prosperity some of these old doorways frowned sullen in the brightest weather that their slave-gain turned to curses, as the Arabian Wizard's money turned to leaves, and that no good ever came of it, even unto the third and fourth generations, until it was wasted and gone."

I had seen a South Yorkshire Development Education pack about the slave trade that centred on local hero, Parliamentarian and slave trade abolitionist William Wilberforce. We could do something similar for Lancashire, I thought; Lancashire had far more connections with slavery, albeit not quite so admirable as those connected to the famous abolitionist from the other side of the Pennines. But we needed our own local hero, which is when I discovered Thomas Clarkson, considered by many to be the architect and founding father of the anti-slavery movement. Okay, Clarkson was born in Wisbech, Cambridgeshire, but he loved the Lake District and took temporary retirement from the campaign near Ullswater, where he built his cottage called Eusemere Hill. That was enough for him to be my Northwest hero for what I named the Fairtrade/Slave Trade project.

At first the link between the two subjects was simple; one was a historical trading system of detriment to the people of West Africa and the other a modern trading system that brought benefits to the people of the same region. As I began to research the subjects, however, I soon discovered there were many other parallels between the Fairtrade and slave trade abolition campaigns.

The abolition campaign was the very first mass political campaign of its kind and many of the tools and techniques used then are still used in campaigning today. An Oxfam article once referred to the 'Am I not a man but a brother to you' abolitionist badge as the 'first white band' when comparing it to the white band worn by thousands during the 'Make Poverty History' campaign in 2005.

Although the work of Wilberforce in Parliament was essential for their ultimate success, the abolitionists directed their campaign at the grassroots, in order to completely change the attitudes of the British public. Thomas Clarkson once rode 7000 miles on horseback in one year gathering signatures for the petition. The greatest strength of the Fairtrade Towns campaign is that it, too, is a grassroots movement that reaches out to all parts of the community.

The abolitionists used the message: "It is simply immoral that people should be allowed to suffer in order to provide us with luxuries such as tea, coffee and sugar" at a cheap price. Unfortunately, that message is still true today and can be just as easily applied to the Fairtrade campaign.

People were asked to boycott West Indian slave-grown sugar and again the message was simple. The slave trade was morally evil, and the people had the power to stop it. Britain consumed more sugar than the rest of Europe put together. If a family using five pounds of sugar a week could abstain for 21 months, the enslavement of one fellow human could be prevented. Abstention by 38,000 families could stop the trade altogether. Parliament might see fit to 'license inhumanity', but the people did not have to be accomplices. This again has remarkable relevance to the modern-day trade justice campaign, only people are no longer asked to carry out a negative boycott, but to show positive support for Fairtrade products. The World Trade Organisation (WTO) might see fit to legislate against bananas from the Windward Islands, but the people could avoid being accomplices by buying Fairtrade bananas.

The year before the bicentenary of abolition in 2007, my son Tom made a short film as part of his Media Production course at Runshaw College near Preston. The film was entitled 'What price are your bananas?' and focused on the Fairtrade / slave trade link mentioned here. It suggested that people 200 years ago were not evil but oblivious to the consequences of their actions. Perhaps in 200 years' time people will look back on us and say the same? The abolition campaign succeeded in exposing the error of their ways and it is the job of the trade justice campaign today to follow their leading example.

Trade justice campaigners in the 21st Century may well believe that today's unfair trading practices are a direct legacy of the past injustices of the Transatlantic slave trade. On a visit to Ghana in 2001 I asked Andrews Addoquaye Tagoe (projects co-ordinating officer for the General Agricultural Workers Union of Ghana) what he thought about the slave trade, and he replied, "After Independence we got what we wanted but did it change our economic status? After slavery, are we better off now than in those days? We have stopped our slave masters from ruling us, but all we have gained is our dignity. You (in the West) get good food to eat, entertainment and a good living and the suffering here (in Ghana) is a legacy of the slave trade. It has left a servant/master relationship due to making blacks depend on whites. People think the solution must come from that angle. We must wash ourselves, change our way of thinking. Now that we have the net we can go fishing and catch the fish for ourselves."

* * *

Racism can also be viewed as a legacy of the slave trade. Before the Transatlantic slave trade slavery had not been about race or colour. There were black and white masters and black and white slaves. The Transatlantic slave traders however, justified their evil deeds by dehumanising Africans, referring to them as 'black cattle'. As the British public became more conscientious, the traders even argued that slaves were better off under the care of 'civilised' whites and the horrific middle passage was perhaps an enjoyable experience to them. Slaves were not considered human and therefore not even allowed to enter a church. Part of what lay behind the evangelical Wilberforce's desire to free the slaves was so they could be fully converted to Christianity.

Following the abolition of the slave trade and eventually slavery itself those who profited and/or were stuck in their ways continued to believe that black people were subhuman, hence the formation of groups like the Ku Klux Klan. Darwin's theory that we all evolved from apes was ridiculed, using a picture of an ape with the words of the abolitionist slogan written below: "Am I not a man and a brother to you?"

A consequence of this was the development of the Atlantean theory (the concept of a superior race descended from the civilisation supposedly responsible for building the lost city of Atlantis and other wonders of the ancient world), which fed the minds of the Nazis and gave rise to the horrors of the Holocaust.

It seemed to me that if you could trace racism back to its insatiable, inhumane, ignorant roots then you could remove the very foundation on which it lies and expose it for what it really is. Andrews also had a message for the racists:

> "Tell them they should travel a little. The world is a global village; there is no inferior person and no better person. Everybody created by God is as important as God wants him to be. So, they should open their eyes, we love them, and we will always co-exist with them."

The more I researched, the more fascinated I became with Thomas Clarkson, and the more I learned about the vital role that Quakers played in the abolition campaign. Once again, the pieces of the jigsaw all came together and fell into place. I studied the definitive Thomas Clarkson biography by Ellen Gibson Wilson, which was the source for much of the content on our website. I had written to the author to obtain her permission and she sent back a lovely postcard of York Minister. She had seen our site and wrote on the card that she was certain Thomas Clarkson would have approved of my work. I was flattered.

I began to relate to Thomas Clarkson. He too had the best ideas in the night, but instead of getting out of bed and jotting notes down on a scrap of paper or even a PC, he kept a quill and note pad by his bed in readiness for those night-time moments of inspiration. He wasn't a Quaker, but while visiting Tsar Alexander I of Russia to gain his support for the abolition, the Tsar asked if he was. He replied,

> "That I was not so in name, but I hoped in spirit, I was nine parts in ten of their way of thinking. They had been Fellow Labourers with me in our Great Cause, the more I had known them, the more I had loved them."[4]

---

4 *Thomas Clarkson A biography* by Ellen Gibson Wilson Page 145.

Together with Granville Sharp, Thomas Clarkson was the driving force in bringing together the Society for the Abolition of the Slave Trade in 1787. This non-sectarian, abolitionist society arose from the Quaker committee that had formed four years earlier and nine of the twelve founder members were Quakers.

During his time at Eusemere Hill, Clarkson became great friends with the poets Wordsworth and Coleridge. Thomas Clarkson was the first person to link Wordsworth's poetry with Quakerism. He also wrote the book 'Portraiture of Quakerism', which was another first to bring Quaker principles to a wider non-Quaker audience.

Clarkson had a strong Anglican upbringing and was convinced his work was driven by God. Coleridge said of him: "He, if ever human being did it, listened exclusively to his conscience, and obeyed its voice." There can be no doubt that for Clarkson God was his conscience and, like Quakers, he listened intently to his message. In fact, it was just such an experience that led him to take up the fight against slavery in the very beginning.

After collecting his Cambridge prize for an essay he wrote on slavery Clarkson made his way back to London. The words he wrote concerned him and he repeatedly got down from his horse and walked for a while. At one point above Wadesmill in Hertfordshire something came to him;

> 'I sat down disconsolate on the turf by the roadside and held my horse.... If the contents of the Essay were true, it was time some person should see these calamities to the end. Agitated in this manner I reached home.'[5]

It continued to haunt him for the next few months:

> 'I walked frequently into the woods, that I might think on the subject in solitude, and find relief to my mind there. But there the question still recurred, "Are these things true?" Still the answer followed as instantaneously "They are". – Still the result accompanied it, "Then surely some person should interfere".'[6]

---

5 *Thomas Clarkson A biography* by Ellen Gibson Wilson p.11 taken from *Clarkson, History, Vol. 1*, p 210
6 *Thomas Clarkson A biography* by Ellen Gibson Wilson p.11 taken from *Clarkson, History, Vol. 1*, p 210-11

It was almost a year later before Clarkson realized that he was that person, and from that point on he devoted his life to the cause. Thankfully, he lived long enough not only to see the abolition of the British Atlantic slave trade, but also the emancipation of slaves in 1833. Clarkson died in 1846 at the respectable age of 86.

CHAPTER 10

Go Global Go Ghana

The basis for the Fairtrade/slave trade project was firmly in my mind, but it would not unfold in quite the way I had initially intended. My original idea was for an exchange between Garstang and Ghana involving different people from across the community in both countries who could explore the issues around Fairtrade and the Atlantic slave trade and, most importantly, share each other's perceptions.

The requirements for the Millennium 'On-the-line' award meant there had to be changes. The exchange was the first casualty, as the grant money was restricted for use by UK participants only; the funding could be used for those travelling from the UK to Ghana, but not in the opposite direction. The 'On-the-line' scheme also focused on young people and I was too old to make the application. So, on behalf of the Garstang Oxfam Group, I joined up with the Garstang Youth and Community Centre and Garstang High School to develop the 'Garstang Go Global' project. Neil Trickett from the youth group and Helen Selby of the Garstang Oxfam Group were young enough to make the joint application. We eventually succeeded in sending a youth theatre group to Ghana for three weeks in July and August 2001. The grant would only fund a maximum of half the budget, so I decided to pay for myself, and the youth group would raise the extra cash they needed.

Even with the help of Neil and two other young adults, I was far from able to handle a group of five teenagers. Fortunately, therefore, I was accompanied by three youth leaders, making a total of twelve people from the Garstang area. We were also to be joined by four others from London. During my research into the slave trade, I had got to know Martine from Antislavery International, the oldest known campaign movement in history. Antislavery International had its roots in the abolition campaign founded by Thomas Clarkson, hence their headquarters is named 'Clarkson House' in recognition of the great man.

Martine had been planning a similar project, which involved taking three London schoolchildren to Ghana to explore contemporary slavery. We decided to combine our projects and make a joint application, much to the dislike of the youth leader, who objected to me inviting Martine without first consulting him. It was then that I began to realise that this was no longer my project and that my original vision was taking a different direction.

The youngsters were not driven by the Fairtrade/slave trade link, for which I had developed a passionate interest and for me was still the heart and soul of the project. The Transatlantic slave trade was history, whereas contemporary slavery was here and now and therefore a far more attractive cause to young eyes. Using the slave trade to better understand the injustices of today was overshadowed by the issue of child labour that, ironically, I had introduced by inviting Martine to join us.

The 'On-the-line' application still went by the name of Fairtrade/slave trade. I was determined to share my research with the world so, in September 2000, the Fairtrade/slave trade project was launched with an exhibition on chocolate and Fairtrade in Garstang Library. All the information from my research was put onto our website and was viewed with interest by many. Our website helped to inspire the Fair Trade Triangle with New Koforidua and Media in Pennsylvania, and proved to be particularly popular during the bicentenary of the abolition of the British slave trade in 2007. Much later, the original Fairtrade/slave trade concept was to lead to the development of The FIG Tree Centre in Garstang and two further projects funded by the Heritage Lottery Fund.

Central to the new-look project was the play 'Hidden Brutality' (on the three issues of fair trade, the Atlantic slave trade and child labour) put together by the 'Go Global' theatre group that was called 'Mission'.

The play was performed in front of 2,800 pupils of the State Experimental Basic Schools in Kumasi. In return, the students of the Ghanaian schools entertained their guests with a full day's program of African singing, drumming and dancing, culminating in their own performance of a play on the Atlantic slave trade as seen through Ghanaian eyes. The idea was for the 'Go Global' youngsters to write their play based on their perceptions from learning in the UK. Following the visit to Ghana, witnessing the play performed by the State Experimental Basic students and sharing the Ghanaian perspective, the play 'Hidden Brutality' would be revised to include the new learning. The outcome of the project would be an education pack to capture that learning for the benefit of other schoolchildren.

Essentially, the visit to Ghana was divided into three parts. The first few days were spent with the charity 'Children in Need' (not to be confused with the better known and much larger BBC charity) in the capital Accra. That was followed by a visit to the slave forts of Elmina and Cape Coast castle and finally we visited the central Ashanti region to explore cocoa farming and Fairtrade. We also visited the banana plantation run by the Volta River Estates Limited (VREL) where Oke Fairtrade bananas are grown. At that time, the VREL plantation was the only Fairtrade banana plantation in the whole of Africa.

The contact with 'Children in Need' was made through Martine and Antislavery International. The 'rescue' centre was run by Ken Amoah, who was later to become a good friend. Ken was a social worker who had a passion for helping street children, and those found working in the nearby stone quarries, by providing shelter and sending them to school. Sadly, Ken crossed paths with a malicious conman some years later and the centre had to close, but at the time of our visit there were 39 happy, smiling children to greet us as our party stepped off the two hired minibuses.

Children as young as five worked in the stone quarries, breaking stones to make gravel to be used in concrete for construction. They worked from 6am to 6pm often six, or even seven, days a week. The work is hard and dangerous with injuries, including the loss of fingers, being a common occurrence. For this work the children were paid between 1,000 and 2,000 cedis (equivalent to between 10 and 20 pence) per day.

The children at the centre entertained the UK students with singing, dancing and drama productions depicting their life before joining 'Children in Need'. Their performances were very powerful and showed a total understanding of their rights as children. What was perhaps most inspiring was the fact that many of the children had great ambitions now that they were receiving an education. Samuel Fianu (10 years old at the time of visiting) wanted to be a veterinary surgeon and he became an instant friend. When the centre finally

Samuel with wife Mary and daughter Aryel.

closed, I took on the role of paying for his education, which did enable him to take up a teaching job. Sadly, however, he had to give it up because it failed to provide a sustainable livelihood. He is now married with a daughter and working as a tour guide and personal driver in Accra.

Samuel's mother, Janet, his sister, Lucy and two-year-old nephew, Derek, also lived at the centre. Lucy is a seamstress and made me my very first Ghanaian shirt. She used shells for the buttons, which she said represented all the love in Ghana, that she wanted me to take back to the UK. I wore that shirt at many events, including Garstang's official declaration as a Fairtrade Town, that took place following this visit. Today I have many Ghanaian shirts, but Lucy's shirt is still very special to me and comes out for special occasions.

I had severely injured my ankle when jumping out of the bus just a couple of days following our arrival in Ghana and had to attend a hospital in Accra, which was an experience in itself. I was immediately put into a wheelchair and taken to a doctor before being given a bed. I soon learned that there was a corpse in the screened-off bed next to me, but I could not complain about the service. My leg was X-rayed and put into plaster, and I was discharged. This was on the same day we had arranged to interview the children at the centre to hear their stories. I obviously had to miss the session, but Ken allowed me to interview Samuel and his family over a meal at my hotel that evening.

Janet was from the rural Volta region of Ghana. Her parents were farmers who could not afford to give her an education. She finally went to Accra looking for work and ended up in the stone quarry where, in 1999, she was found working with Samuel and Derek. At that time Derek was only six months old. Janet hardly spoke any English, so Lucy was acting as my interpreter. When I asked Janet if her problems would have arisen had her parents been able to afford to provide her with an education, she didn't wait for the translation. She adamantly shook her head and gave a very definite 'No' for an answer. I will never forget that response and testimony to the need for Fair Trade.

The second stage of our journey took us along the coast to visit the slave forts at Cape Coast and Elmina to enable the students to see for themselves the true horror and brutality of the Transatlantic slave trade. Cape Coast was a fort used by the British to trade in slaves whereas Elmina, the oldest fort in Ghana, was used by the Portuguese and Dutch. Elmina was later captured by the British, but never used by them for the notorious trade in slaves. The connection with Britain's largest slave port was evident, however; the road leading up to Elmina castle was named Liverpool Road.

The church at Cape Coast castle was deliberately built above the men's dungeon where male slaves were so inhumanely kept. The site of the dungeon was likewise built upon the shrine to the old gods worshiped by the native Africans. This demonstrated how some Europeans not only used religion to justify the trading in humans, but also used it as a symbol of their power and so-called 'superiority'.

Finally, the group visited Kumasi, the cultural centre of Ghana and the capital of the Ashanti region. There we were hosted by the cocoa farming cooperative Kuapa Kokoo, co-owners of Divine chocolate. This was the first time I was to visit the Kuapa Kokoo Society of New Koforidua. Mr. Ohemeng, the then Director of Kuapa, had selected the town for our visit. With a population of about 3,000 people, it lies either side of the main Kumasi to Accra highway, just 40km east of Kumasi. New Koforidua provided the ideal location for a quick, convenient visit for our students, who were shown how cocoa is grown and processed into cocoa beans that were sold to the European market to make chocolate. It was only a brief visit, but friendships were made that day that would last a lifetime and the seed was sown for our link between Garstang and the Ghanaian community.

Nuruddin Boateng worked for Kuapa and was our guide while in the Ashanti region. Nuruddin came from a large family of teachers and his father had been the regional director for education before retirement. I had been with Nuruddin for a few days before he took us back to his father's house, and it was only then that I learned he was a Muslim. Not that this mattered, but it did make me think that things may have been different in the UK. Nuruddin's family was a mixture of both Christians and Muslims and they had no problems living and even worshipping together. It was less than two months before the Twin Towers in New York were destroyed in 9/11 yet still Nuruddin felt it necessary to quickly defend his faith by pointing out that he and his family were not fundamentalists.

To my delight, I discovered that Nuruddin and his father founded and ran the Foundation for Learning And Merit Education (FLAME), which provided support for school links between Ghana and the UK. When Nuruddin had been away he left his Christian friend and colleague, Harry, in charge of recruiting new supporters. He called Harry his 'fisher of men' because of his Christian faith and recruiting skills. It was great to see these two men of different faiths working so closely together.

Nuruddin had gained specialist knowledge and experience from linking with schools and he was about to help me develop the link between Garstang and New Koforidua. We had a free day that was to be spent relaxing by the lake, but early that morning Nuruddin arrived at our hotel and asked me to go with him. I didn't even have time to let the others know what was happening, but Nuruddin assured me all was okay. He took me to see Maxwell Jumah, the chief executive of the Kumasi Metropolitan Assembly, but we didn't go to his office, nor did we have an appointment; we just turned up at his house. Despite being an obviously busy man, he was able to spare an hour of his valuable time.

It is a tradition in Ghana for a visitor to make known their reasons for the visit before they are accepted into the community or home. This makes good sense and I proceeded to explain why I had come and what

I wanted from him. As a supporter of the Nestle boycott, a result of the multinational promoting the use of powdered milk over breast milk in poorer countries, I expressed my frustration at seeing nothing but Nestle coffee and Nestle condensed milk in Ghana and how Fairtrade chocolate was not even available to visitors or those Ghanaians who could afford to buy the luxury. He just leant towards me and said, "Bruce, you must remember that Christianity started with just twelve good men." This was such a typical response in Ghana, where patience was a necessary lifestyle as well as a virtue. I imagined what it might be like if senior officials back home took on this same positive, relaxed and friendly attitude.

I told him about the friendship that had developed between our group and the people in New Koforidua and whether he would approve a link between our two communities. "You have a friendship," he replied, "that is all that matters. Why do you need my approval for you to have a link?" I explained that to have a community link in the UK, approval from the authorities was required: something I was to learn many years later is simply not true. "Okay, then, you have my blessing," was his warm response.

When I returned to the UK and approached Garstang Town Council, as expected the proceedings were very different. The Garstang town councillors had already rejected the idea of forming a twin town relationship with somewhere in Europe, on the grounds that they wanted to avoid any links that may be viewed as simply an excuse for local authority 'jollies.' I admired and respected this decision but explained that our proposal was quite different; it involved young people and a friendship with New Koforidua had already developed. Astonishingly, the council agreed to the link on condition that it was to remain a community-to-community link and not one that just involved the local authorities. I was delighted and fully supported their reservations. The decision was recorded in the minutes of the meeting and reported in the *Garstang Courier* on 22nd February 2002. Unfortunately, many years later when the council rescinded this decision, I was to learn that, apparently, it meant nothing at the time.

* * *

The youth groups were in Ghana to perform and revise their play as part of the Millennium 'On-the-line' project, but that was not what lay behind my visit. What brought me to Ghana in 2001 was the same motivation that took me to Nicaragua in 1989; I needed to see for myself. I wanted to hear the views of the Ghanaian people, especially about the slave trade, but also about Fairtrade and trade justice. I was aware that this may not necessarily be the views written up in the museums at Cape Coast castle or Elmina, as these were heavily financed, and therefore influenced, by American dollars. I wanted the views of ordinary people and I first received them as I was walking on my crutches towards the fort at Cape Coast.

Everyone else in our group had gone to visit the canopy tree walk at Kakum National Park and were to join me at Cape Coast castle in the afternoon. Due to my ankle injury, I accepted I had to miss the tree walk, but was glad that I was now able to spend a full day for my first visit to a slave fort and I would be on my own.

I saw the castle ahead of me when I met two Ghanaians who, seeing my leg in plaster, asked how I had acquired my injury. They were horrified to learn my accident had taken place in Ghana and apologised profusely. On hearing I was British they told me how they believed Ghana had been so much better off under British rule and the country had only deteriorated since gaining independence. "You gave us so much," they claimed. As I looked upon the symbol of British dominance and cruelty that stood behind them, I felt no pride, only shame. This is what Britain gave to Ghana, I thought.

The view expressed by these two Ghanaians was not what I expected or, indeed, wanted to hear, but it was a view none-the-less and perhaps I shouldn't blame them for choosing to focus on the positives of colonisation? Thankfully, however, as I heard more and more from people like my friend Andrews from the Agricultural Workers Union, I began to realise that this was not the view shared by the majority of the Ghanaian people.

* * *

A year later, during the summer of 2002, Nuruddin Boateng was in the UK on business with Kuapa Kokoo and spent some time visiting Garstang. We had a very full itinerary planned for him but had allowed one day of rest when I'd decided to take Nuruddin to the beautiful village of Haworth in West Yorkshire, the home of the Bronte sisters and the Keighley and Worth Valley steam railway. The intention was to give Nuruddin a day off, but I was to learn at this early stage that there was no rest in the world of Fairtrade Towns.

Rita Verity co-owned a fair trade shop called 'Sonia's Smile' and she called me just a couple of weeks before Nuruddin's visit to ask my advice on making Haworth a Fairtrade Village. The Brontë museum was selling 'Dubble' bars made by Divine Chocolate and in no time at all I'd agreed to a photo call with Nuruddin and I outside the famous Parsonage.

Bruce with Meg and Rita (left to right).

Haworth was declared the world's first Fairtrade Village just weeks later on 22nd November 2002, exactly a year after Garstang had been officially recognised as the world's first Fairtrade Town. Amongst many other things, the unrelenting Rita went on to persuade the steam railway to use Fairtrade beverages. I had long since overcome my fear of steam engines experienced as a child and now loved the sights, sounds and smells of anything powered by steam. Rita once organised a Fair Trade event in one of the engine sheds appropriately named 'Chuffin Fair'. It included a real ale bar. I was very quick to accept an invitation to speak at this event. How could I possibly resist my three favourite delights: Fair Trade, steam engines and real ale? Rita was great at using puns to name her Fair Trade events. As well as 'Chuffin Fair' she organised an outdoor event called 'Fair Intents'.

In 2009, inspired by the Garstang and New Koforidua link, Rita also succeeded in developing a twin town relationship between Haworth and Machu Picchu in Peru. Our own community link was already having an impact on promoting Fairtrade and inspiring others, but we needed an exchange visit to bring us closer together.

At Garstang's Fairtrade Town celebration, held at the high school the year before, John Whitaker had drawn a parallel between my life and vision and that of his friend and colleague, Nick Maurice. Nick had gradually reduced his hours and finally given up his job as a general practitioner to focus on his work supporting links between the UK and developing countries. Following the publication of the Brandt Report in 1980, Nick founded the link between his hometown of Marlborough in Wiltshire and the fishing village of Gunjur in the Gambia. Nick was also the founder and director of the UK One World Linking Association (UKOWLA) and, much later, the Building Understanding through International Links for Development (BUILD) coalition.

I first met Nick at the 2002 Oxfam Assembly in Loughborough. I distinctly remember telling him about our 'Go Global' project while queuing for dinner and my disappointment at not fulfilling my original vision of a community exchange. "So why don't you do it now?" Nick responded and I took his advice. Nick continued to support and inspire our link and it wasn't long before we became paid-up members of UKOWLA.

Our exchange was arranged for ten days in Ghana and ten days in the UK during August and September 2004. The UK party of six were to include myself, a school child (which for ease was to be my son Ben), a dairy farmer, a businessperson (who was the proprietor of a local art shop), a teacher from Ben's school and a town councillor. Our Ghanaian partners were a Kuapa Kokoo staff member, my friend and school child Samuel from the 'Children in Need' centre in Accra, a cocoa farmer, a teacher, a hairdresser and the chief from New Koforidua, Nana Agyekum Sarpong II.

When he visited Garstang, Nuruddin had told me about his dream of building a play area for the children in Ghana. He said he only knew of two play areas in the whole country, and both were in a very poor condition. As a part of the exchange, a landscape design lecturer and a student from Myerscough College were to supervise the building of a play area in New Koforidua. It was funded by Churches Together in Garstang and built as a token of our friendship.

We were also joined by Salford poet Robin Graham and a *BBC North West* TV presenter who would, in their own ways, report and document the two exchange visits. Our MP, Hilton Dawson, had planned to travel to New Koforidua but unfortunately, due to time commitments, he had to pull out just a couple of weeks before departure. He offered to donate the cost of his ticket, but we were unable to obtain a refund.

In the earlier stages of planning, the dairy farmer from the UK had decided that he was unable to leave his farm unattended for such a long period. He withdrew from the visit although still agreed to host his partner. It occurred to me that perhaps we had been presumptuous in thinking that the cocoa farmer in New Koforidua could leave his land, but on making the enquiry I was told that his neighbours would tend to his farm while he was away. When you have a link between a community in the 'rich North' and one in the 'poor South' the false assumption is always that the 'poorer' community will learn from the 'richer' one. This was the first of many examples, however, where the reverse was true. Perhaps British farmers could learn something from the cooperative spirit of farmers in developing countries like Ghana, or perhaps they just needed reminding of something that we once had, but had long since lost, in this country?

The UK participants were not only responsible for covering their own expenses, but also for raising the money to fund their partners. I had received funding from my Quaker Meeting, which had provided tremendous support morally as well as financially. We were to provide the accommodation for our Ghanaian guests and likewise were given food and shelter when in Ghana.

To save on travel expenses we had booked our flights with Ghana Airways, which turned out to be a mistake. Two days before our planned departure we learned that Ghana Airways had gone bankrupt and all flights had been grounded. Although the return of stranded passengers had to be the priority, due to the special circumstances of our exchange our travel agent managed to find substitute flights. It meant delaying our departure by three days, however, thus reducing our time in Ghana to just one week and delaying our guests return home, thus extending their stay in the UK to twelve days. It also meant that we would now fly from London instead of Manchester, so we had to make alternative travel arrangements to and from the airport.

We had an early morning flight from Gatwick and therefore travelled from Garstang the day before and tried to get some sleep overnight at the airport. Our arrival in Accra was immediately followed by an eight-hour bus journey to New Koforidua. Kuapa Kokoo had arranged a meal and reception at their central office, so frustratingly we had to drive through New Koforidua on to Kumasi before finally travelling back to our host village. Robin wrote at least one poem for each day of our visit and, appropriately, his first poem was entitled 'Did Anyone Sleep?"

Our time in New Koforidua had been severely restricted to just four days, to allow for the now-obligatory visit to Cape Coast castle that accompanied every trip to Ghana. I was also very keen to go to Kakum National Park for the tree canopy walk, having missed out during my first trip to Ghana three years earlier. It was also Samuel's first visit to the National Park as it was to Cape Coast, which proved to be an invaluable and emotional history lesson for both Samuel and Ben.

Amazingly, we were able to complete the building of the play area and still found time to visit the palace in Kumasi. We had previously arranged to have an audience with the Ashanti king, although realistically we understood that this might not be possible. In anticipation, we passed

from ceremonial room to ceremonial room, each room becoming more elaborate as we got nearer to the king. I held on to my House of Commons bag that contained the two bottles of House of Commons whisky given to us by our MP; according to Ghanaian tradition, one is expected to present a king or a chief with a bottle of spirit or two. Unfortunately, after several hours of waiting, we were told that there had been an emergency in the north of Ghana and, therefore understandably, the king's attention was needed elsewhere.

By the time we returned to New Koforidua we were a little late for the durbar, held to honour our visit. A durbar is a meeting involving the whole community held in the square with speakers, drummers and plenty of singing and dancing. The chief, queen mother and sub-chiefs were wearing their ceremonial dress embellished with gold jewellery.

It is often a surprise for visitors from the 'rich' North to see African chiefs being carried through a procession wearing their enormous pieces of solid gold jewellery, but then, Ghana had been named the Gold Coast for good reason. I was told that in days gone by gold would come to the surface of the ground during heavy rain. Even now, one will often see the sides of roads cascaded with rocks and stones that reflect the sun's shimmering golden light, but today it is only 'fool's gold'. What gold does remain in Ghana doesn't seem to provide any benefit to the people living there. As I have so often heard when visiting developing countries, Ghana is another "rich country full of poor people".

On taking my seat at the durbar and reading the program I was surprised to learn that I was to be made a Nkosoohene (a sub-chief) and would be expected to give no fewer than two speeches during the proceedings. Nervously, I sat working on the content of my speeches in my head, when someone tapped me on the shoulder to tell me that the local press were here and wanted to interview me to find out what I was going to say. In answering their questions, the words of my speech came to me. Due to the stress and busyness of the evening, I was unable to take in the sheer joy and pleasure of the event, so I was delighted to discover next morning that Robin had captured everything in the writing of another poem entitled 'The Durbar Day'.

The following day, they held the enstooling ceremony to pronounce me Nana Kwadwo Osafo 1st, Nkosoohene of New Koforidua; Nana was the title given to a chief or sub-chief, Kwadwo meant I was born on Monday and Osafo meant I was a pathfinder. At first, I was a little apprehensive about any false expectations that may have accompanied the title of 'pathfinder', but with time everyone understood our link was one of equality and mutuality and I therefore accepted the honour with pride. To this day I can think of no greater honour and recognition for my work than being made a sub-chief in New Koforidua.

I had been given my ceremonial robe, crown, sandals and gold (sadly no longer real gold) jewellery at the durbar, but now I was to be seated on my very own stool. In Ghana a stool, rather than a crown, is the symbol of authority; therefore chiefs and kings are enstooled as opposed to crowned. Although I returned to Garstang with my ceremonial dress, my stool has always remained in New Koforidua.

The ceremony itself was a joyous occasion, again with the usual drummers and dancers, but I was expected to keep a stern face and posture in line with my new chief's role. I was carried on my stool while talcum powder was thrown over me amongst the celebratory shrieks of joy.

Then I was given a cushion and seated on the left side of New Koforidua's chief and the Queen Mother, with a crate of beer and soft drinks beside me. I was instructed to sit with my legs apart and keep a

straight face, not something that came easy to me amidst all the smiles and laughter.

In the UK, we had another packed itinerary even though this part of the exchange had been extended by two days. Our visit to the slave fort in Ghana was reciprocated by a visit to the slave trade section of the Maritime Museum at Albert Dock in Liverpool, later to be made into the International Slavery Museum. This proved to be another valuable history lesson for the two boys. Samuel did have plenty of leisure time, however, including a trip to Blackpool Pleasure Beach and the famous illuminations as well as watching Manchester United play Everton at Old Trafford.

Despite all the initial problems, our exchange was a success. *BBC North West* TV ran a serial called *Fair Trading Places* during the evening news on four consecutive days and we had good coverage of our exchange on the regional edition of *The Politics Show*. Robin published a book of his poems called *The New Koforiduan*, which also contained other Fairtrade poems, including '100 Fairtrade Towns' written especially for the joint declaration of Manchester and Salford as the 100th Fairtrade Town in March 2005.

The exchange had provided a solid foundation to build on and it was clear that our link with New Koforidua was going to be the heart and soul of our Fairtrade campaign in Garstang and, in later years, The FIG Tree.

CHAPTER 11

Fairtrade Towns Coordinator

By the start of 2003 I was working regularly at only two veterinary surgeries; three days a week at a surgery in Blackpool and three half days and an evening on-call in Garstang. One morning while working in Blackpool the proprietor of the practice left me a letter informing me of my three months agreed notice before my contract would be terminated. No previous discussions had taken place and, having worked there for the last eleven years, the news came as quite a surprise. It was, perhaps, appropriate that this took place on April 1st, although I am not sure who was the greater fool; myself for believing that all was well and my job secure, or the proprietor for making what seemed to me to be a rash, poorly thought-out decision. I had built up several of my own loyal clients during my time at the surgery and had a very good working relationship with the two nurses there. Both nurses had worked there far longer than I, but on hearing my news they decided it was time for them to also leave the practice; one left even before my departure and the other soon after.

I was still working as a self-employed veterinary locum and set out to replace the three days of work lost. My heart was not in it, however, and perhaps my lack of enthusiasm on touting for further hours was one reason that no work was forthcoming. I explored all possible options and even seriously considered starting my own practice. Both the nurses from the practice in Blackpool were keen and willing to work for me and for a while this option looked the most likely; that is, until another thought came to me that fortunately bore fruit and was to take my life in a whole new direction.

Earlier that year I had been telling Bob from Divine Chocolate about my dream to eventually retire as a vet and take up paid work for Oxfam or another likeminded organisation. My main concern was the fact that neither Jane nor I wanted to live and work in London or Oxford, where I assumed most of these jobs would be located. Bob remarked that the success of Fairtrade had meant the creation of more and more jobs and not necessarily in and around London; Traidcraft, for example, was based in the Northeast of England and, he suggested, it may even be possible to get a job not too far from Garstang.

I rang Sarah, the campaigns officer for the Fairtrade Foundation, in order to obtain some phone numbers to enable me to make some Fairtrade job enquiries, but the unexpected response she gave me could not have been better. It turned out that very same week the Fairtrade Foundation had created the new post of Fairtrade Towns coordinator and were about to advertise the position. "The only problem," Sarah commented, "is that the job is only part time for three days a week." I couldn't believe my luck. This would replace the hours I'd lost in Blackpool and the job was more than I could have hoped for, but it would be located in the Fairtrade Foundation office at Baldwin's Gardens, London. I pointed out that Garstang was just ten miles west of the central point of Britain and, as the post involved a considerable amount of travel to Fairtrade Towns around the country, perhaps I could take on the role while remaining in Garstang. As the founder of Fairtrade Towns, I was the obvious candidate and was delighted when they offered me the job without the requirement to move to London.

My income as a veterinary locum was sufficient to enable me to carry out many of the roles of a Fairtrade Town coordinator in my own time and even at my own expense, long before such a post was created. During Fairtrade Fortnight that year I had already run a workshop at the Oxfam 'Food for Thought' Conference where it was debated whether the FAIRTRADE mark could and should be applied to British produce. The following day I shared a platform with Sarah to speak about Fairtrade Towns at another conference in Aberystwyth. Just under three weeks before I started my new job, I gave a presentation at the launch of the Keswick Fairtrade Town campaign; Keswick was later to become one of the best examples of a Fairtrade Town that I know. Although my attendance in Keswick was still carried out in my own time, it was now considered work and my expenses were covered. "The question now is when are you able to start?" Sarah asked, when I'd accepted the position as Fairtrade Towns coordinator. "No, the question is not when am I able to start, but when are you able to start paying me?" I replied audaciously.

Monday 30th June was to be my last day at the Blackpool surgery, so I arranged to travel to Baldwin's Gardens for my induction the next day. I was thrilled to not only be visiting my 'Fairtrade Mecca' but also to be working there. The Fairtrade Foundation was growing rapidly, but at that time everyone managed to crowd into the kitchen for the weekly staff meetings. The offices may not have been worthy of the 'Fairtrade Mecca' status that I'd granted it, but the friendship and working camaraderie that I was to experience more than surpassed my expectations.

When I was working in Blackpool, I would regularly find time between surgeries to visit my mother, who lived in Knott End less than half an hour's drive away. She usually cooked me lunch with a choice of two or even three desserts. My mother suffered from rheumatoid arthritis and had great difficulty getting around. I therefore felt guilty as I sat there watching her prepare my meals, but it was a long time before I realised that this was something she took joy in doing. For most of her life she had cared for my father and our family, and she did not want to stop.

My father had died during Fairtrade Fortnight the year before. My mother rang me in the morning to give me the news. I of course took the day off from the vets and went straight over there to support her in any way I could, but my mother was tough when she needed to be and, although I am sure she was glad I was there, she was more than capable of dealing with the situation on her own. That evening, I had arranged to attend a Fairtrade event in Lancaster. Sarah and a producer were coming up from London and Sarah was to stay overnight at our home. Out of respect, I felt I should cancel my contribution and stay at my mother's for at least one night, but she insisted that I continued as normal and convinced me that I was no longer needed.

With my job in Blackpool terminated I no longer went to my mother's for lunch. Combined with the loss of my father, I realise with the benefit of hindsight that my mother now felt redundant and this was made worse when I repeatedly and foolishly tried to suggest that the time had come for me to look after her.

Just one week after I'd started to work for the Fairtrade Foundation, I called on my mum on the Wednesday morning. She told me she had taken a fall just a couple of days before and her leg was hurting. As always, she underplayed the situation and therefore I did too, but I did tell her that she must seek medical advice. It turned out she had broken her leg and was admitted into Blackpool's Victoria Hospital, ironically very close to the surgery where I no longer worked.

Mum spent several weeks in hospital and was never to return home. She contracted Methicillin-resistant Staphylococcus aureus (MRSA) during surgery and deteriorated from then on. I was unable to get regular updates from the hospital. They had both my mobile and landline telephone numbers but even when she was moved to another ward, I cannot recall them ever phoning me. My wife was a nurse and I a vet so we both understood, and indeed sympathised with, the pressures put on the NHS, but looking back I can't help thinking that they were more concerned with protecting their liability than they were in telling it as it was. I went on a family holiday in August to South Wales. It's strange how sometimes taking time away from work provides the opportunity for stress and anxiety to fill the niche, as it did in this case. On returning home I managed to fix up an appointment to speak to the hospital consultant. I just wanted the truth so we would know how to respond, perhaps even asking to take my mum home to spend her last days there. By this time my mum kept asking me to take her out of hospital and saying she was just going to get up and walk out of the hospital door. But I didn't, and nor did she. On Thursday 25th September 2003 I received a phone call telling me mum had died early that morning. It's still hard to come to terms with the fact that the emotion I felt most was one of relief.

I could not sleep that night and found myself writing the words for my mum's eulogy; they just flowed and there was a need to write it down on a scrap of paper. Once finished, I took a walk in the dark and watched the sun rise. It occurred to me that this would be the first sunrise my mum would not know, and it was beautiful.

Like my father, mum had shown a desire to be cremated. She had wanted a cardboard coffin; being a Yorkshire lass she hated waste and unnecessary expense, but this was not to be possible. Likewise, it was considered inappropriate at a funeral to read her favourite parable, that of the widow's offering (Mark 12:41-44), but I did it anyway, reading out word for word what I'd written during the night after she died. I also managed to prevent her Yorkshire white roses from being burnt along with the coffin. That is what mum would have wanted.

* * *

I was now working part time for the Fairtrade Foundation as Fairtrade Towns coordinator and for a practice in Garstang as a locum vet. The two jobs could not be more different. With the Fairtrade Foundation I was to learn about strategies and workplans. As a vet there were no such things; you don't plan your day but just deal with what comes through the door. I had avoided having to move to London but still had to make regular day trips to the capital to attend meetings. I was finding it hard to be creative in this environment; the best ideas and thoughts always came to me in the night or while showering and not at meetings where we were told to "think outside the box". I struggled to 'think outside the box' and then it occurred to me why; I was never in the box in the first place. I was expected to conform and enter the box only to be asked to think outside it when we needed to be creative. That said, I did manage to deliver.

My first creative task was to come up with an idea for Fairtrade Fortnight 2004, which was also the 10th anniversary for the FAIRTRADE mark. I managed to come up with two. On Friday 5th March, five pairs of 'rival' cities were to declare as Fairtrade Cities on the same day to demonstrate communities coming together in support of Fair Trade. The idea for the 'Ten Cities Declarations', as it was called, struck me after I discovered Aberdeen and Dundee were competing to be the first to declare and I

The Fairtrade Bus visits Garstang.

suggested that in a spirit of unity perhaps they could declare together. For the most part this idea was welcomed, but I was surprised to learn that two cities in Wales just refused to cooperate. I even received a letter from the council in one of the two cities concerned telling me I did not understand how deep this 'rivalry' was and should not meddle in matters that did not concern me.

The second event involved cyclists converging on Garstang (now established as being at the centre of Britain) from the four compass points around the country. Like spokes of a wheel, the cyclists set off from the Fairtrade cities of Newcastle in the north, York in the east, Oxford in the south and Liverpool in the west. Each day they would pass through other Fairtrade Cities where more cyclists would join them on the journey to arrive in Garstang for the FAIRTRADE mark 10th anniversary celebrations on Friday 12th March.

The bike ride idea was resurrected for the celebration of 500 Fairtrade Towns in 2010. To mark this occasion, cyclists rode 500 miles from Aberfeldy, the joint first Fairtrade Town in Scotland, to Cardiff, the first Fairtrade Capital City. I even managed to get permission from The Proclaimers to use their song, 'I'm Gonna Be (500 miles)' for the event. The ten day journey passed through the prominent Fairtrade Towns of Strathaven – joint first Fairtrade Town in Scotland; Dunscore - first Fairtrade Town in Dumfries and Galloway; Brampton on Hadrian's Wall - the first Fairtrade Heritage Trail; Kendal – the first Fairtrade Town in Cumbria; Garstang – the world's first Fairtrade Town; Chester – the first Fairtrade City; Bridgnorth – the first Fairtrade Town in Shropshire; Hay-on-Wye – the site of the first Fairtrade School in Wales; and Ammanford – the first Fairtrade Town in Wales. A parchment was signed by the cyclists during the celebrations each evening and carried in a baton passed from one group of cyclists to another. During the planning stages we did not know which place would become the 500th Fairtrade Town so it was left a mystery until the day. On 1st November 2010 the cyclists rode into Cardiff and a video link was made with Bicester in Oxfordshire, which had declared as the 500th Fairtrade Town on the same day.

For the 'Ten Cities Declaration', Manchester was initially chosen as a possible 'rival' to Liverpool, but they were just not ready to declare so soon, so in line with the old Yorkshire and Lancashire rivalry Leeds took part instead. Manchester was ready a year later, however, so for Fairtrade Fortnight 2005 I suggested they could declare jointly with neighbouring Salford as the 100th Fairtrade Cities. Sarah and I worked together to create a Fairtrade Towns logo that was to be unveiled at the event taking place at the Cooperative Group's HQ, then at New Century House on Corporation Street in Manchester. But for reasons I never quite understood the unveiling was not to take place. A month later Sarah left the Fairtrade Foundation.

As the Fairtrade Foundation grew and replaced Baldwin's Gardens with larger office space at Ibex House, I suppose somewhat inevitably it seemed to be losing some of the close camaraderie that I'd experienced when I first visited the office back in 2003. I was not used to working for an institution and was blind to any office politics that may or may not be taking place. My visits to the office were infrequent, which exacerbated any isolation I felt, but I thoroughly enjoyed visiting Fairtrade Towns, helping to inspire and support the campaigners and speaking at events.

I particularly enjoyed the Patron Roadshows. The BBC newsreader George Alagiah had become patron of the Fairtrade Foundation in the same year I joined, 2003. His wife, Fran, had got the job as head of fundraising also at the same time but they did not make their marriage known to anyone until they were both accepted and established in their positions. I was given the job of selecting the Fairtrade Towns that should host a Patron Roadshow, writing the briefings for George and accompanying he and Fran on the visits. I had the enormous pleasure of arranging and attending twelve Patron Roadshows in the four and a half years from 2003 to 2008. George spoke at the events about his time as Africa correspondent, which as a sad reflection of the time was so often mistaken for war correspondent. George had travelled through some of the most war-torn areas of Africa and had learned that people were far more likely to go to war if they were poor. That was why he wanted to support Fair Trade and become the Fairtrade Foundation patron. Despite hearing it many times, I was always struck by this and it reaffirmed my view as a Quaker that there can never be peace in the world so long as poverty and inequality exist.

I also enjoyed my time visiting and supporting campaigners with Windward Islands banana producer Simeon Greene. We travelled the length and breadth of the country, mainly visiting places that were just starting their Fairtrade Town campaigns. In January 2004 we went to speak at the launch of a campaign in Hamilton, just outside Glasgow. Simeon had to travel all the way from Southampton and an overnight stay was necessary for both of us. The event was in a church hall attended by just three people. But neither Simeon nor I were thwarted. The campaigners were enthusiastic and further enthused by our visit, which we both felt was more than worthwhile. Hamilton was declared a Fairtrade Town just 13 months later.

On another occasion, I was driving with Simeon to an event when suddenly he said, "When I was talking with Fidel Castro," (as one does), "he told me that where there was a genuine will, a world leader could eradicate poverty in any country regardless of what political system they were running." That was really something else coming from Fidel Castro, but it was so true and again reaffirmed what I'd always believed.

Despite once being told that members of our local council called me the "Che Guevara of Garstang" I never wore my political or religious beliefs on my sleeve. Their intended insult reflected more their political leanings than mine; I took it as a compliment.

Once, when we were standing on an overcrowded train, Simeon said to me, When we have 100 Fairtrade Towns, we will have the largest campaign movement this country had ever seen." I thought about the campaign to abolish the British Transatlantic slave trade and the women's suffragette movement and doubted his claim. But Simeon recognised how Fairtrade Town campaigns involved all aspects of the community and therefore a network of communities was something far greater than just a network of local authorities or schools, for example. In time, we would see over 500 Fairtrade Towns in the UK and more than 2000 Fair Trade Towns worldwide. Some were to call it the largest campaign movement the world had ever seen.

Bruce with Simeon Green.

CHAPTER 12

Branching Out Around the World

The Fair Trade Towns movement started with the grassroots and essentially has remained as such. We were never proactive in trying to start up new Fairtrade Town groups in the UK; there was never a need. Likewise, the movement spread beyond UK borders without us having to encourage it. Besides, the Fairtrade Foundation only had the remit to promote Fair Trade within the UK.

The Republic of Ireland was the first country outside the UK to start its own Fairtrade Town campaign. As in the UK it was run by the Fairtrade Labelling Initiative and therefore focused on promoting the FAIRTRADE mark and associated products. They used the same five basic goals but added an extra sixth one based on education and schools. It was good to see another country adapt the goals, but I have always believed that if the five Goals were fully met all aspects of the community should be involved and therefore never really understood the need for an extra, specific goal on education. I felt the same when new campaigns were set up such as Fairtrade schools, universities and faith groups. A school could play a major role in a Fairtrade Town campaign without itself being a Fairtrade school. In this way they would still be very active in promoting Fairtrade but save themselves the extra administration needed to become a Fairtrade school. I saw many examples of schools taking this approach and believe they served their purpose just as well.

Clonakilty became the first Fairtrade Town in Ireland on 22nd September 2003.

Belgium was the next country to come on board but due to their geo-political nature one campaign wasn't enough; they had to run two. The Flanders region was the first to start with what they called Fair Trade Gemeenten run by a coalition of organisations: Fairtrade Max Havelaar (the Fairtrade Labelling Initiative), Oxfam Wereldwinkels, and Vredeseilanden (a sustainable farming organisation). French speaking Wallonia had their own campaign called Communes du Commerce Equitable.

Belgium also added a sixth goal focused on promoting local farmers and local produce. Although the original Garstang campaign had initially focused on local farming, this was something not officially taken up by the Fairtrade Foundation in the UK following the debate at the Oxfam 'Food for Thought' Conference in 2003. That said, some British Fairtrade Towns did choose to include local produce in their campaign as well as other issues.

Ghent became the first Fair Trade Gemeenten in Belgium on 1st July 2005. The Belgian campaign was so successful they went on to become the country with the largest density of Fair Trade Towns per capita, with more than half the population living in one. This achievement was surpassed, however, when Luxembourg started their campaign in 2011.

* * *

My oldest brother, Graham, was taken ill with pancreatic cancer in 2005. He and his wife Pat lived in Hemel Hempstead, and I often stayed with them when making my visits to London. Now he was in a London hospital I was able to visit far more often than if I had not had my job with the Fairtrade Foundation. In October that year I was invited to speak about Fair Trade Towns at a fringe meeting at the USA Fair Trade conference in Chicago. I flew from Heathrow on the Saturday and after the weekend conference had an overnight flight back from Chicago on the Monday night. For two nights away it just was not worth trying to reset my body clock and, not normally being an early riser, I thoroughly enjoyed my early morning swims in an empty hotel pool. I was fortunate enough to be sharing a room with Mr. Ohmeng, the director for the Kuapa Kokoo cocoa farming cooperative in Ghana, whose idea it was to visit New Koforidua during our Go Global project in 2001. He was on the same body clock as I, so we both enjoyed an early dinner and early night after taking the time to discuss the pros and cons of Garstang having a link with the Ghanaian community.

The conference was run by, and for the benefit of, a coalition of Fair Trade organisations, of which there were many. Few people knew about Fairtrade Towns in the US and my presentation was not well attended but, as I often find with conferences, the networking that took place was far more productive than the actual presentation. David Funkhouser, the representative from Transfair USA (at that time the US Fairtrade Labelling Initiative), invited me to have breakfast on the Sunday morning with representatives from the other Fair Trade organisations that were interested in Fairtrade Towns. The problem seemed to be who should take ownership of any campaign that they might adopt. It was clear from the start that this was not going to be a campaign run solely for the benefit of the Fairtrade label but would instead involve the wider Fair Trade arena: what was later to be called the 'Big Tent' approach. Belgium had already managed to do this, but without the same level of controversy. I understood the problems they faced and explained that, although the severity of the problems may be greater in the US, they were not that much different to the problems faced initially by the Fairtrade Foundation and other organisations thinking of starting a national campaign.

Having an overnight flight left me with a free day on the Monday; David suggested that I visit the famous Art Institute of Chicago. Graham had told me I should visit the Chess Records studio on 2120 South Michigan Avenue, made famous by the Rolling Stones record of the same name. As the art museum was at 111 South Michigan Avenue and I didn't know my way around it made sense to visit the museum with David first and then just walk along the avenue until I reached the studio.

After saying goodbye to David, I proceeded to walk past the 1,000 plus buildings on the opposite side of the long avenue. I started to become aware that the buildings were becoming much poorer in appearance and I soon became the only white man around but, being a seasoned traveller who always loved to get away from the usual tourist spots, this did not bother me.

When I finally arrived at the studio, it was much smaller than I'd imagined and it was closed. I peered through the window and saw someone inside. I wasn't going to go back now and was keen to get a special gift for my sick brother, so I knocked on the window. Not only did the man let me in but when I told him why I'd come he took me on a tour of the studio. The walls were adorned with gold and silver discs from some of the greatest blues artists the world had ever known, including my own guitar hero, Eric Clapton. There was a narrow staircase leading to the upstairs studio and I was asked to imagine how many great stars had carried their guitars up and down that stairwell. I bought a T-shirt to give to Graham as proof of my visit and then, having completed my mission, left to walk back down the avenue.

I arrived back at Heathrow on Tuesday afternoon and immediately called Pat to get an update on my brother, but Graham had died. It turned out that he passed away on Monday evening and, allowing for the five-hour time difference, it was precisely the same time I was visiting Chess Records studio in Chicago on Monday afternoon. I gave the T-shirt to Pat.

Graham had been working on a model railway before being taken ill and Pat did not feel able to even enter the room after his death, so she asked me if I would take it down and remove it. It was one of the hardest things I have ever done. I had my own railway, albeit nowhere near the standard Graham was working to, and I wanted so much to incorporate what I could of Graham's model into my own in memory of him. It was impossible to reuse the track, but I was able to rescue the locomotives, station house, engine shed and put his precious Ford Escort RS Cosworth dinky model outside the house that represented my own in Garstang on my layout. It was as if Graham was always visiting.

* * *

Following the conference in Chicago, discussions continued between the US Fair Trade organisations regarding if and how they should run their Fair Trade Town campaign. Then, out of the blue, I received a phone call from Elizabeth, who lived in Media, Pennsylvania. Elizabeth worked for Untours travel agents and her boss was an elderly man called Hal. Hal was a remarkable man who had set up the travel company because he felt "American's needed to travel more". He once not only gave a lift to a hitchhiker but ended up giving him his car as well. He had somehow heard about what Garstang had done and wanted Media to follow suit so had asked Elizabeth to contact me. It turned out Elizabeth was also a Quaker and Media had two Quaker meeting houses but when I asked her if she had used the local Quaker community to drive things forward, she replied, "Oh no, that would have taken far too long." I had always admired Quaker work throughout the centuries, but knew precisely what she meant.

I explained to Elizabeth how Garstang had originally made its self-declaration long before being formally recognised by the Fairtrade Foundation and how discussions were taking place in the US following the conference in Chicago. I suggested that, rather than wait for anything to develop, perhaps the campaigners in Media should also make a self-declaration once they had met the five goals used in the UK. This they did on 8th July 2006. They even wanted to send their application into the Fairtrade Foundation, but I did not think that would be such a good idea. As

Hal at Media's declaration.

expected, Media's self-declaration as not only the first Fair Trade Town in the USA but the whole of the two American continents, served to kick-start the campaign in the USA. Transfair USA agreed to resource the campaign, but it would be run in cooperation with the other US Fair Trade organisations and so would not solely focusing on the Fairtrade label, becoming known as Fair Trade Towns USA. As we'd seen before, the campaign soon spread across the US, and both Chicago and San Francisco were later to become Fair Trade Towns.

Media is just outside Philadelphia - in fact, just a tram ride away - and I finally got to stay there when I was invited to speak at the Fair Trade Towns USA and Fair Trade Universities Conference in Philadelphia from the 9th to 11th September 2011, exactly 10 years since the infamous terrorist attack on the Twin Towers. There was total mayhem at Heathrow airport with people being turned away for no apparent reason except, perhaps, that they resembled the 'stereotypical terrorist'. Despite being a white Caucasian I almost missed the flight myself due to the large amounts of administration and checks in place.

While passing through security at the airport I had a missed call and could not access the voicemail until I had finally settled in Media. Although the information was not yet in the public domain it was to tell me that Transfair USA were about to break away from the International Fairtrade Labelling Organisation (or FLO as it was known then). Unlike most of the Fairtrade family, Transfair had never adopted the new FAIRTRADE mark (the blue and green roundel) and were now to become a totally different organisation – Fair Trade USA. As a representative of the Fairtrade Foundation, I anticipated problems, or at least some embarrassment, but it was not to be.

Media had a rather cheesy slogan: "Everybody's hometown". However, it turned out to be true. I made many new friends who made me feel so much at home there. I learned how becoming America's first Fair Trade Town had transformed the community. They had Fair Trade shops on the high street and held many Fair Trade events and it was hard for me to believe that it wasn't always like this. Drew ran 'Earth and State', a wonderful gift shop that was the home of Fairis the Frog, as in 'Fair Is The Frog". Fairis was used in children's Fair Trade hunts, when he was hidden around the town for children to find him. But now he wanted to broaden his horizons and I was asked to take Fairis back with me to Garstang and then send him out visiting Fair Trade Towns across the world.

For my return trip I had far more luggage than on arrival and so had to carry Fairis through security, which was still on high alert because of the 9/11 anniversary. I was walking past a very large, robust policeman when he shouted to me, "You can't take the frog." For some reason that

I'll never understand, I just went up to him, gave him a slight pat on the back, and said, "Okay, good one, mate." He just laughed and let me through. Fairis was free to travel the world.

Two months later I took Fairis to the International Fair Trade Towns conference in Malmo, Sweden from where he could continue his international travels. Since collecting him from Media in the USA I had travelled in the UK to Stratford, Birmingham and to Oxfam House in Oxford. Fairis had accompanied me on these visits but, now with his Garstang Fairtrade Town badge, it was time to pass him on. Fairis made regular appearances at conferences thereafter until he went missing, only to be found again sitting on a desk at the offices of Fairtrade Sweden during my visit to Stockholm in 2015.

Bruce with Fairis the Frog and other Media friends.

* * *

In 2006 the Fair Trade Town message was spreading far and wide. As well as Media declaring in the US, Yarra in Australia became the first of their Fair Trade Communities and Scandinavia was going to hit the ground running. In March I was asked to speak at a conference organised by the Norwegian Ideas Bank to help kick- start Fair Trade Towns in Norway. As I walked through the streets of Oslo on my first day, I was amazed to see a poster with the photograph of the Garstang road sign and the words below in Norwegian, "150 Fair Trade Towns in Britain; what about Norway?"

I first met Stale at the conference, who was keen to make his hometown of Sauda a Fair Trade Town and just 5 months later - 23rd August 2006 - Sauda became the first Fairtrade-Kommune in Norway. Before that, on 17th May, Malmo had become the first Fairtrade City in Sweden, and with Copenhagen declaring in 2008 and Tampere in Finland in 2009, all four Scandinavian countries were to have Fair Trade Town campaigns and eventually Fair Trade capital cities. Malmo hosted the International Fair Trade Towns conference in 2011, and Oslo in 2013.

Norway ran its own national Fair Trade Towns conference in 2008 and where better to have it than the beautiful town of Sauda? That said, Sauda may have been ideologically well placed but certainly was not geographically. Sauda lay at the end of a fjord; the mountainous terrain made it difficult to reach inland and it was a good three-hour road journey, criss-crossing the fjords from Stavanger to reach Sauda from the coast. Sauda was also lacking in 'ideal' conference facilities but choosing it as a venue for this national event was a good example of what can be done when there is a genuine will to do it. I fondly remember walking along the beautiful Sauda streets to the restaurant for lunch following presentations held in the historic Trade Union Hall. It made a change from walking through the bland corridors of a conference centre. My wife, Jane, was able to join me on this visit and I'll never forget the day we were just sitting and relaxing enjoying the calmness and tranquillity of the fjord when she turned to me and said she could never think of when she had been in a more beautiful setting.

Sauda was twinned with San Juan del Sur in Nicaragua and, like our campaign in Garstang, they used the link to strengthen their Fair Trade Town campaign. It was no coincidence, therefore, that they chose to run the conference alongside a visit to Sauda by their Nicaraguan friends. At the start of the conference, we were entertained by a combination of Norwegian choral and Nicaraguan folk music: an example of how two contrasting cultures can come together to produce something original and quite outstanding. If that was not enough, I had the great pleasure of drinking Nicaraguan Flor de Caña rum with Stale and his friends, the first time I had enjoyed the beverage since I visited Nicaragua almost 20 years earlier. For the journey home, Jane and I took the much longer, but even more scenic, route by boat all the way along the fjord from Sauda to Stavanger.

Two years later I was back in Sauda again for their own local Fair Trade Town conference, but this time I travelled alone. There was some construction work going on at the Sauda quayside so I was to get off the ferry at Ropeid, where Stale would meet me and take me the remaining 27km to Sauda. As the boat was drawing up to the quay, I thought I'd nip to the bathroom before taking the car journey but when I came out the ferry was now drawing away from the jetty and I could see a bemused Stale standing on the shore. I could not phone him and thought perhaps I could get off at the next stop along and get a bus to Sauda. I eventually plucked up the courage to tell the conductor about my plight. But the next stop was Marvik, another 14 km in the opposite direction and it was going to be too late to get a bus to Sauda. Next thing I knew, they were turning the boat around and heading back to Ropeid. I was beginning to feel like a 'pork pie' once again despite my fellow passengers appearing all forgiving. I sheepishly debarked, but there was no longer any Stale to be seen; in fact, there was no longer anybody to be seen anywhere. I walked up to the main road, managed to hitch a lift, and arrived in Sauda just in time for dinner followed by my presentation 'Garstang to the world'.

Stale & his wife Ellen later moved to Kopervik on the island of Karmøy at the entrance to the fjord opposite Stavanger. They remain good friends and Jane and I visited them again in 2013.

* * *

Right from the start it has always proved difficult to find the funding for any organisation to run a Fair Trade Town campaign. Not having the available resources was often given as the primary reason for not starting a campaign. My argument, however, was that whatever resources could be found would be more than paid back as the campaign rapidly grew; that had certainly proved true for the Fairtrade Foundation and their National Fairtrade Town initiative in the UK.

In 2006 the Fairtrade Foundation secured funding from the European Union to run a three-year project entitled Fairtrade Towns in Europe. In partnership with Max Havelaar Belgium and Max Havelaar France, the project would support existing Fairtrade Town projects in Europe, as well as facilitate the development of new projects in places where a Fairtrade Labelling National Initiative already existed. As well as funding my position as Fairtrade Towns coordinator for three years, the project would include the running of an annual International Fairtrade Towns conference to be hosted by each of the three partners. The first of these conferences was to be held in the UK in November 2006.

Liverpool was my preferred choice of venue. The city had become a Fairtrade City as part of the 'Ten Cities Declarations' two years earlier and we already had good relations with John Moores University, which had become a Fairtrade University earlier in 2006. Despite both Liverpool Council and John Moores University welcoming the approaches we made, the venue was changed, and the conference was now set to take place at London South Bank University. Participants would be attending from across the globe, and I was told that Liverpool would not be as easy to reach. This was such a contrast to the choice of Sauda for the national conference in Norway despite lying at the end of a fjord. And even if people could not fly directly to Liverpool's international airport, they could fly to Manchester and get to Liverpool in less than an hour by train; it took at least as long to get from Heathrow to central London. London was not to declare as a Fairtrade City until 2008 and the South Bank University was not a Fairtrade University; but still, London was to be the final choice.

Because the funding came from the European Union and was received by the three Fairtrade Labelling Initiatives, the conference was promoted as the first European Fairtrade Towns conference. In time, however, they would become known as the annual International Fair Trade Towns conferences.

The second European Fairtrade Towns conference was held in Brussels in January 2008 and the third in Lyon in February 2009. Nick Maurice, director of the UK One World Linking Association (UKOWLA) gave a workshop on community links at the conference in Lyon and I travelled with him on the train for the journey home. As Fair Trade Towns spread across the world, I was being asked to do more and more to support the international movement, but my part time job as Fairtrade Towns coordinator with the Fairtrade Foundation was primarily focused on supporting the UK initiative, and this was even more true now that the funding for the three year European project was coming to an end. I was also still working part time as a vet and therefore finding the time to support the international movement was becoming a real challenge.

Nick understood this, as he had previously made the decision to give up his profession as a general practitioner in order to devote his time to promoting community links through UKOWLA. As the founder of UKOWLA, he also had the skills and confidence to start up his own organisation. It was perhaps no surprise, therefore, that he suggested I should do the same. Although that was precisely the action I would take just two years later, it was not something I could consider at that time. Our discussions did, however, lead me to start seeking funding to enable me to better support the international movement and eventually my position as International Fair Trade Towns ambassador. This was a task that would continue to challenge me for the next seven years until the annual conference in 2016, when I was reluctantly forced to step back from my international role.

In 2009 the Netherlands, Germany, Finland, France and New Zealand declared their first Fair Trade Towns, and Perez Zeledon in Costa Rica became the first Fair Trade Town in Latin America. This was also the year of my 50th birthday and I had learned that Jain monks would sometimes mark their fiftieth year by setting out on a long walk, relying on the generosity of strangers to support them. I had spent my childhood in Chester, now the first Fairtrade City, and I came up with the idea of walking from Garstang to Chester, staying overnight at the homes of Fairtrade supporters on the way in the Fairtrade cities of Preston and Liverpool.

My friend and GOG chair, Graham Hulme, was a keen rambler and he suggested that instead of walking south to Chester that he would join me for a walk if it took a more scenic route heading north through the beautiful Lake District to the Fairtrade Town of Keswick. On Sunday 25th October 2009 Graham and I, along with other supporters, set out on the 88 mile trek from Garstang to Keswick, staying overnight with Fairtrade activists where possible in the Fairtrade Towns of Lancaster,

Arnside, Kendal, Bowness and Grasmere. Each day we would start and finish at a site related to our three historical themes: Fair Trade, the slave trade and Quakers. The Fair Trade Way was born.

Before setting off on the Fair Trade Way I was contacted by Professor Tatsuya Watanabe, who was organising a symposium in Tokyo to help launch Fair Trade Towns in Japan. He wanted me to attend the symposium as well as visit potential Fair Trade Towns in the country. The problem was, my visit to Japan would need to take place during Fairtrade Fortnight 2010 and as Fairtrade Towns coordinator my services would also be needed in the UK. Tatsuya pressed me for a response, and as I had heard nothing from the Fairtrade Foundation by the day before setting off on the Fair Trade Way, I told Tatsuya I would make the visit even if I had to take annual leave from both the Fairtrade Foundation and the vets to do it, which ultimately is what I did.

I spent ten days in Japan from 25th February to 5th March 2010, travelling across the country in the way that Japanese tourists love to do in Europe. One morning I woke up in Nagoya and had to give a presentation at a conference in Osaka at 1pm. I was told we would break the 200km journey to do some sightseeing in the ancient capital of Kyoto on the way. That was equivalent to waking up in London, having to give a presentation at 1pm in Birmingham but deciding to stop off in Oxford. I would not even consider that in the UK but the bullet train, or Shinkansen as it's known in Japan, made it just a 45 minute journey and, perhaps most importantly, it was 100% reliable.

144

We arrived in Osaka after midday, but sure enough I was on the stage to give my presentation in good time.

It was a great joy and privilege to meet with the campaigners in Japan. As I'd experienced listening to Japanese visitors to Garstang, they had this idea that it was so much easier to campaign on Fair Trade in the UK. Perhaps they were right, but I shared their frustration and despair more than they could ever realise and that message served to inspire them.

Nagoya had a population of over nine million and they had no more than twenty activists in the Fair Trade group there, working to make Nagoya a Fair Trade City. They believed their group was too small to work in such a large city, so I told them what Maxwell Jumah, the chief executive of the Kumasi Metropolitan Assembly, had told me during my first visit to Ghana: "You must remember that Christianity started with just twelve good men." I added, "There are more than 12 good men and women here in this room, so anything is possible." Nagoya became Japan's second Fair Trade City in 2015.

The ten days in Japan were the hardest I'd ever worked in promoting Fair Trade, but in helping to bring Fair Trade Towns to the world's third richest economy it was also going to have the greatest impact. Every day, I was faced with new audiences at new venues and, on at least one occasion, having to prepare my presentation with just a couple of hours' notice, something I was just not used to. Ironically, although I'd taken annual leave during Fairtrade Fortnight in order to make the visit, on my return I was so exhausted that I was forced to take a couple of days off as sick leave.

As a grassroots movement, the campaigns that led to the first Fair Trade Town in many countries were so often driven by the vision, enthusiasm and determination of one extraordinary activist and, in Japan, Shoko was the person behind the Kumamoto campaign. Kumamoto declared as the first Fair Trade Town in Japan and Asia on 4th June 2011 and the city hosted the annual International Fair Trade Towns conference in 2014.

Kumamoto's declaration was made jointly as the world's 1000th Fair Trade Town. As with the 'Ten Cities Declarations' held in 2004, ten towns and cities around the world all declared at the same time on the same day. Due to the different time zones, however, the declarations would occur sequentially from East to West with Kumamoto being the first followed by Madrid, Herne in Germany, Delft in the Netherlands, the towns of Kontich and Bilzen in Belgium and finally in the UK with the declarations of then Prime Minister David Cameron's constituency of Witney, Aberaeron in west Wales, and the Scottish towns of Rutherglen and Cambuslang.

Our linked community of New Koforidua in Ghana was meant to be a part of the celebrations as Africa's first Fair Trade Town. After years of joint campaigning, not just with us in Garstang, but also our friends in Media PA as part of our 'Fair Trade Triangle, they also wanted to be a part of the Fair Trade Town family. They asked me to help; how could I possibly refuse? We devised five goals for a 'producer community', which were based on the original UK five goals but had to be considerably adapted for use by a community that, although they grew Fairtrade cocoa, had no way of selling or purchasing any Fairtrade products. To make matters worse, there was no Fair Trade organisation in Ghana that had the time or resources to help them. But this was a people's movement, so we persisted. The five goals were met, and New Koforidua was ready to make their own self declaration, just as Garstang and Media had done, as part of the 1000th Fair Trade Town celebrations.

The press release was about to be launched when I received a phone call from my superiors at the Fairtrade Foundation telling me in no uncertain terms that New Koforidua must not be included in the event, because there was no 'official' body to recognise their declaration. My heart sank; I was both shocked and horrified. I had no choice, however, and instead of seeing Fair Trade Towns in 22 countries across six continents, the press release for the 1000th Fair Trade Town read: "Fairtrade campaigners will celebrate the growing people's movement, now present in 21 countries across five continents." I felt I had betrayed my friends in New Koforidua and immediately called them to say so.

CHAPTER 13

Emponchey Ane Encoco

Emponchey ane encoco: 'goats and chickens' in the local Twi language spoken in New Koforidua, Ghana. After becoming a sub-chief in New Koforidua in 2004, there was an expectation from some that I should learn the language of the Ashanti people. Goats and chickens were to be found throughout New Koforidua and, despite real efforts on my part, my Twi vocabulary has never extended much beyond this along with the simple greeting *ete sen*.

As someone who loves to travel and experience different cultures, learning languages has always been an obstacle for me. Now, I understand I have some form of verbal dyslexia. I had to have speech therapy lessons for my own native language as a child and French was by far my worst subject at school. After switching to German, I found that no easier, although I did scrape a Grade 1 CSE, albeit with the aid of a dictionary. Out of school, I have made several attempts to learn Spanish; it's such a beautiful language and I have found Spanish-speaking people to be more forgiving and accepting of my faults.

In 2006 I travelled to Ghana for the third time, primarily to develop our Partnership Agreement between Garstang and New Koforidua. The Garstang and New Koforidua Linking Association (GANKLA) held its inaugural meeting earlier that year, meeting in the back room of a local pub to discuss what the link should mean to us in Garstang and what we wanted to get out of it. I have to confess to feeling quite smug with the democratic process we had gone through and our attempts to get the whole community represented. New Koforidua was headed by an unelected chief so we would have to tread carefully to try and ensure they went through a similar process; but we could not have been more wrong.

During our visit, our sister organisation, the New Koforidua and Garstang Linking Association (NKGALA) held their meeting in the Catholic church, the largest building in the village. A truck with a megaphone was driven around the village early that morning to encourage the residents to take part in what they saw as a very important meeting for everyone. The church was full and the NKGALA committee had representatives from the local carpenter right up to Nana Agyekum Sarpong II, the village chief, and the queen mother. Much of their discussion focused on the desire that the link should be led by the whole community and not just by the chief, queen mother and the village elders. Nana was a wise man and, although he fully supported the link, he also fully understood that it had to be community-led. That was to be our first, but by no means last, lesson in humility.

We had benefited tremendously from working with the UK One World Linking Association (UKOWLA) and later with the organisation Building Understanding through International Links for Development (BUILD). Both were founded and led by Nick Maurice, who had first inspired our own link, as he had done with many others before and since. Nick had a vision that everyone in the UK should at some point

meet someone from a developing country through linking. Linking was a formidable tool to help build up understanding around the issues of poverty and inequality and lead us to a better, fairer and peaceful world. "All wars started from fear of oppression" or so the New Internationalist had taught me. As Yoda stated in the original Star Wars Trilogy: "Fear leads to anger, anger leads to hate, and hate leads to suffering" and I would go further to say that it was a misunderstanding of people that first leads to the fear.

The 2003 UKOWLA conference in York was focused on links between the UK and Ghana. Nick had asked me to give a presentation on the work we were doing with Fair Trade and the slave trade that came from our Go Global Go Ghana project. Just before our visit to New Koforidua in 2006, the UKOWLA conference was held in Swindon. There I heard a participant from Tanzania say: "The problem with links between a rich country and a much poorer one is that the people in the poor country are too humble to feel they have anything to give and the people in the rich country too proud to know how to receive."

This learning provided us with a strong foundation for developing our Partnership Agreement, and the balance between pride and humility formed a central part with the wording: "Both parties recognise that the inequality and injustices of our present trading system are a legacy of colonialism and the transatlantic slave trade of the past, which did nothing for the self-confidence of the West African people. We hope, through this partnership, to bring balance to the individual pride and humility of those involved. We hope to bring pride and dignity to those who feel they have nothing to give and humility to those who do not know how to receive. We aim to build a grassroots development for global change – a change for which justice is required and not the perpetuation of aid."

The calligrapher Dorothy Bicknell, who had proposed that Garstang became a Fairtrade Town at the public meeting in April 2000, volunteered to hand-write two ceremonial copies of our Partnership Agreement, and Gail from Kwik Kutz paid to have them professionally bound by Lancaster University. Both copies were each signed by the members of GANKLA and NKGALA at ceremonial events held simultaneously in Garstang and New Koforidua on Sunday 3rd June 2007, rather appropriately the same year that saw the 50th anniversary for Ghanaian independence from British rule and 200 years after the passing of the act to abolish the British Transatlantic slave trade. I was proud to be the only person to sign both copies, as chair of GANKLA and Nana Kwadwo Osafo, 1 Nkosohene of New Koforidua. Less than four weeks later, Archbishop Desmond Tutu launched the UKOWLA Toolkit for linking, making it possible for anybody to benefit from the knowledge and experience built up by UKOWLA.

Despite formally agreeing to support our link at the council meeting in February 2002, Garstang Town Council would never sign the Partnership Agreement with New Koforidua. When discussing it, one councillor asked: "What can a country like Ghana possibly offer a place like Garstang?" My immediate answer was humility. I remembered what Maxwell Jumah, chief executive of the Kumasi Metropolitan Assembly, had said when I met him in 2001 at his home in Kumasi. "You have a friendship," he told me, "that is all that matters." Our community link was strong, and even endorsed by Archbishop Tutu when I had a brief email dialogue with him while asking him to support another Fair Trade event. To have the approval of our town council was not only of no importance, I actually believed to have them sign our Agreement now would be a blot on something most beautiful.

Media PA had declared as America's first Fair Trade Town in July 2006 and, on learning about our link with New Koforidua, wanted to be a part of it. Elizabeth asked me if Media could form a link with Garstang. I told her how our town council had responded to our link with New Koforidua and said that, although we would welcome Media to join with our campaigning, if they wanted an official link involving the local authorities, they would need to approach our town council separately. This they did and, to my surprise, some, if not all, councillors were keen to support any link with Media.

Sometime later, a councillor informed me that the reason some opposed our link with New Koforidua was that they objected to supporting a link with a community in a country that spent £10 million on celebrating independence. I pointed out that our link was with the community of New Koforidua and did not in any way endorse the actions of the Ghanaian government; besides, why shouldn't they celebrate independence in any way they chose? I was told the problem was they were spending £10 million on "celebrating fighting the British." I could not believe what I had just heard. They had a problem supporting a link with New Koforidua and yet embraced the prospect of a link with Media, which lies in a country that every year spends millions of pounds celebrating giving the British a good thumping. Then it hit me like a brick; one was a link with rich, white Americans, the other a link with poor, black Africans. I went to my desk and started to write an article for our local paper that started with the line "The arrogance and ignorance of our council will never cease to amaze me.". It made the front page and the battle lines between the council and I were firmly drawn in the sand. This led to difficulties and challenges down the line, but I will never regret writing those words.

An official link between Garstang and Media failed to materialise, but we welcomed the US Fair Trade campaigners to join with us and New Koforidua in what we unofficially called the 'Fair Trade Triangle', which coincidentally but beautifully lay on the same three corners as the historic slave trade triangle. Schoolchildren took part in the Fairtrade Fortnight 'Go Bananas' event in 2009 by eating Fairtrade bananas together via webcam in three schools in Garstang, New Koforidua and Media PA. Fairtrade bananas were not available to purchase in New Koforidua, but the Volta River Estates Ltd. (VREL) kindly donated the bananas. VREL was set up in 1988 as Ghana's first commercial banana export operation and Africa's first Fairtrade banana plantation. We visited VREL as part of our 'Go Global Go Ghana' project in 2001. The bananas eaten by children at Garstang Community Primary school were donated by the Co-op.

Our Partnership Agreement between Garstang and New Koforidua listed several projects that we aimed to fulfil, including the building of a community house and continued joint campaigning against poverty and promoting Fair Trade, which now included Media as part of our Fair Trade Triangle. We also wanted to explore the ambitious project of building a footbridge over the main Accra to Kumasi highway that cut New Koforidua in two. The busy highway dipped dangerously as it passed through the village and a number of children were killed each year attempting to cross it, which many were forced to do just to get to their school. We soon realised, however, that there were no bridges on the 160 mile stretch from Kumasi to the capital. It seemed that, with the dangerously high-loaded lorries in Ghana, bridges were not an option. The highway was also firmly under the jurisdiction and the responsibility of the Kumasi Metropolitan Assembly and something we rightly had little control over. In time, the road was flattened and, although a great deal of care is still needed when crossing it, thankfully there are no annually reported deaths today.

In June 2008 we were to visit New Koforidua again in order to begin implementing our project aims and, in particular, start building the community house. In the spirit of cooperation and equality we wanted this to be another exchange visit as we had in 2004. Raising the funds for our friends to visit Garstang from New Koforidua was becoming increasingly difficult,

Jocelyn with Garstang schoolchildren.

however, as was obtaining visas for their visit; an all-too-frequent problem for links like ours. We succeeded in securing only one visitor to Garstang: Samuel Ofori, a teacher from D.A. JSS school in New Koforidua and our main contact person at the time. His visa was initially refused, but with the help of our MP his delayed visit did go ahead, albeit later that year in November. By chance, we were also visited by Jocelyn and Stephen, who were pupils at Samuel's school. As children of Kuapa Kokoo farmers they were known as the Kuapa Kids and they had been invited by Divine Chocolate to tour the UK to promote Fairtrade. We were able to welcome them to Garstang on Friday 13th June, just three days before our group left for Ghana.

There were six people from the UK joining me on this visit: my son Tom; Robin, joining us for the third time; Richard Watts, a lecturer from Myerscough College who had also been on the 2004 exchange; and his team of three students who would start work on building the community house. Tom was an excellent photographer and produced a book of photos from the visit that became a valuable resource for our work with schools. My friend Samuel Fianu, who I met when visiting Children in Need in 2001, would also join us for the visit to New Koforidua.

Building a house in Ghana would be far cheaper than building the equivalent in the UK and we had set ourselves a fundraising target of £10,000. We eventually raised more, with donations coming in from individuals, faith groups, schools, community groups and businesses not only in Garstang and New Koforidua but also from across the globe. The full list of donors was put up on permanent display on the wall of the house once completed. The Co-op in the UK was by far the largest donor and, since the building of the house was made possible due to the cooperation of so many groups and individuals, it was to be named the 'co-operative house'.

Laying the foundations for the house was hard work under the hot sun but Richard and his team had made a good start. The house was not completed until 2011 when Richard and I were able to visit again to attend its ceremonial opening and although not yet properly furnished I was to be able to sleep in my own room facing the DA JSS school for the very first time. I had to give a short speech at the opening ceremony which, thanks to Samuel's help, I was able to deliver in Twi.

The co-operative house included a library that later was to be equipped with laptops for use by the schools. The house was also to be used to hold meetings and host visits to New Koforidua, which self-declared as Africa's first Fair Trade Town just two months after the house was opened.

During our exchange in 2004 our guests were welcomed by Garstang's mayor as "our Christian friends" but it was essential that our link, and therefore the co-operative house, was not in any way seen to be affiliated with any one religion or even political group. Many of the faith groups in New Koforidua had made donations towards the house, including the

Muslim community. I had remembered the comedian Dave Allen and his parting words at the end of his shows: "May your God be with you." We wanted people from all faiths to be made welcome at this house so above the 'co-operative house' sign we had painted the seven religious symbols representing the major world faiths and the words "Welcome – May your God be with you". At the centre of all the symbols we placed the Ghanaian Adinkra symbol *Gye Nyame*. This symbol appears throughout Ghana, from sandals to gate posts and purses to the backs of lorries. *Gye Nyame* means "Except for God" in Twi and represents the supremacy of God, but not specific to any one faith.

I was to visit New Koforidua again in 2015 and 2019. In 2015 I also travelled north to visit Bolgatanga, which was inspired by New Koforidua to become Ghana's and Africa's second Fair Trade Town.

In 2019 I had the great joy to be able to present my hand-made bean-to-bar chocolate to Frederick, Patricia and Madam Ferida; the cocoa farmers in New Koforidua who had grown the beans I used to produce it. I had planned for my seventh visit in 2019 to be my last, but while I was there

Frederick Gamor Wilson

I could not imagine never going back to what has become my second home. Who knows what the future will bring?

* * *

While working for the Fairtrade Foundation I was continuing to work in a voluntary capacity with Oxfam. My work with Oxfam and our community link often

Presenting FIG Tree chocolate to Patricia Adwubi.

overlapped with my paid job and sometimes it became difficult to see where the line was drawn between them.

I attended all eight Oxfam assemblies between 1994 and 2006, when I came off the association and became an Oxfam Friend. I consider it an honour to be made a Friend despite a part of me thinking it a little comparable to a horse being put out to graze to live out its last years.

The first Oxfam Assembly in 1994 was something quite special, attended by 250 stakeholders from every corner of the globe who had gathered to debate how poverty should be defined and, consequently, how it should be tackled. At that time, Oxfam was debating whether it should work to alleviate poverty at home in the UK. As well as raising vital funds for Oxfam, the second-hand shops already provided a service to those disadvantaged in the UK, but up to this point Oxfam had never run a UK program. I went with an open mind, but my initial thought was that Oxfam should continue to work with the world's poorest outside the UK. My mind was altered, however, after listening to Stan Thekaekara describe poverty as a 'disease' and a lack of empowerment that affected people living in the Gorbals of Glasgow in the same way it affected the 'untouchable' Dalit class of India.

After three days debating poverty, someone told a joke. "How many Oxfam stakeholders does it take to change a lightbulb? Well, it depends what you mean by change." I got the point but felt the three days were more than worthwhile. I came away transformed, moved and motivated by the whole event.

The debating process I experienced at Oxfam assemblies was, and still is, the best I have known. You were assigned to workshop groups and remained in them throughout the whole assembly. You stayed in your group over coffee breaks which, I discovered, is often when the best discussions take place. The facilitators facilitated rather than presented to the participants. I learned then that a good facilitator need not know anything about the subject being debated; their job was to get the best out of the people attending the workshop. As my friend, and best facilitator I know, Joe Human told me many years later, that was the difference between a workshop with a facilitator and a seminar with a presenter. I have attended many 'workshops' over the years that turned out to be seminars. Not a problem, as long as the participants know they are going to attend a seminar and not a workshop.

I first met Joe at the Oxfam Assembly at Loughborough in January 2000 when I was asked to give a presentation about my work as a campaigner. This was the first time I was to address an international audience of this size and I was terrified. Joe had the job of taking me through the rehearsal and he did it brilliantly. He is a fantastic people person, so it is only right he should be named Joe Human.

My legs were like jelly, and this was just the rehearsal. Joe could see this and somehow managed to calm my nerves, at least to the point that it did not show for the main event. Because of my own difficulties learning languages I have nothing but great admiration and respect for the interpreters at these events and told Joe how I really wanted to thank them as well as apologise for speaking too fast. "Then why don't you?" he replied. I did and made a point of doing so whenever I could at the many international conferences I was to speak at thereafter.

My presentation went well and was well received, even more so when I was able to demonstrate my commitment to Oxfam by informing my audience that I was giving the presentation on my wife's birthday. So many people came up afterwards to wish Jane a happy birthday and one kind person even passed on a gift for her: a small painted papier-mâché egg.

I am still nervous when public speaking today, but with some thanks to Joe I have learned to live with it. A few years later, Joe was to retire and move up from Oxford to Keswick in the nearby Lake District. He contacted me before the move to say he wanted to start up a campaign group in Keswick to make it a Fairtrade Town. Keswick went on to become one of the best examples of a Fairtrade Town that I know. If that wasn't enough, Joe also went on to lead the campaign to make Cumbria a Fairtrade County and the Lake District National Park a Fairtrade Region.

The first job I undertook in any official capacity with the Fairtrade Foundation was to give a presentation at an event in Keswick. I told the audience I was more nervous than usual partly because it was my first official Fairtrade Foundation task, but also because I would be speaking in front of my presentation 'guru'. After the event I asked Joe how it had gone, and he said perfect and gave me ten out of ten. During the car journey home, I kept reflecting on what he'd said; there is no such thing as perfect, least of all in Joe's eyes. There was always room for improvement and if anybody could see how to improve a presentation, it was Joe. The next day I received an email again congratulating me on my talk but also listing several bullet points on how it could have been better. I owe whatever presentation skills I have to Joe and will always be grateful.

Following the success of the shanty house built by local Scouts for the Oxfam Fast during my time in Northern Ireland, I had decided to do the same in Garstang in 2002 for the proposed Oxfam Overseas Challenge. Again, I enrolled the help of the local Scout group and a shanty house was built in the enclosed area outside Garstang Arts Centre. I'd managed to get hold of an award-winning Oxfam bucket, albeit slightly damaged, which I used to promote Oxfam's work and, after fixing the small hole, to collect clean water from my home just 100 yards or so up the road. I spent 48 hours living in the house, not setting foot in my own home, and living off nothing but Fairtrade Geobars and water.

My mail was brought to the shanty house and one of the letters was from Oxfam providing more information on the Oxfam Overseas Challenge. The idea of the Challenge was to invite supporters to raise funds for Oxfam's work and then take part in an endurance test followed by a visit to an Oxfam project. The letter was asking potential participants to

Ben and Anna at the Garstang shanty house

name their preferred choice of destination; mine had to be Machu Picchu in Peru. I had raised £1,701 by living in the shanty house, so was well on my way to reaching the target of £2,500 that had to be met before walking on the Inca Trail to Machu Picchu two years later in May 2004. The director of the Fairtrade Foundation, Harriet Lamb, had suggested that I visit the Fairtrade coffee farming cooperative, COCLA, while I was in Peru, so my planned ten-day visit with Oxfam was extended by an extra four days.

On Friday 14th March 2004 I awoke at 3.30am at Heathrow airport after just three hours sleep and with fourteen hours of flying ahead.

I needed coffee but there was no Fairtrade option; it was Costa Coffee or nothing. As I drank, I read the Costa slogan: "The pleasure of coffee is in its sensual appeal." With no thought for the farmers who grow the beans, this was in stark contrast to the slogan in the newly-launched Oxfam 'Progreso' café I had visited in London the day before: "Sin café no hay manana". This was a beautiful Spanish pun; for the coffee drinker, meaning: "Without coffee there is no morning", just as I felt that morning, but for the coffee producer it had a more profound meaning: "Without coffee there is no tomorrow"; in other words, without coffee there is no future for the producers and their families.

One day later, after an overnight stay in Lima, we were finally touching down in Cusco, the ancient capital of the Inca Empire. I have this theory that every person has a liking for food and drink as a consequence of their culture; for example, because I am English, I like fish and chips, tea made with plenty of fresh milk and warm beer. But I also believe that deep within every person there is also an innate liking that cannot be explained. For me this was Peru and as we landed in Cusco to the sound of pan pipes, I felt a genuine sense of coming home.

Cusco was quite simply the most beautiful city I had ever seen. At 3,400m our two nights in Cusco gave us a chance to acclimatise, as well as time to get to know the rest of our group. Altitude sickness affects some people more than others and luckily for me its severity is not in any way linked to one's physical fitness. I was going to do everything to avoid it and promised myself that I would not touch a drop of alcohol until I had completed the Inca Trail and arrived safely back in Cusco. I drank plenty of coca leaf tea, however, and tried chewing on a coca leaf the day I set out on the Trail, but could not keep that up for long.

Day one of the walk was easier than expected, leaving me with just a slight headache. I thought I had a passing glimpse of a hummingbird when I visited Central America fifteen years earlier, but now I caught sight of many of the tiny creatures and, in stark contrast, also saw a condor soaring high above us. As we slowly ascended from Ollantaytambo to Huayllabamba, the porters came running past us carrying everything from cooking pots to tables and I swore I even saw one with a fridge on his back. They were just amazing; setting up camp and digging out toilets before we arrived and then taking everything down again after we set off each day.

Day two was the hardest, starting at 3,000m and climbing up to Warmiwanuska, or Dead Woman's Pass as it is appropriately named. At 4,250m above sea level, this was the highest point of our journey and the highest point on land that I have ever reached. I trailed at the back with another team member and one of the guides as the rest of the team hurried on towards the top of the pass. "They'll be sorry," the guide told us, as slowly but surely is the best way when dealing with altitude sickness. It was a steep ascent, which I would have found hard going even without the rarefied air, forcing me to stop for breath every 50 yards or so. At each stop I turned around and took time to take in the beautiful scenery, the likes of which I had never seen before or since. The images I saw were embedded in my brain as surely as a camera captures a photograph; I'll never forget them.

The feeling on reaching the top of the pass was fantastic and on the other side we could see our campsite for that night near to the River Pacamayo. It was a difficult descent but far better coming down than going up. I had survived with nothing more than a slight headache which, although it got worse as we came down, soon went away with painkillers. Some of the others paid the price for their haste; altitude sickness can be delayed and severely debilitating. My quote for the day was: "Fundraising with altitude".

The views from both the front and back of our tent when we awoke the next morning were just out of this world. We had an eleven-hour trek ahead of us, the longest out of the four-day trail, but there was never a dull moment. Another, but less formidable, climb up to Runku Raccay, which was a tower used by the Incas to observe the stars and enable them to predict the coming of the rains. It is said that the Incas never suffered from famine as they were always well prepared for any oncoming drought. The mountainous Inca path took us through the cloud forest with abundant vegetation including orchids, mosses and creepers living off the permanently moist air. We stopped for lunch at Phuyu Pata Marca, the 'town above the clouds', before taking a steep descent down over 2,000 steps to catch site again of the famous Urubamba River that flows like a sacred snake below Machu Picchu.

We could now see Wayna Picchu, which means young mountain, along with our goal of Machu Picchu (old mountain) although the ancient city was hidden behind it. Thanks to the porters, who also doubled as great chefs, we enjoyed flambé bananas with chocolate sauce for our last meal on the trail and then went to bed for an early start the next day.

We woke at 3.30am to the sound of a cockerel crowing and had a three-hour trek to Intipunku (sun gate) if we had any chance of seeing Machu Picchu at sunrise. On arrival, however, the ancient site was obscured by cloud, so we made the gentle descent towards it. When the cloud did clear it was like experiencing an eclipse; words just cannot describe the feeling on first seeing the ancient city ruin.

Contrary to popular belief, the site of Machu Picchu was not chosen or kept secret because of its altitude; in fact, at just 2,430m it is lower than Ollantaytambo at the start of the Inca Trail (which sits at 2,792m) and is far lower than the ancient capital, Cusco (which sits at 3,399 m). The Machu Picchu site was chosen because of its sacred location lying above the Urubamba River, below Wayna Picchu (which forms the shape of a puma) and beside another mountain shaped like a skull that looks towards Intipunku. Intipunku itself is positioned so that the sunrise on the summer solstice will shine directly through the gates onto Machu Picchu. Although the Incas gave up the locations of many places to the Spanish, the sacred site of Machu Picchu was never revealed and thus it was not found until Hiram Bingham re-discovered the 'lost' city of the Incas in 1911.

Eventually we had to leave Machu Picchu to have lunch at the nearby inhabited town of Aguas Calientes, or Machupicchu Pueblo as it is known today. I stood at the exit, not being able to take my eyes off the site knowing it would be for the very last time. The train was the main mode of transport used to reach Aguas Calientes and the railway runs straight down the middle of the main street. It was a bizarre feeling having lunch while a train passes your table. I enjoyed the thermal baths at Aguas Calientes, hence its name, and then bought souvenirs at the central Mercado Artesanal craft market, including a beautiful dark blue shoulder bag, which I still use with fond memories today.

The next day we took the train back to Ollantaytambo and the bus to Cusco. The mountainous train journey is one of the most scenic in the world, but somehow after walking the Inca Trail the scenery viewed from the valley floor was nothing compared to that seen from high above. Back in Cusco, we met with the new group about to do their walk the next day and enjoyed a celebration meal that included my first alcoholic drink since arriving in Peru: Pisco Sour.

Next there was a return flight to Lima to visit two Oxfam-funded projects at San Juan de Lurigancho. The projects were simple, requiring relatively little funding but providing considerable impact: a set of steps and a path enabling local residents to negotiate the steep banks and difficult terrain in all weather conditions throughout the seasons. We visited the women who ran the community kitchens, who then took us into their homes and fed us: such a humbling experience.

It was the last day of the Overseas Challenge and time to say goodbye to the rest of the team who departed for the airport and their return flight to the UK. I, however, had arranged to visit the Fairtrade coffee farming cooperative, COCLA, which grew the beans that went to make the Cafedirect Machu Picchu coffee. That meant another flight back to Cusco and a long bus journey to the valley neighbouring the ancient site of Machu Picchu. But for now, I had a day in Lima, and it was the day of the FA cup final: Manchester United versus Millwall.

I had to miss watching the game with my son Ben and, as I was now six hours behind UK time, the match had already taken place. In the hope of catching some highlights, however, I visited an English pub and discovered United had won 3 – 0.

The bus journey from Cusco to visit COCLA at Quillabamba was yet another remarkable experience. Unlike the journey between Cusco and Aguas Calientes, this was off the tourist trail. The long, twisting and narrow road over the Andes was barely wider than the bus and was frequently crossed by mountain streams. We were often driving through cloud and, as it got dark, I started to feel a little concerned. I was told, however, that it was safer driving at night on this road as the headlights made it easier to see oncoming traffic. Just when I thought things couldn't get any worse, they did: the bus stopped in the middle of what could only be described as a jungle. No problem; they just had to change the inner tube of a tyre.

I only had one full day with the farmers at COCLA, who could not understand why I had made such a long journey for such a short stay. Their warmth and generous hospitality made me feel so welcome but despite their requests that I should stay longer, it was sadly not possible. It was great for me to witness the benefits of Fairtrade first-hand and an enormous honour to be given the opportunity to deliver a presentation on the development and spread of Fair Trade Towns, making Garstang famous in this small corner of Peru. I presented the farmers with Fairtrade footballs and their own Cafedirect Machu Picchu coffee purchased from my local Co-op store in Garstang – the world's first Fair Trade Town. We shared the same love of football and in return they gave me a COCLA football shirt and treated me to roasted guinea pig in garlic sauce cooked by Maria, the wife of COCLA president Guillermo. The guinea pigs and Cusquena beer were donated by Hermenegido, the president of the Huadquina cooperative. I had previously eaten guinea pig in a restaurant in Cusco and must confess to not being at all impressed; it lacked flavour, was dry and looked like roadkill. But the guinea pig cooked by Maria was something quite different: incredibly moist, full of flavour and the most memorable meal from my time in Peru.

I was sorry to leave so soon after my arrival in Quillabamba but had to travel for the fourth and final time to Cusco. On my final day, I went on a mega shopping spree for souvenirs and family gifts and enjoyed my last meal in Peru; ceviche de pescado (a traditional Peruvian fish dish marinated in citrus juice, primarily lime and lemon), alpaca with Andean sauce, followed by pecan pie and accompanied by Pisco Sour, half a litre of Peruvian white wine and a liqueur coffee, all for just the equivalent of £13.20. The next day I was flying back home to the UK.

* * *

The 'Make Poverty History' campaign was to be launched by Nelson Mandela at a rally in Trafalgar Square on 3rd February 2005. Mandela had recently announced his retirement from public life so this would likely be my last opportunity to see the great man. I took the day off work with the Fairtrade Foundation and went to London by train. I was invited into the Oxfam enclosure to one side of the speaker's platform, so ended up just yards away when Mandela spoke. I could almost cut with a knife the awesome atmosphere created by his legendary charisma.

Our Fair Trade/slave trade campaign had already drawn comparisons between slavery and poverty and Mandela was to endorse this with his speech. He said that poverty and inequality was "to rank alongside slavery and apartheid as social evils" and "like slavery and apartheid, poverty is not natural. It is man-made and it can be overcome and eradicated by the actions of human beings." He thanked "the people of Britain for their support through those days of the struggle against apartheid" stating that, "Many stood in solidarity with us, just a few yards from this spot." I remembered with pride the couple of hours I spent alone, keeping the vigil outside the South African Embassy before going on my journey to Central America.

After the rally I met my good friend and fellow Oxfam campaigner Pushpanath, better known as Push in campaigning circles. Push introduced me to David Taylor. Like me, David was a Fair Trade campaigner, Manchester United fan and was born in Tring, less than seven miles from my birthplace in Wendover. He was a student at Warwick University and was about to attend their declaration as a Fairtrade University. He had asked the Fairtrade Foundation if they could send a representative to the event, but nobody was available. I had taken a day off work but was able to break my return journey home to attend the Warwick University declaration. David was delighted and I had managed to see Nelson Mandela and put in some time at work after all.

I had another great day out with members of the Garstang Fairtrade Group to visit the Edinburgh Make Poverty History rally in July. In the same month, I collected my Beacon Prize for Creative Giving for my work with Fairtrade Towns at an event at the Foreign and Commonwealth Office. David Miliband presented the award. I was told he was likely to become a future prime minister, but it was his brother Ed that was to lead the Labour Party five years later, and neither of them were destined to become prime minister. The day after collecting my award, my son Ben was the first pupil to receive the Halford Award for Global Citizenship at his primary school leaving assembly. Ben was recognised for taking part in our Ghana Exchange the year before at just ten years old and following his visit he had given several presentations in the school and for the local community.

On the day it was announced that Gordon Brown would succeed Tony Blair as prime minister in 2007, the story was all over the news. You can imagine my surprise, therefore, when I received a phone call on that same day asking if the prime minister-elect could speak with me the following morning. He wanted to include my story as one of 30 in his upcoming book titled 'Britain's Everyday Heroes', recognising the achievements of ordinary people whose commitment to a cause or a community had inspired him. Gordon Brown was still chancellor of the exchequer when I was invited to 11 Downing Street along with some of the others featured in his book for an informal group consultation. Nineteen days later, on 27th June 2007, Gordon Brown moved next door and became prime minister and on 24th July, Jane and I were invited to his book launch at the Methodist Central Hall in Westminster.

Just one week before the book launch, Jane and I were also invited to the Queen's Garden Party at Buckingham Palace. We were to visit Buckingham Palace again in February 2009, where I was awarded an MBE for services in support of Oxfam and Fairtrade.

On this occasion we were joined by the whole family, Tom, Ben and Anna. Later that same year, I visited 10 Downing Street as part of a delegation from the Fairtrade Foundation by invitation of Gordon Brown's wife, Sarah. Gordon Brown was not at home on that occasion, but thanks to David Taylor I was to meet with him for a third and final time when I saw him speak following his election defeat in 2010.

When we formed the Garstang Fairtrade Town Steering Group in January 2002, with Alex as chair, it superseded the work of the Oxfam Group, which still exists today, albeit in name only. In 2007 we were facing our third renewal as a Fairtrade Town and we needed a new chair. I semi-reluctantly took on the role and decided we would relaunch our campaign.

After the relaunch, we hosted a visit to Garstang by my line manager, Hannah Reed, Windward Islands banana producer Simeon Greene, and Emma Rung, the Fairtrade Towns coordinator for Fairtrade Sweden. Emma had asked to meet up with me when I could spare some time on a visit to London. However, my work visits to London always had full agendas so I persuaded Emma to come and see me in Garstang instead. We all had dinner at the former Jacobite restaurant where the meal that gave rise to our first Fairtrade Town status took place. The restaurant was now under new ownership and called 'Pipers'. Emma and Simeon joined me to visit some of Garstang's schools the next day. After returning to Sweden, Emma told me that she was pleased that she had to go to Garstang as it made a big difference hearing the 'Garstang Story' on location as opposed to being in London. That was when I realised the importance of hosting visits to Garstang as well as taking the message far and wide.

As part of our renewal, Garstang Town Council updated their Fairtrade Resolution in May 2007, which now stated: "The Council agreed to renew its commitment to include the use of Fairtrade products at Town Council meetings and functions." But Wyre Borough Council was the local authority that had real influence in Garstang and although they had welcomed our visitors from Ghana and sent representatives to the occasional event, up to now they had never passed any formal resolution in support of Fairtrade and it was clear that opposition existed in some parts.

I was invited to give a presentation to the Wyre Borough Fairtrade Task Group in March 2008. I made many references to how we also supported local farmers alongside Fairtrade farmers and mentioned the way we had linked our campaign to that of the historic slave trade abolition. It was not well received. "You do yourself no favours mentioning the slave trade," one of the members said and asked why I had not talked about local farmers. But they did finally budge and from October 2008 all hot drinks served in the council's Breakaway canteen became Fairtrade. Vending machines, however, were locked into a five-year contract until 2012, which would cost £16,500 to break. I'm not sure what happened after the contract ended. On 4th December 2008 Wyre Borough Council passed the following resolution: "This Council supports the principle of fair trade and seeks to promote fair trade within the Wyre Borough. The Council will seek to use fairly traded products (as certified with the FAIRTRADE Mark) whenever possible and will work with the Wyre Strategic Partnership to promote fair trade across the borough. We also support local production and will work with relevant organisations to strive to promote local products and a fair deal for Lancashire producers."

The Fair Trade Town concept of a whole community declaring support for a specific issue went on to inspire other initiatives, including Social Enterprise Towns. Hebden Bridge became the first Walkers are Welcome Town in October 2007 and the following year BUILD launched their Gold Star Awards, recognising the best community-based partnerships between the north and south hemispheres. The way we had used our link between Garstang and New Koforidua to promote Fair Trade inspired Joe in Keswick to develop a similar link with the coffee farming community of Choche in Ethiopia. We were honoured to have coffee farmers from Choche, who were visiting Keswick, attend our showing of the film 'Black Gold' at our 'After Black Gold' event in 2008. And I'll never forget urging Rita to go ahead with her grand idea to form a link between Haworth and Machu Picchu. Their link was strengthened with support from the Peruvian ambassador at their tenth anniversary celebrations in 2019. Both Cusco and Machupicchu Pueblo are now working towards becoming Fair Trade Towns in their own right.

The FIG Tree

The Lorna Young Foundation is a remarkable organisation that has always punched far above its weight. Named after one of the founders of Cafedirect, the Lorna Young Foundation is a UK registered charity that works towards the eradication of poverty by helping disadvantaged groups through the medium of ethical trading. Christina Longden is the director and her husband, Ian Agnew, the chairperson. They make a wonderful partnership. The Lorna Young Foundation began its life working from their kitchen table and, although still very much mindful of not wasting money on expensive overheads, the charity works across various African countries as well as in the UK, supporting disadvantaged people to become ethical entrepreneurs.

It was just a year after Nick Maurice had suggested I start my own organisation on the return trip from the Lyon conference in 2009 when Christina approached me with her vision of an international Fair Trade Visitor Centre. This was to be a place that focused specifically on fair trade and the inheritance of trade injustice, and the grassroots movements and organisations that had been working to redress the balance in the past and which are still making waves today. It would be somewhere for people to find out specifically how trade injustice affects the lives of 'the poor', the historical ties that the vast majority of British people have to the creation of the grossly unfair trade system that exists today and the measures which can be applied in modern day society in order to redress this imbalance – those are the benefits offered through fair trade. There was no such a place; we needed one and Christina thought there could be no better location than Garstang, the world's first Fair Trade Town.

She was right, but at first I reacted in the same way as I did to Nick; a great idea, but beyond my abilities and not something I could do. But, as so often happens in my life, things started to fall into place and I felt almost reluctantly guided towards taking an action; I was unsure about what to do but somehow very sure that I must do it. The demands to support Fair Trade Towns internationally were increasing and, as my visit to Japan had shown earlier that year, these demands could not always be met through my role as UK Fairtrade Towns coordinator.

One day, while walking to work at the vets, I passed the old Garstang Council Offices just yards away from my home. This used to be the site of the Tourist Information Centre where we held the ceremony to officially declare Garstang as a Fairtrade Town in 2001 and was also the starting point for our Fair Trade Way walk. Wyre Borough Council had relocated the Tourist Centre to a modern rented site in the new Cherestanc Square in Garstang. The old location was now lying empty. With our Fair Trade campaign linked to the past injustices of the slave trade and its abolition, and Garstang being the world's first Fair Trade Town, something told me this could be the site for the International Fair Trade Visitor Centre that Christina spoke of and that I would be the person to build it.

The seed had been planted and, like it or not, it would grow. I could choose to nurture it or let it die: was there really a choice? The place would have to have a café and Rita suggested we should visit 'Cobbles & Clay' in Haworth to get some ideas on how a café could be run. I never needed much excuse to visit Haworth so together with Jane, my friend Graham and his wife Belinda, we spent a day exploring the world's first Fair Trade Village. Enthused by our visit, we started to think up names for the centre and on the way home Graham came up with The FIG Tree – FIG standing for Fairtrade In Garstang. Over the Christmas period, and with thanks mainly to Jane and Tom, we developed The FIG Tree logo; a fig tree growing around the world with the branches joining at the top. I came up with the strap line 'Branching out around the world'.

I was on a very steep learning curve and needed all the help I could get, so it was back to the Lorna Young Foundation and Ian Agnew to discuss what business model we should use. We would clearly become a social enterprise and I wanted to steer away from becoming a charity. Ian recommended we became a community interest company but with the caveat that if The FIG Tree was to be a great success I would not get rich from it. I replied, "If The FIG Tree was a great success, I would be the richest man on the planet." The FIG Tree (Garstang) CIC was incorporated on 22nd February 2011.

Now the real work would begin, and I was still working part time both as a vet in Garstang and for the Fairtrade Foundation as Fairtrade Towns coordinator. I knew at some point I would have to give up one, if not both, jobs if I was to run The FIG Tree, with the expectation that my new role would make up for any loss in income. As it turned out, any difficult career moves were decided for me; the proprietor for the veterinary practice where I worked in Garstang had decided to sell up and retire and my job at the vets ended. My dream to give up vetting and work full time in some Fair Trade capacity at the age of 50 had been fulfilled, but just one year late.

The FIG Tree would also enable me to fulfil another dream. Before my first visit to Ghana in 2001, I'd watched a documentary in which a cocoa farmer was forced to store his five bags of cocoa until the price of cocoa was high enough to provide he and his family with a sustainable income. His family went hungry while he waited, and I wondered why he never resorted to eating his own cocoa. I knew that cocoa was a rich source of energy and if the Aztecs could make it into a drink surely he could, too. When I visited New Koforidua for the first time, I asked a cocoa farmer why they never ate their own cocoa and the answer I received still angers and motivates me today. "It is not our cocoa," he said, "we grow it for the British." I understand that as a producer he would see the cocoa as something he grew for his buyers and not for his own consumption, but it was almost 50 years after Ghanaian independence, and he still considered the cocoa he grew as belonging to the British. There and then I had a vision and a dream that one day we could run chocolate-making workshops for British children to learn about Fair

Trade and how cocoa is grown, and for the children of cocoa farmers to learn what happens to the cocoa grown by their parents and, most importantly, that the cocoa belongs to them and they can do with it whatever they wish. We have still to hold the workshops in Ghana, but the chocolate workshops for British schools was to be one of the main sources of income for The FIG Tree along with the café, shop, tourist and school visits to Garstang, and any additional income I could earn through supporting the International Fairtrade Towns movement and giving presentations.

Wyre Borough Council had already agreed in principle to allow us a three-year lease to rent the building with an option to renew and we had plans to open on World Fair Trade Day - 9th May 2011. I was still foolishly optimistic that we could reach our deadline when I travelled to New Koforidua to attend the opening of the Cooperative House in April, but it was going to take far longer.

It was clear that there were people on both Wyre Borough Council and Garstang Town Council who were against us, or at least me, and obstacles were constantly put in our way. Through the Freedom of Information Act, the deputy editor for our local paper had gained access to internal emails circulating across Wyre Borough Council and he told me, "Do you realise how much they hate you?" On more than one occasion did we get the go ahead from our solicitor only to find it meant nothing, baffling all of us. Wyre Borough Council even sent officials to the site demanding that our builders left the premises. Our solicitor said, despite working with many councils, he had never come across a situation as difficult as this.

We needed planning permission to run a wastewater pipe outside the building. We understood this would involve a lot of paperwork at a cost to us, for a pipe that could barely be seen from the road, but it became a real eye-opener for me personally. A senior planning official had absolutely no objection to our application, but it needed to be passed by Garstang's Town Council. He rang me at home to explain that this could be a problem and, perhaps on sensing my naivety, told me I did not understand the situation and that it was all about brown paper bags passed under the table. He then referred to a previous planning incident that I'd read about in the local paper. A local town councillor was responsible for refusing planning permission for a house that was built just a few inches higher than specified in the application and the builder was told the house had to be demolished. The case was referred, resulting in the local council ruling being overturned and the council receiving a fine at considerable cost to residents. The senior planning official went on to tell me this was all because the councillor making the objection had a personal vendetta with the builder concerned. He supported us and said he would have no hesitation in referring our case if it should be refused by the town council. I left the call feeling considerably shocked but somewhat reassured. The senior planning official retired from his post just a few months later, which may have been the reason he felt able to openly confide in me in the way he did.

Our opening date was constantly pushed back until finally, more than six months after our initial date, we looked set to open on Monday 21st November 2011; one day before the tenth anniversary of Garstang's official recognition as a Fairtrade Town, and The FIG Tree was to be located on the exact same site. The International Fair Trade Towns conference in Malmo, Sweden took place the weekend before. Just hours before my flight I sent in yet another signed document and our solicitor confirmed the deal was finally sealed, but when I left for Malmo I had still not received the keys.

It was down to Graham, Belinda and Jane, along with some of our other supporters, to collect the keys and get the place ready for opening over the weekend. As well as setting up the café they also had to set up our exhibition on Fair Trade Towns and the abolition of the Transatlantic slave trade. I returned from Malmo on the Sunday evening accompanied by a delegation from Brazil, which included the mayor of Poços de Caldas that was to become a Fair Trade Town the following year. As we drove around the final corner approaching my house, I was relieved and overjoyed to see the sign over the entrance to The FIG Tree. We opened as planned the next morning with an exhibition on display. It was, in my view, nothing short of a miracle achieved by my family, our closest friends and supporters.

Our successful, albeit delayed, opening also required funding as well as committed supporters, and we received funding from right across the globe as well as individuals locally. Donations came in from Japan, Germany, the USA and Dubai as well as Bolton, Brampton, Cumbria, Garstang and, of course, the Co-op. Such support always was, and still is, our greatest strength and I was determined to ensure we recognised it. We had a plaque made listing all our initial donors "who helped to fund The FIG Tree when it mattered most; at the start." We were most proud to display the plaque alongside the 'welcome rug' that had been specially made for us by the Claughton on Brock Women's Institute.

Support also came in from higher places. Earlier in the year someone had suggested I wrote to Gordon Brown, MP and former prime minister, following his recognition of my work in his book 'Everyday Heroes'.

As I started to draft a letter my expectation was low but there was nothing to lose in trying, and then something remarkable happened. I received an email from my friend and fellow Fair Trade campaigner David Taylor, who I had not heard from for a considerable amount of time, but who was now working as a PA for Gordon Brown. I couldn't believe it, and immediately called him up. I went ahead with the letter and, thanks to David's support, we received the following response: "The town of Garstang has been a pioneering force in the Fairtrade movement. From being the world's first Fairtrade Town, to their special community link with the Kuapa Kokoo society of New Koforidua in Ghana, they provide a best practice example of how communities can work together for the benefit of society as a whole. The establishment of the FIG Tree international visitor centre is the logical next stage in maintaining Garstang as a beacon for Fairtrade. I wish them every success and support their efforts to raise the necessary funds to make their dream a reality."

We needed a patron and Rita suggested we approached the author of Chocolat, Joanne Harris, who had recently attended a successful Fair Trade chocolate event in Haworth. We were delighted when she accepted our invitation and even more so when she visited The FIG Tree in 2013. It was then that we realised the similarities between our struggle with the establishment in Garstang and that of Chocolat heroine Vianne Rocher in the French village of Lansquenet-sous-Tannes.

* * *

Losing my job at the vets in Garstang was perhaps a good thing as it freed up the time critically needed to get The FIG Tree up and running. I was now on The FIG Tree payroll and, ironically, I continued to do some veterinary locum work on behalf of The FIG Tree to help raise the money needed to pay my salary. I worked my last day as a vet, however, in July 2012 and came off the veterinary register.

I was still working part time with the Fairtrade Foundation although I was increasingly spending more and more time supporting the International Fair Trade Towns movement than Fairtrade Towns in the UK. I had always received positive annual reviews but in 2011 I was told I only 'partially met' my passion and commitment for Fairtrade.

My passion for Fairtrade, or Fair Trade, was in my view my greatest and perhaps only strength. My newly-appointed manager ensured I received a very positive review in May 2012, but two months later I was made redundant and told my job would finish at the end of September. It was made worse by the fact that, despite having worked nine years for the Fairtrade Foundation, I would not receive full redundancy pay as most of that time was spent working on a contract in a self-employed capacity. Even though I was not a member of the union, the union rep fought hard for my cause, but her efforts were in vain.

The year before, the Co-op had funded a website for the Fair Trade Way and markers to fix along the route, so a few of us had arranged to walk the Fair Trade Way again in August 2012 to raise money for The FIG Tree, Oxfam and a sustainable coffee grower's project in India, recommended by friend, fellow walker and Oxfam campaigner Pushpanath, or Push. We were joined by Nicola from the Manchester Oxfam office, who had arranged for us to walk into Keswick on the last day with a couple of llamas. Harriet Lamb also joined us for one day of the walk.

During the walk I received a phone call from the Fairtrade Foundation asking me if I would be willing to extend my time working with them for an extra three months until the end of the year. This presented me with a real dilemma; I was already burning the candle at both ends and there was lots more to come in the pipeline. It was Hobson's choice, however, and I accepted their offer.

Joe in Keswick was suffering badly from depression and, on listening to his account of the problem, I began to realise I was suffering from the very same signs. I had previously suffered from depression while working at the vets in Liverpool in 1987 and experienced another breakdown when I went on a family holiday to Wales while my mother was in hospital, before she died in 2003. I went to see my GP and, sure enough, he confirmed the diagnosis and this time I was prescribed, and accepted, the anti-depressant Citalopram.

I went on sick leave almost to the day my three-month work extension with the Fairtrade Foundation was to start. Apart from the three International Fair Trade events already arranged, I did nothing in my Fairtrade job throughout those three months. I went into the London office for the last time on 14th December and then took annual leave until the end of the year.

My work with the Fairtrade Foundation was over, but my work supporting International Fair Trade Towns would get even busier. It is hard for me to recall how I managed to do so much for The FIG Tree and in support of Fair Trade Towns in the state I was in, but my depression was to continue for most of the time The FIG Tree was running in Garstang.

Depression hits people in different ways; some may go into isolation, yet I was travelling the world. Despite having a loving family around me and meeting with so many good people on my travels, I often felt alone. I have always felt despair at the poverty and injustices in the world but when I was depressed this just came to a head. It felt like I was the only one in the world who cared, although clearly this was not true. But even today I question, in a world where a small child dies needlessly from poverty every three seconds, why the whole world is not protesting about it?

There were times when I wanted to leave home, not because I wanted to be away from the family but because I genuinely thought they would be better off without me. The one positive thing I can say is that this time around suicide was never an option. I hated myself for what I was doing to those I loved, which further fuelled the depression; it was like spiralling down into a bottomless pit with no return. I cannot even start to imagine how Jane felt. Did she worry about me when I travelled alone? I know on occasions when I was at home she found it difficult to cope, which sent me further down the spiral. But she stood by me none-the-less.

Getting on a plane was a form of escape, literally taking me to another place where nobody knew what was going on in my world and how I was hurting myself and others. I did not consciously make the decision to travel; most, if not all, of the time I was responding to requests and just did what I felt I had to do. I didn't question it, nor worry about how my flights were contributing to climate change. I just knew people wanted me to do a task and I just did it because this was something I could do. Now, post-Covid, we have all learned that we can still do so much without needing to travel, but rightly or wrongly this didn't cross my mind at the time.

On hearing about my problem, a Quaker Friend from my local Quaker Meeting told me about the excellent work carried out at the Tuke Centre in York, which offered a residential retreat and mental health clinic. It was highly recommended, but as well as having to make regular 200-mile, four-hour round trips to York, the therapy was expensive. I was extremely fortunate to have the costs covered by my Quaker Area Meeting and travelling to York each week was more than worthwhile. I attended a total of 20 therapy sessions that started in June 2014 and finished in April 2015. Although I accept that chronic depression is never cured, I was able to come off the anti-depressants and the sessions left me fully equipped with the necessary 'tools' I needed and a good understanding of what underlies my condition, thus enabling me to prevent further depressive episodes. I will always remain grateful to the Tuke Centre, my Quaker Area Meeting, my friends and family who stood by me, but most of all to Jane for staying with me throughout that terrible ordeal.

Just a few days after my depression was diagnosed, I attended and spoke at the European Parliament Fair Trade Breakfast run by the Fair Trade Advocacy Office in Brussels. Soon after that, on my 53rd birthday, I visited Eck- ernforde as part of the German 100th Fairtrade Towns celebration. Several German Fairtrade Towns declared jointly as their 100th, as we had done with Manchester and Salford seven years earlier. With Saarbrück- en declaring as the first Fairtrade Town in 2009,

Bruce with Kathrin celebrating 100 German Fairtrade Towns.

Germany was a bit of a late starter, but over dinner on my birthday I told Kathrin, the German Fair Trade Towns coordinator, that I believed one day there would be more Fairtrade Towns in Germany than in the UK. She asked if that bothered me and I replied, "As an English football fan we are more than used to creating something only to be beaten by the Germans some years later." My prediction came true.

The third and final event I attended during my last three months with the Fairtrade Foundation was the 6th International Fair Trade Towns Conference held in Poznan in November 2012, which also saw the declaration of Poznan as the first Fair Trade Town in Poland.

This conference fully embraced the wider Fair Trade movement rather than just the Fairtrade label and, like the Malmo conference the year before and all international conferences since, it was correctly named a 'Fair Trade Towns conference' with Fair Trade as two words. On arrival, I was delighted to also see The FIG Tree recognised as an international entity, with our logo included on the poster as one of the partner organisations.

Fair Trade Towns is a grassroots movement and, although it needed to be facilitated and funded by international and national Fair Trade and Fairtrade organisations, it should be driven, if not led, by the activists. The Poznan conference provided a real opportunity for grassroots debate and discussion and, as a result of participants asking for more international coordination, led to the formation of the International Fair Trade Towns Steering Committee (IFTTSC).

During a panel discussion, the question was asked time and time again: "Who do you go to if you want to start up a Fair Trade Town campaign in your own country?" Without exception, all responses said they would contact me. Up to this point I had been able to carry out this role partially through my work with the Fairtrade Foundation and partially, as when I visited Japan in 2010, in my own time. Having lost both sources of income as a vet and with the Fairtrade Foundation, I now needed funding for my international work more than ever and thankfully this was the conference where things started to happen.

I became one of the members of the newly formed IFTTSC as a representative of The FIG Tree, which was set up precisely for that purpose – to support the International Fair Trade Towns movement. The six other IFTTSC members included four from Europe, one from the USA and one from Japan. Yes, it was Eurocentric, with only the northern continents represented, but when you consider that at that time over 95% of Fair Trade Towns were in Europe and campaigns had only just been established in South America and Africa, this was an inevitable consequence. Apart from that, it was not as if loads of people were putting their names forward to go onto the committee; on the contrary, it was hard to find any representatives at all and most of them had to be persuaded.

I was given the title of International Fair Trade Towns Ambassador simply in an attempt to clarify my role and I would be the only committee member paid for that role. All the others were in some way employed by a Fair Trade organisation, which allowed some of their work time to be taken up to fulfil their international roles. I would act as a consultant on behalf of The FIG Tree, with The FIG Tree being paid for my services. Ideally this would help The FIG Tree be fully sustainable, including the payment of my salary.

The IFTTSC would require an annual budget of around £20k; mainly to cover my services. We would appeal to national Fair Trade Town organisations, but our hope and expectation was that eventually the full amount would be covered by the three major Fair Trade organisations: Fairtrade International (previously known as FLO), the World Fair Trade Organisation (WFTO) and Fair Trade USA (previously known as Transfair USA before breaking away from Fairtrade International in 2011). Although Fairtrade International did award the IFTTSC with a grant to develop a website in 2015 they were never forthcoming in providing a regular contribution. At the 2013 WFTO conference their members voted unanimously to support my work by funding the IFTTSC, but despite a contribution made that year, a much smaller one in 2016 and WFTO Europe making contributions in 2013 and 2014, no regular reliable contributions were forthcoming. Fair Trade USA, however, provided a regular substantial contribution for the next four years. The other main donors came from Germany, Austria and Belgium but perhaps the most touching were the regular donations coming in from places with far smaller campaigns such as Poland, Switzerland, the Czech Republic, Japan, Taiwan and Hong Kong. On one occasion we even received a substantial donation from an individual campaigner.

With the formation of the IFTTSC there was now a body that could unite the International Fair Trade Towns movement. Our first task was to write the International Guidelines for Fair Trade Towns, which included a definition of Fair Trade & Fair Trade products based on the Charter of Fair Trade Principles; our Mission and Objectives; Recommendations for the movement; and perhaps most importantly it was stated that Fair Trade Towns was a grassroots movement with ownership at those grassroots. Although I liked to think of the national campaigns being facilitated by the national organisations responsible, it was perhaps more realistic to appreciate that they were in fact run, and therefore controlled, by those organisations. But Fair Trade Towns in countries where no national organisation could facilitate or fund a national campaign, such as Ghana, could now be recognised by the IFTTSC. This meant that New Koforidua's self-declaration as Africa's first Fair Trade Town as part of the 1,000th Fair Trade Town celebrations in 2011 would now be recognised and this would open the door for other communities in Africa and elsewhere to make self-declarations, even if there was no national body to officially recognise them. The International Fair Trade Towns Guidelines were presented at the 7th International Fair Trade Towns conference in Oslo in September 2013.

By 2013 the FIG Tree café and workshops were in full swing, but my international work was also making massive demands on my time. In May I visited Seoul to attend the launch of their campaign and, less than two weeks after my return, I was flying in the opposite direction around the world for the WFTO conference in Brazil. Later that year I made two visits to Norway, visited Bremen in Germany, and Brussels in Belgium in the space of just 26 days and for six of the remaining twelve days I was at home I hosted a Japanese visitor to Garstang.

As well as attending the Oslo conference in September, I travelled with Jane to visit our Norwegian friends and fellow campaigners, Stale and Ellen, who had moved from Sauda to Kopervik on the island of Karmøy. The main purpose for the trip was to deliver a FIG Tree chocolate workshop to a local school, but there was time for fun, which included being stranded offshore when Stale's boat broke down and having my first and only go at fishing. One day we visited the quiet town of Skudeneshavn on the south coast of the island. We were taken to a small café with the words "we serve the best waffles in the world" displayed in the window. The café was run by a wonderful man called Johannes and all he served were Norwegian waffles, jams and coffee, but that was enough. Despite empty streets outside, the café was packed full of local people and the waffles were delicious. Johannes had a map on the wall with pins indicating where all his many customers had travelled from. We were proud to put our pin in Garstang, the world's first Fair Trade Town. We told Johannes about the FIG Tree and he allowed us to use his very own special waffle recipe, and Stale and Ellen donated a Norwegian waffle maker. Norwegian waffles, with local ice cream topped with melted chocolate that instantly set into 'chocolate armour', soon became a regular favourite in the FIG Tree. We discovered sometime later that Johannes had not given us the full waffle recipe used exclusively in his café; he had held back at least one of his secret ingredients. But perhaps we could call our waffles the second-best waffles in the world?

The 2014 International Fair Trade Towns conference took place in Kumamoto, Japan, the first Fair Trade Town in Asia. This was the first International Fair Trade Towns conference to be held outside Europe and, like the Poznan conference two years before, was not afraid to challenge the contentious issues around Fair Trade Towns and what became known as the 'Big Tent' approach embracing the wider Fair Trade family.

This was my second visit to Japan and, realising it could be my last, I made sure that I would find time to visit Hiroshima. The peace gardens and the museum there were a life-changing experience I'll never forget. One cannot imagine the horror unleashed at 8.15 am in Hiroshima on 6th August 1945; truly hell on earth! And it was all a lie!

Nobody can deny that dropping the bombs on Hiroshima and Nagasaki brought a swift end to the war with Japan, but there were other reasons behind dropping both bombs and in the museum there are copies of the letters to prove it.

I had always wanted to spend a night in a Japanese pod, and I only had one night in Hiroshima so stayed in a pod hotel. This was an experience that was very different to my time at the museum, but an experience none the less.

* * *

To be sustainable, the FIG Tree could not rely solely on the income from our café, shop and workshops and, thanks primarily to the work of our fundraising volunteer Emma, we were achieving a good success rate in our grant applications. Our first attempt at applying for a Heritage Lottery grant was not successful, however, because we had included funding for our chocolate workshops. Our intended project was based on four themes: Fair Trade Towns, the British Transatlantic slave trade and its abolition, Quakers and chocolate. All these themes were central to our work but only three of them involved our local heritage, which obviously was a condition for a successful Heritage Lottery Fund bid. The funders took time to explain this and with their help and support we resubmitted the application around the three local heritage themes: Fair Trade Towns, with Garstang being the world's first; the slave trade and its abolition, with nearby Lancaster having been Britain's fourth largest slave trade port; and Quakers, with Garstang lying within '1652 country' where Quakers were founded. This time we succeeded.

Our project ran for a year from July 2012 to June 2013 and was primarily focused on building up our exhibition on the three heritage themes. Initially we purchased three display cabinets, including a tower case that housed the plaque that was unveiled by the comedian Tony Robinson at Garstang's official ceremony in November 2001. The plaque had previously been displayed on the exterior wall outside the Tourist Information Centre and was a little worse for wear, but we had it remounted on a special piece of imported Fair Trade wood and it now stood on the exact spot where the unveiling had taken place.

Central to the project was the production of eight display panels

covering the slave trade abolition campaign: how Fair Trade Towns started, what they mean and how they spread across the world; the historic slave trade triangle and how it relates to our current Fair Trade Triangle; and our Fair Trade Way walk. The panels were researched and written by an excellent team of local volunteers supported by Global Link, the Lancaster Development Education Centre. We also had the support of Steve Miller, then the chief executive for the Ironbridge Gorge Museum Trust, a World Heritage site. Our team of volunteers visited Ironbridge to see how a museum is run, but in particular to learn how to put together a display and how to write the content for the panels. Steve Miller later said that the process we had gone by to produce the panels would put most museums to shame. He had also written in an email: "I have had the pleasure of working in the museums and heritage sector for nearly 20 years and I can honestly say that I have never witnessed a more impressive project than The FIG Tree."

As part of the project, volunteers also visited Wisbech, the home of the abolitionist Thomas Clarkson; the International Slavery Museum in Liverpool together with the archives; the Quaker Tapestry in Kendal; and two volunteers took part in a Fair Trade course at Liverpool Hope University.

Visiting Wisbech to see the Clarkson memorial, his home and, most of all, the Clarkson display at the Wisbech and Fenland museum was the highlight for me. We saw Clarkson's famous treasure chest containing seeds, textiles and other goods from Africa that he had collected on his travels to demonstrate the advanced African culture. Clarkson's chest also contained many items that demonstrated the cruelty of the slave trade, such as handcuffs, leg-shackles, thumbscrews, whips and branding irons. The chest became an important part of his lectures and one of the earliest examples of a visual aid.

The Wisbech museum also holds the original manuscript of Charles Dickens's Great Expectations and to celebrate this we saw a fascinating replica of Miss Havisham's decaying wedding dinner set out on a long table. We later learned that this was made by a craftsman called Fred who worked with the museum. He had also made a 3D model of the Brookes slave ship taken from the plan developed by Clarkson to demonstrate how slaves were packed onto the ship in the most inhumane conditions. We decided we would contact Fred to help us with our project.

Later in the project we produced two additional panels with accompanying artefacts: one entitled 'Thomas Clarkson Motivator and campaigning pioneer' and the other 'Quaker belief and convictions'. We asked Fred to make a replica of Clarkson's chest and another 3D model of the Brookes ship that could be taken apart to show how the slaves were packed onto each deck. Mainly aimed at school children, those viewing the Clarkson panel were asked what they would put into a modern-day chest to promote fair trade and demonstrate the injustices of our present trading system? They were also asked to count the number of slaves in the Brookes model. We had marked an area on the floor to represent the amount of space given to a slave on a slave ship (40cm wide by 180cm long) and asked people to sit in the area and try to imagine what it would have been like to spend several weeks in this space, in the hold of a ship sailing through storms in tropical heat. Fred also made some replica shackles and working hand cuffs to put

The original Clarkson chest with The FIG Tree replica.

into the chest and reproduced a drawing of his of slaves on the deck of a ship which we had made into a 145cm square backdrop.

Fred had made all these objects in Wisbech, Cambridgeshire and we had to find a way to transport them 200 miles to The FIG Tree in Garstang. Fred offered to deliver them personally, which gave us an idea for a publicity stunt. Clarkson had travelled over 35,000 miles, setting up

1,200 groups for the abolition of the slave trade. Fred would of course be travelling by train and not on horseback but, in memory of the great man, Fred agreed to dress up as Thomas Clarkson and ride into Garstang to deliver the chest on horseback. It was an amazing sight.

The Darby family in Ironbridge were Quakers and the Darby Houses make up part of the Ironbridge museum complex. At Rosehill House visitors are given the chance to dress up in period costume and compare the fancy, flamboyant clothing typical of that Georgian period with the simple dress Quakers were advised to wear. Guidelines stated the maximum number of buttons Quakers should wear on their sleeve, and lace and fancy trimmings were not approved. I was struck by a comment made at the museum declaring that over time the modest Quaker dress almost became a vanity in itself that people wore with pride. So, later in the 19th century these guidelines were no longer adhered to. This need to act according to their convictions, rather than set rules, may explain why Quakers both past and present are often compelled to campaign against things they consider immoral even if they are legal and acceptable within society, which may explain why Quakers pioneered the abolition of the slave trade at a time when it was generally accepted as the norm. This was the message we shared on our 'Quaker belief and convictions' panel. The panel was accompanied by replica Quaker period dress made by the Ironbridge costume department which, as at Rosehill House, visitors to The FIG Tree could try on and wear.

One morning when discussing this panel with Jane I said it was a shame that, again like Rosehill House, we couldn't have any typical Georgian period dress for people to compare with the Quaker dress. Instead, we would use photographs but then, remarkably, Jane pulled out an original Georgian waistcoat of the period that she had stored safely behind our bedroom dresser. I could not believe it. It was in a poor state, so could not be handled, but we were able to mount it behind glass and put it on display next to the panel.

Perhaps the most special items we purchased as part of our Heritage Lottery Fund project were three original slave trade leg irons. They were in the USA and to save postage we had them sent to our friends in Media who then delivered two of them when they made a visit to the FIG Tree. They kept one and another was presented to our friends in New Koforidua. The three were put on display at the FIG Tree, UK, The Cooperative House, Ghana and in Media PA, US. They were all displayed unlocked and open to form a broken chain, symbolising how the Fair Trade Triangle community link between Garstang, New Koforidua and Media PA sets out to reverse the legacy of the historic slave trade triangle that existed between the same three communities.

Education is key to the FIG Tree and as another part of the project the volunteers produced and delivered a lesson plan on our three heritage themes to year six children at the local Garstang St Thomas Church of England Primary School. During our project a senior staff member from Blackburn-based Promethean, which specialises in providing interactive boards and displays for schools, approached us while enjoying a cup of coffee in our café. He was most impressed with our work and offered to donate a state-of-the-art Promethean Interactive ActivBoard, which we were able to use for our workshops and as a permanent interactive display regularly updated to show the number and location of Fair Trade Towns on a world map. With the replica Clarkson chest and the Promethean Activboard, we were proud to be using both the earliest and the latest educational visual aids.

* * *

At the FIG Tree we didn't just sell Fair Trade products but were proud to form relationships with the producers and hold events to promote the products. Like our Cafedirect challenge that we ran as the Garstang Oxfam Group twenty years earlier, we offered the Ubuntu challenge, inviting people to blind taste the Fair Trade cola Ubuntu alongside regular Coca Cola. Again, it was perhaps a surprise to learn that I was not the only one to prefer Ubuntu. We held a 'Tea at the FIG Tree' event to promote Just Change tea sourced from the Dalit community in India and a 'Coffee at the FIG Tree' event to promote our Oromo Coffee. Our friends at the Lorna Young Foundation helped to set up the Oromo Coffee Company, run by Ethiopian refugees in Tameside, to roast and sell excellent ground coffee sourced from the Oromia Coffee Farmer Co-operative Union in Ethiopia. Members from Oromo held an Ethiopian coffee ceremony as part of our 'Coffee at the FIG Tree' event. We also hosted a Co-op Fairtrade wine tasting and of course held many chocolate events to promote our vast range of Divine chocolate.

As well as our own permanent exhibition, we also hosted a Quaker Pacifist Exhibition and an Oikocredit Photographic Exhibition -

Investing in People – consisting of photographs taken by my son Tom. Evening events included two music evenings when young local musicians performed free of charge to help raise funds for the FIG Tree. I was amazed by the abundance of so much local talent around a small town like Garstang. They were well attended and, with the poor ventilation in the building, I proudly considered the FIG Tree to be Garstang's answer to Liverpool's 'Cavern'.

By the time we left Garstang at the end of 2014 we had sold over £125,000 worth of Fair Trade and local produce in our café and shop, delivered 27 Fair Trade chocolate workshops and hosted numerous visits including delegations from Ghana, the USA, Brazil, Japan, Korea and Lebanon. We had created something special and unique and, following our successful Heritage Lottery project, had high hopes of eventually gaining Museum status.

Yet, when our three-year lease came to an end, Wyre Borough Council told us we were not in the public interest. They had initially agreed in principle to allow us a three-year lease to rent the building with an option to renew and I, perhaps foolishly, believed that once they saw how successful we would become they could not possibly refuse to let us stay, but they did. In our final year we were paying Wyre Borough Council almost £13,000 in rent and had refurbished and utilised a space they had left empty and neglected. We had put Garstang onto the world map and attracted international visitors and investments into the town. I could not see how we were not in the public interest. The FIG Tree ceased trading in Garstang on Monday 10th November and some years later the whole building was demolished to make way for luxury flats.

The FIG Tree in Garstang had employed six staff and recruited over 60 volunteers, providing opportunities from being a barista and/or serving in the café to running workshops and/or producing and displaying our exhibition. In reversing Kennedy's famous quote when volunteers asked how they could be of help I used to respond, "Don't ask what you can do for the FIG Tree, but what the FIG Tree can do for you." Whatever skills they possessed we could always find something for everybody, and providing these opportunities was a central part of our service.

Then there were our amazing team of volunteer directors: Graham, Rita, Danny and David.

But none of it would have been possible without the hard work and input from my family. Despite having no previous experience Tom did a remarkable job as café manager. Ben and Anna were volunteers in the heritage project and in the café, with Ben employed as café assistant in the final year. And Jane? Well, what didn't she do? She was always there supporting all of us in times of need in so many other ways, not to mention making it possible for the FIG Tree to be selling the very best Tiffin in the world as well as the second-best waffles.

CHAPTER 15

The FIG Tree at St. John's

The representative from Wyre Borough Council made it clear to us as early as 2013 that our lease in Garstang would not be renewed. The FIG Tree could not remain in Garstang, so we had to look elsewhere and, with our focus on the slave trade, nearby Lancaster was the obvious choice. A few Lancaster Green Party councillors welcomed our move and suggested possible venues. We explored several options, including the old Assembly Rooms on King Street, but ended up at St John the Evangelist's Church on the corner of North Road and Chapel Street.

St. John's is a designated Grade II listed building under the care of the Churches Conservation Trust, and they had hopes of restoring it but needed to find a good use for the building. Conversely, we had so much to offer and needed a building, so it seemed like a good partnership, and they agreed to let us utilise the church rent free.

The church was built by wealthy Lancaster traders in 1754–55 as a chapel of ease to Lancaster Priory. The town was growing rapidly at this time and the wealthy elite wanted somewhere to 'worship' away from the crowds of 'common folk' that attended the Priory. There would have been a hierarchical seating plan in St. John's, with the wealthiest at the front and the 'free' pews for visitors at the back. The mayor and corporation had their own spacious double pew. Lancaster's wealth in the 18th Century was generated by the lucrative West Indies trade, heavily linked to the trading of slaves and the notorious slave trade triangle. As I laid out the Ghana flag as part of our exhibition, I felt a shiver down my spine. It somehow felt right that all these years later the flag of what is now a free, independent, West African nation should be displayed in a church built from the blood of slaves taken from those very same shores. St. John's would make a fitting home for the FIG Tree and our exhibition.

Perhaps because of the nature of our work we were always attracting good people. Jane had found a 'man with a van' to help make our move from Garstang into St. John's. He went by the name Simon but later told me his real name was Imran and that 'Simon' was just the name he used when meeting white people like me. I shared Simon's political views and related to him in many ways, especially when he told me about his previous jobs and how he now felt he was 'unemployable', explaining why he took on his own business. He was keen to learn about the FIG Tree and why we were moving from Garstang and after doing so he wanted to support us by offering his services free of charge. We had already made an agreement, however, so I thanked him but declined his offer. Simon went on to become a much-needed volunteer for the FIG Tree during our time at St. John's and thereafter; he fitted our barista coffee machine and pretty much did all the work converting the original vestibule at St. John's, containing just one cold water tap, into a fully-functional commercial kitchen.

We were also extremely fortunate to have Christine on board during our time at St. John's. Christine was the daughter of the Reverend Peter Haywood, who had supported us when the Oxfam Group was first set up in Garstang. She applied for our six-month post of marketing intern to start when we were still in Garstang in March 2014. Although she had previously worked as an Oxfam shop manager, she had stated in her application that she had very little marketing expertise but that she believed it was more important to have a passion for Fair Trade as the marketing skills required could easily be learned following on from that. As someone who had always been driven by my passion rather than anything I'd learned, she had my full backing and the other directors agreed.

Following the end of her internship, Christine stayed with us in a voluntary capacity as our volunteer coordinator. We were able to put her back on the payroll in that capacity when we were awarded a second grant from the Heritage Lottery Fund to facilitate our move to Lancaster.

The project entitled 'The FIG Tree relocating to St John's Lancaster' would run for 18 months from April 2015 and enable us to adapt our exhibition and workshops to our new home. It would also focus on the history of St John's Church in Lancaster and Dodshon Foster, a wealthy Quaker slave trader. We

recruited a team of eight volunteers who would create three new exhibition panels on these two themes and one specifically looking at the abolitionists in Lancaster as a slave trade port. The volunteers would also develop new heritage workshops to be delivered to five schools in and around Lancaster.

The FIG Tree at St. Johns opened for business on Saturday 7th March 2015. There was no heating and the large interior surrounded by thick stone walls meant it retained a stable temperature; once cold it stayed cold, and we were at the end of winter. Our attempts to heat the place with stand-up heaters were futile and I experienced a cold like I had never known before. Few people knew the church was now open and many of those that popped their head across the threshold soon turned around when met with the cold, dim interior. But we still had something special to offer and, aided by our excellent coffee, Jane's tiffin and our unique exhibition, slowly but surely people started to wander in. Some kept coming back as they enjoyed the 'special ambience' and we were often visited by our old regulars from Garstang.

Spring came and the heating was fixed, but despite feeling warmer it was still much colder than we appreciated. Part of the bean-to-bar chocolate-making process involves mixing the ingredients (cocoa beans, cocoa butter and sugar) in a chocolate melanger consisting of two stone rollers that grind the ingredients together to produce a chocolate paste. Although we managed to run chocolate workshops at St. Johns, where the ingredients were mixed in food processors, we could not mix chocolate in the melanger as it was still so cold, and the chocolate just solidified in situ.

In May 2015 Christine took on the additional part-time role as FIG Tree centre manager overseeing the general running of the café, shop, exhibition and events. She did an excellent job despite the many challenges to overcome. St. John's was not built to be a Fair Trade Centre with a café; even though we shared a vision with the Churches Conservation Trust to restore and convert the building they were in no rush to do so and were reluctant to put any funding in at this stage. We weren't even able to fit new electrical sockets in the kitchen area but, with Simon's DIY skills, Christine's creativity and ingenuity and the help of the rapidly expanding volunteer team that she was recruiting, we were again achieving great things.

As part of our application for Heritage Lottery Funding we carried out a survey in central Lancaster to see whether people knew about St. John's and how they would like to see the space used. It was clear we had local support and, although it is impossible to please everybody, we tried our best to do so.

Once a church is put into the care of the Churches Conservation Trust it is no longer consecrated and services no longer take place. St. John's was a rare exception to that rule, however, and a service did take place in the church every Thursday morning. We of course respected this and delayed the opening of the café each week until after the service. Various priests would come down from Lancaster Priory to give the service and that is how we met the Revd Canon Chris Newlands who was the vicar at Lancaster Priory. I enjoyed his sermons, which were a little bit more unorthodox than the norm and delivered with a large chunk of humour. It was clear that Chris supported our work and understood what we were trying to do, which was to become even more apparent when we had to leave St. John's.

By far the biggest and best event we held during our time at St. John's was 'Fair Trade Live'. July 2015 would see the 30th anniversary of Live Aid. In 1985 it was a remarkable achievement to run simultaneous concerts across the world, but 30 years on surely we now had the technology for the FIG Tree to be able to host such an event, albeit much smaller? On Saturday 18th July seven Fair Trade Towns across five continents would take part to provide non-stop live entertainment across all time zones by at least one location throughout a 24-hour period. We aimed to run a 24-hour live stream on You Tube and I was assured by our website host that this would be possible, but sadly he did not deliver on the day; in fact, we even failed to make contact with him. It turned out he ran into some personal problem, and we were never able to speak with him again after that. But the event was a success starting at 3am GMT in Kumamoto, Japan and finishing at 3am GMT the next day in Media, USA, with live concerts taking place in between at St. John's in Lancaster; in Saarbrücken, Germany; Pays de la Loire, France; Ebolowa, Cameroon; and Poços de Caldas, Brazil. The pews were full of people there to see local musician Alex Hulme headline our event at St. John's and we even made a special celebratory chocolate bar to mark the anniversary.

We had been warned that, once the weather became colder, rats would start to enter the building and sure enough, when opening one Friday morning, I noticed that something had nibbled at the corner of a bar of Divine milk chocolate with almonds. There were no other signs whatsoever, but this had to be the rats. I immediately contacted the local council for advice. They arranged for a visit by the rat catcher and advised that we could remain open. Feeling reassured, I moved all the edible items onto the higher shelves, foolishly thinking they would be out of a rat's reach and carried on as normal. I must confess I did not even think of telling Christine. You can imagine her shock and, even more understandably, her exasperation with me, when she discovered two live rats after opening the premises the following Wednesday morning. I'm so sorry, Christine.

I was intrigued to learn more about the rats when the rat catcher visited and soon shared his palpable respect for the vermin. He told me that there used to be a pit for making tallow just beside St. Johns Church, which had left a large cavern under the road inhabited by rats. Although you can remove them from the building for long periods, possibly a whole season, it would never be possible to permanently get rid of all the rats. The most remarkable discovery, however, was finding the rats had attacked another bar of Divine chocolate despite moving them to the top shelf. It wasn't the fact that they had managed to reach the shelf that amazed me, however, but the fact they had again chosen to attack a bar of milk chocolate with almonds. We were proud to stock the complete range of Divine chocolate, which at that time consisted of over fifteen varieties, and the almond chocolate was by no means the easiest to reach. The rat, or rats, must have chosen to go past many other varieties before deliberately selecting this bar. Assuming they could not read the label, they must have been able to detect the flavour through the foil and paper wrapping. The rat catcher was not surprised by this feat but felt it was perhaps a good idea to use the remainder of the bar as rat bait: an excellent example of recycling and Fair Trade for extra measure.

In November I went on my sixth visit to Ghana, which included visiting Bolgatanga, Africa's second Fair Trade Town located in the far north of the country. Bolgatanga was famous for its coloured baskets, and as part of their Fair Trade Town activities they were now hosting an annual International Fair Trade Craft Fair. Along with the drums and other musical instruments I usually bought from Jah Bwai at the Arts Centre in Accra, this was an opportunity to stock up with Fair Trade crafts to sell in the FIG Tree.

Jah Bwai presenting his FIG Tree bowl.

Just nine days following my return from Ghana on Saturday 5th December 2015 we held our event 'Sustainable Development Goals @ The FIG Tree' to increase awareness on climate change and how it most affects the poorest people on our planet. Ironically, this would be a day to remember.

The event started on a positive note by showing a film of the lecture by Hans Rosling: 'How to End Poverty in 15 Years'. This was followed with presentations by Kelly Mundy from Oxfam Campaigns, Cat Smith MP, the Mayor of Lancaster Jon Barry and Julie Ward MEP. We were delighted to have such a great line up and it made such a pleasant change when the Green Party mayor asked us whether we had a bike rack for his bicycle. This contrasted with the requests made by Wyre Borough Council when in Garstang, informing us on the correct protocol required when greeting the mayor's limo.

Lancaster's mayor publicly signed the Bristol Declaration that was put together by the Fair Trade Advocacy Office and first signed by the mayor of Bristol at the International Fair Trade Towns conference five months earlier. The aim was to get mayors from Fair Trade Towns across the globe to sign up in support of the post-2015 Sustainable Development Goals and commit to taking one step in support of Fair Trade before September 2016. This was a chance to mobilise all Fair Trade Towns across the world in support of one common cause, but it was sadly only taken up by a handful.

On the morning of the event Christine had sent me an email to say that water was leaking onto the toilet floor and we must get the Churches Conservation Trust to repair the roof as soon as possible. It had rained throughout the whole day, but as our guest speakers talked about how climate change affects the most vulnerable people on the planet, we thought nothing of the weather outside our window.

We finished at 5pm but I stayed behind to get the place set up ready for a school chocolate workshop we had planned for Monday morning. That extra hour was to have a large bearing on what was to unfold, for better or for worse. The rain was falling hard now but I made it to my car and drove out of Lancaster along the A6 to Garstang, only to find the road blocked due to flooding. I didn't realise the extent of the flooding and thought I knew a back route beside the canal that would take me to Garstang via Cockerham, but I took a wrong turn and found myself in the wetter lowlands on the east bank of the River Lune, only managing to get away by driving through over a foot of water. I made my way back into Lancaster, aiming to go along Caton

Road and get onto the motorway; with hindsight this should have been my first choice. My car stalled and had to be abandoned at the bottom of Caton Road. I thought it best to spend the night in St. John's and retrieve my car in the morning.

Ben and Anna were now studying at Lancaster University and Anna was living with her boyfriend, Matthew, close to St. John's on the other side of the main bus station. When they heard about my dilemma, they came across to see if I needed help, lent me a sleeping bag and offered me a spare bed at their place. But I had bought something nice to eat, was comfortable, now had a sleeping bag and rather liked the idea of spending the night on the long-padded cushions in the mayor's pew. They also offered to help me move shop stock and exhibition items onto the balcony to keep them from harm's way if the water should rise. That was an offer I would regret not taking up but, again, somehow didn't anticipate any problem.

While working on my laptop the electricity suddenly cut off. Still unconcerned, I decided to go to the pub for a pint before settling down for the night. St. John's lies on the southern bank of the River Lune on what was formerly known as the Green Ayre and as I walked back from the pub, I noticed the flow of water flowing down the hill towards the church and the adjacent bus station. I unlocked the door to St. John's and was aware of the vast amount of water draining away into the area below the church, which would include the rat-infested cavern that was once the tallow pit of old. There were many large spaces available to fill, so I remained undeterred.

I got into the sleeping bag borrowed from Matthew and laid down for the night on the cushioned mayor's pew. I awoke to the soft sound of stirring water and opened my eyes to see flood water just below the level of my pew. I was dry for now but surrounded by two feet of cold water. My immediate and only initial reaction was that the FIG Tree was finally over.

CHAPTER 16

After the Flood

Dawn had broken and I was just able to see many of the FIG Tree exhibition items that I treasured floating in the water. There was nothing I could do. My shoes and socks were below water, but I was dry, and my clothes were dry. It was still early morning, so I lay down and went back to sleep.

When I awoke the second time I could see far more clearly, and the water had subsided by a foot or more. I was able to get dressed and, with my trousers turned up, I could wade though the water. It was heart-breaking to see the damage. I took what I could out of the water and lay it on the balcony stairs and over the pews. Losing the shop stock wasn't too bad; at least that could be replaced. But seeing the exhibition items and many of the artefacts I had built up over the years destroyed was soul destroying; gifts from Jane, such as the books written by Thomas Clarkson, gifts made from our friends in Ghana and presented to the FIG Tree, and the large amount of magazines, posters, directories and action guides telling the story of Fair Trade Towns: many of them sent to me from across the globe over the last ten years or more. All were now totally ruined. Our iPad was immersed in water. It was under guarantee so could be replaced but it contained all my photographs taken during the Ghana visit nine days before and they were lost forever. At least most of our workshop equipment had been set out on the stage in preparation for Monday morning so much of it was safe, but that was small consolation, if any at all.

Photos courtesy of Richard Davis

I went outside and could not believe what I saw. It was like a scene from an apocalyptic movie, with cars abandoned and the occasional person wading through the water like zombies. There was a man taking photographs and he came across to talk with me. He took four photographs of the flood damage at St. John's, including one of me standing outside the door still wearing my brightly coloured Ghanaian waistcoat that I'd worn at the climate change event the day before.

Anna and Matthew came to mind and I wondered how they were coping and started to make my way across the bus station towards their flat. The water became deeper until it reached the level of my turned up trouser legs. I was just about to turn back when some firemen pulling a dinghy shouted to tell me not to move. They pointed out the dangers of walking around in dirty, possibly contaminated, water; there could be open manholes underfoot and perhaps most startling was the possibility of treading on hypodermic needles left by drug users.

The firemen had come across from Bradford to help in the crisis. I later discovered, rather ironically, that the Lancaster fire station just around the corner from St. John's had also been flooded, making some fire engines inoperable. The firemen asked where I was going and pulled me across to my destination in the dinghy. Anna's flat was on the 2nd floor, so they were okay, and my thoughts now focused on how to get home.

There were no phone signals and I had no idea what was happening in Garstang. The firemen took me over the road to higher ground where I could walk into the city centre and, if necessary, the ten miles to Garstang. I came across a crowd of people at the bus stop, mainly students trying to get back to the university. I went to inform them that the bus station was flooded and there would be no bus coming, when to my surprise a bus came into view heading for Preston via Garstang.

The bus was almost empty once we had passed the university, but the driver kept going along the normal bus route. Halfway to Garstang the A6 was flooded, forcing the driver to deviate from the route and try the side roads, but to no avail. Apart from me, the few remaining passengers were heading for Preston, so the driver chose to get to Preston using the M6 motorway, which was a success. I was the only remaining passenger and the driver had already gone beyond his duty, but I had paid my fare to Garstang and he was determined to get me there. The A6 from Preston to Garstang was much clearer and the driver finally dropped me off before heading back to Preston for what I hoped would be the end of his working day.

Garstang had escaped severe flooding and it seemed strange walking down the High Street to my house wearing my Ghanaian waistcoat and sodden shoes. It was a joy as well as a relief to see Jane again and then it hit me; I felt stunned and shaken and, with hindsight, I now understand I was suffering from delayed shock.

On Monday morning Jane and I drove to Lancaster to check on Ben and Anna, retrieve our other car and salvage what we could from St. John's. Ben and Anna were fine, although the university was greatly affected, and they soon came back home to Garstang for Christmas. Our car had gone, and Jane thought she might have seen it on the back of a trailer as we parked at St. John's. Despite contacting the police and various breakdown services we were never able to retrieve the vehicle. We took the damaged exhibition items home and Jane did a remarkable job at saving some of them, including painstakingly inserting paper towelling between each page of the sodden Thomas Clarkson books.

The response from the Lancaster community following the flood was outstanding; everybody rallied round to help those most affected.

Spending the night of the flood sleeping in the mayor's pew at St. John's was a great story and I found myself giving media interviews as early as the following Monday and for several weeks after that. A local radio station asked me to present an award to the Lancaster Fire Brigade. They did of course deserve it, but it seemed to escape their notice that the firemen who helped me were from Bradford.

Our team of volunteers, organised by Christine, did a tremendous job of cleaning up the mess at St. John's, bagging the rubbish and storing the undamaged items safely on the two balconies. We were later able to move the display cases and other heavier items for storage in the Dukes Theatre warehouse due to their kind offer to help. The greatest problem, however, was a large heap of second-hand clothing that filled up most of the pews on one side of the church. We had agreed to act as a collection point for a local refugee charity as far back as September and had received a tremendous response, but then the charity had not collected. I had expected to find it all removed when I came back from Ghana and in time for our climate change event, but now most of it was soaked through and ruined. The council offered to remove flood damaged items free of charge, and thanks to our volunteers we had made good use of this service in clearing out all the damaged FIG Tree items, but there was not the time to bag up the enormous pile of clothing on top of everything else.

Four days after Christmas I received an email from the Churches Conservation Trust informing us that they wanted the clothing removed by New Year's Day. The refugee charity were nowhere to be seen nor could we ask our volunteers to come back into the church at such short notice. I had a day to do this, but Churches Conservation Trust were asking for the bagged clothing to be completely taken away and the free removal service offered by the council in response to the flood was no longer available to us; we now had to purchase marked bags from the council if they were to be removed at all.

Several Green Party councillors had welcomed us to Lancaster and supported us during our time at St. Johns. It was now one of those councillors who saved the day. Gina Dowding had not only offered to help Jane and I bag the clothing in the pouring rain but even paid for the council bags with her own money and made sure they would be collected.

As is often the case when making these sort of charity collections, people had donated all sorts of other items as well as clothing, including pans and other kitchen equipment. Gina had contacts enabling us to pass on most of the undamaged clothing and other items to various charities where they could be used, including a homeless charity in central Lancaster. We were so grateful to Gina and delighted that many of the items could be utilised by good causes even though they did not reach the refugees for whom they were originally intended.

We had lost £1,800 worth of uninsured stock and over £1,000 in flood-damaged kitchen equipment, not to mention the loss of income due to closure of our café and shop in the busy run-up to Christmas. We had a lot of undamaged stock, but nowhere to sell it. Thanks to the media coverage, however, we received offers to sell our items on stalls at Lancaster Girl's Grammar School, the Methodist Cornerstone café and St. Nic's shopping arcade. The latter offered us a prime position in the arcade for the four busy shopping days before Christmas and two stalls each week up until the end of February. These stalls were a much-needed lifeline enabling us to sell over £2,400 worth of stock before Christmas

and half as much again in January and February. We continued to run stalls at the Cornerstone and grammar school regularly thereafter and St. Nic's let us run Christmas stalls for the next two years.

We were also approached by a filmmaker called Ray who made a short film about our plight to help us raise funds. We received over £2,800, with donations coming in locally, nationally and internationally, including the British School in Prague. They heard about our disaster during a Fair Trade Christmas party being held in Seoul and raised almost £500 as a response. We also received a £1,000 Lancashire Flood Recovery Community Foundation Grant that was paid promptly into our account before Christmas.

I contacted the Heritage Lottery Fund about our project. Since it was named 'The FIG Tree relocating to St John's' I naturally expected them to cancel the grant unless we were able to stay at St. John's, but they were remarkably understanding. Providing we were able to deliver our approved purposes as outlined in our application they were more than happy for the project to continue regardless of whether we returned to St. John's or even if we failed to find new premises. We were able to adapt the project and they gave us a six month extension, even covering the extra costs involved. This meant that although we had to end Christine's job as centre manager in February 2016, we were able to keep her on as volunteer coordinator for the project until the end of March 2017.

When I had first awoken to see the flooded church that tragic night in St. John's, my first reaction was that the FIG Tree was finished. But now, despite great losses, the FIG Tree would survive, but we had to decide what path we'd take. It was thanks to our supporters, volunteers and the local community that we were able to go on, so it made sense to consult them all when deciding our future. We held this important stakeholder meeting at the Friend's Meeting House in January 2016 and anybody with an interest in the FIG Tree was able to take part in the discussion, which would inform the directors and help them to make the final decision. Twenty-seven people attended, with as many apologies.

We were to consider three possible future options for the FIG Tree:

1. Remain at St. John's and build up a stronger relationship with the Churches Conservation Trust to ensure a more sustainable future.

2. Work closer with Lancaster City and Lancashire County councils to explore using one of the three museum sites: City Museum, Maritime Museum or Judges Lodgings.

3. Move back to the original site in Garstang if the building could be secured by the community away from the control of either Wyre Borough Council or Garstang Town Council.

On reflection these were not options actually available to us, but it was clear from the discussion that the vast majority of our stakeholders did not want us to return to St. John's or Garstang. We would need to look for another site in Lancaster. I was immensely uplifted by the support we received following the flood and the enthusiasm of our stakeholders at the meeting. The FIG Tree and our international work was to continue.

* * *

Just four days after our stakeholder meeting, I flew to Lithuania to help support a proposal to make the capital Vilnius a Fair Trade City.

Hiiu District in Estonia had declared as a Fair Trade Town two years earlier, but to my knowledge the Lithuanian campaign never did succeed.

The tenth International Fair Trade Towns conference was in the Fair Trade Village of Baskinta in Lebanon in 2016. Benoit and Lory had visited the FIG Tree in October two years before to find out more about Fair Trade Towns. Benoit was the projects director for Fair Trade Lebanon and Lory was to become the Lebanese Fair Trade Towns coordinator. The mayor of Menjez had self-declared Menjez as the first Fair Trade Village in Lebanon in May 2013. Fair Trade Lebanon wanted to recognise the declaration and had sent Benoit and Lory to Garstang with the aim of starting the first National Fair Trade Town campaign in the Middle East.

I was invited to Lebanon to support the launch of the Lebanese Fair Trade Town campaign, with nine Fair Trade Villages declaring in June 2015. I always considered it an enormous privilege to be able to support the launch of Fair Trade Towns in any country, but the Lebanese campaign was something quite special again.

Our Garstang campaign included supporting local farmers and local produce right from the start, but the national campaign in the UK was first and foremost focused on promoting Fairtrade products, with support for local farmers in some cases following on as a secondary consideration. In Lebanon, however, they would do it the other way around, with an initial focus on supporting local producers and helping them integrate into the fair trade network in Lebanon and elsewhere, and then when the consumer understood why this was important the message would widen to asking them to consider farmers in other countries that were also struggling to get a fair price for their produce.

It was felt, in Lebanon at least, that this would be a better way to get consumers to understand Fair Trade and the reasons why they should support it.

During my week in Lebanon, I was able to visit seven out of the nine Fair Trade Villages, starting with Saidoun, where they produced honey and thyme. I was fascinated to learn how the taste of the honey is affected by the crops grown in the village and to such an extent that a true connoisseur can identify the village of origin just by taste alone, in the same way that one can identify the origin of a fine wine. For this reason, the beekeepers in Saidoun were seeking to see an end to the growing of tobacco in the area.

In Ferzol, I met with members of the woman's cooperative who produced jams, pickles and other processed foods. Then onto the wine region to the north appropriately near to the temple of Bacchus and the world's largest rosary beads that would only be complete when 1,000 people had prayed there.

Thanks to its remarkable, high-spirited, enthusiastic and visionary mayor, Menjez had become Lebanon's first Fair Trade Village two years earlier. Georges Youssef is a proud mayor, claiming that Menjez was the oldest village in the Middle East and very quick to point out he had evidence. The village lays in the north of Lebanon next to the Syrian border, and with 60 megalithic stone circle burial grounds dating to

5,000 BC was one of only two locations in the Middle East with such sites. Other historical sites in Menjez included a crusader castle and a Roman temple built by the Emperor Hadrian.

The next day I travelled to the south of the country to the Fair Trade Village of Kfar Tebnit to meet with another very supportive mayor and members of another women's cooperative that made jam. Benoit took me to the ancient Beaufort Castle where I could see the Israeli border and the much-troubled Golan Heights. On the return journey to Beirut, we called in on Abra, a suburb of Saida where there was another women's cooperative making jams and handicrafts and I met with yet another supportive mayor who would attend the International Fair Trade Towns conference to be held in Bristol the following month.

On the first day of my Lebanese visit I went to the World Fair Trade Day Rural Lunch at the 'Waterfront City' in Beirut. All nine Fair Trade Villages would hold their own events as a part of gaining their status. A week later, on my last day, I visited Mhaidthe for the first of these events, which included a marketplace of stalls, entertainment and, perhaps most memorably, a delicious Lebanese banquet with so many different dishes that I could not possibly sample them all, despite the efforts by the locals who did their very best to make me do so.

In sense of area, the largest Fair Trade Village was Baskinta, a popular holiday resort up in the mountains where you could smell the cherry blossom in the clear, clean mountainous air. Lory and her friend and Fair Trade colleague, Tala, took me to meet the mayor. I was reminded of some of the councillors back in Garstang who just could not see the benefits of being a Fair Trade Town, let alone begin to understand and support Fair Trade. He just did not get it and dismissed any potential for Fair Trade tourism with the belief that no tourists would want to visit Lebanon anymore. This was the only time I experienced opposition from any of the mayors I'd met in Lebanon and when Lory and Tala asked me what I thought I had to speak my mind. "That is why we took you to meet him," they responded. They had wanted me to see how difficult things were for the campaigners there and, following my own encounters in Garstang, they knew I'd understand.

The Fair Trade Steering Committee in Baskinta was set up by the environmental group Baskinta Baytouna Association (meaning 'Baskinta our home') led by Elie Karam, a lawyer who is passionate about sustainability and Fair Trade. They had already started a recycling scheme at source using different coloured bins, which at that time was a real rarity for Lebanon and introduced despite an extremely 'backward' and unsupportive mayor.

I was and still am most impressed by the Lebanese Fair Trade Town campaign and all this in a country seven times smaller than the Republic of Ireland, but with a population almost one and a half times greater; a third of which consists of refugees fleeing war-torn Syria. I felt even more ashamed by the ever-growing anti-immigrant sentiment that existed in my own country. We still needed to find a country to host the international conference in 2016 and I suggested that, despite the logistical problems, perhaps it could take place in Lebanon. I'd always believed that where there is a will there is a way and it seemed there was a will, because at the 2015 Fair Trade Towns conference in Bristol the Lebanese delegation responded to the call for a 2016 venue by proposing Lebanon.

There were those who said it could not happen and/or nobody would attend, but it did, with participants from 18 countries. The theme was 'Building bridges through Fair Trade' and I was delighted when I heard it was to be held in Baskinta. I recalled my meeting with Baskinta's mayor and his negativity towards welcoming people to the village but learned that he had been replaced by a new mayor who was far more supportive and, coincidentally, also went by the name Elie Karam.

Anna and Matthew were to join me on this visit as Anna needed to undertake an internship related to politics and global development as part of her history and politics degree. They were both keen cooks and Anna ran her own business baking and decorating celebration cakes. The Lebanese Fair Trade campaign focused on local production and much of the catering for the conference would be provided by local producers, thus providing the ideal opportunity for Anna to focus on agricultural development in Lebanon while exploring and enjoying Lebanese cuisine.

We shared an overnight flight that arrived in Beirut in the early hours of the Monday morning ahead of the weekend conference. I was to stay in Beirut for a few days whereas Anna and Matthew went straight on to Baskinta. Everything had been arranged by our Fair Trade friends so I knew they would be safe, but it still felt strange leaving my daughter and her boyfriend in a taxi in Beirut during the dead of night. I saw them again at the opening fair when I arrived in Baskinta late on the Friday evening. I was given a room in a convent just outside Baskinta whereas Anna and Matthew were staying at a home in the village, which meant I saw little of them.

When I arrived at the fair, I was greeted by so many people including Elie (the lawyer), who gave me a microphone and asked me to say a few words. I genuinely never enjoyed that sort of attention or pressure, but always considered it a privilege to be asked to support any event in any way I could. Samir was the president of Fair Trade Lebanon and he was to make the opening speech at the conference the next day, with me to follow. As always, I was nervous and not entirely sure what I would say but knew my role was to inspire and motivate fellow activists. It was not a role I wanted but with my experience was something I could do well; indeed, I often think it is the only thing I can do well and again saw it as a privilege to be given that role. On returning to the convent, I was both shocked and hurt to be confronted by one of the UK participants asking me what I was going to say at the conference and accusing me of focusing my speeches on myself. I genuinely did not know where this came from and, even though they apologised soon after, any confidence that I had was shattered.

The MP Jo Cox was brutally murdered by a far-right extremist just two weeks before the conference and this was followed a week later by the Brexit leave vote in the EU Referendum. I was deeply saddened by both events and did not like nor understand what I saw as a steady shift to the nationalist right, not just in the UK but throughout Europe. Jo Cox had done a lot of work in support of Syrian refugees and I had suggested to Samir that perhaps there was a way to remember her at the conference. Samir told me that he had lost many good friends and colleagues to the hatred of the far right and said he would do what he could. I was warmed and heartened when he announced during his opening speech that the conference would be dedicated to the memory of Jo Cox. I can't remember what I said in my presentation, but it was an honour to follow Samir.

It was seven years since I had had the conversation with Nick Maurice on the train heading back from the 2009 conference in Lyon and much of that time was spent writing funding proposals and giving presentations in an attempt to secure some sort of role enabling me to continue to support Fair Trade Towns internationally. The ever-increasing demands on my time had forced me to cease working as a vet and I now felt like a beggar in trying to secure an income. I never wanted to be a leader or even ambassador, but just wanted to do what I could to support Fair Trade, Fair Trade Towns and ultimately the fight against poverty. It was far easier in my early days when I had a reliable income as a vet and was able to give my time freely as a volunteer, but as the founder of Fair Trade Towns I had been thrown into a position where I could do so much more, but still needed to make a living.

I had become frustrated with institutions generally; with their focus on strategies, reports, their own agendas and restricted budgets rather than just getting things done and making things happen. I had still failed to secure regular funding for my role as Fair Trade Towns ambassador from the two largest Fair Trade Organisations: Fairtrade International and the World Fair Trade Organization. I was growing tired, weary and demoralised and, despite my usual persistent optimism, could no longer handle the constant rejections and occasional accusations that I was somehow striving to gain control over the international movement. I had no choice but to reluctantly stand down as Fair Trade Towns ambassador and come off the International Fair Trade Towns Steering Committee. I would still do what I could to support the international movement through the FIG Tree whenever I could and whenever asked, but at least now I would be my own man again.

The events had left me in a state of low self-esteem, but I was no longer taking anti-depressant medication and my therapy sessions had finished over a year ago. I had learned how to cope, so did not spiral down into the pit of depression as I had done on so many occasions before. On Sunday 3rd July 2016 I attended my last International Fair Trade Towns coordinators meeting, but this time as a guest and no longer as Fair Trade Towns ambassador.

* * *

As with Lebanon, it was a privilege to play a role in supporting Fair Trade Towns in South Korea and in particular for the capital city of Seoul. Mr. Won Soon Park visited Garstang with his wife and daughter in April 2010. Mr Park was the founder of the chain of ethical shops in Korea known as 'Beautiful Store' and he was visiting the UK to learn more about Oxfam shops and Fair Trade Towns. I remember his visit well because we spent most of the day talking in my living room and afterwards Mr. Park told me what an impression it had made on he and his family. Two years later I discovered that he had become the mayor of Seoul and went on to launch the campaign to make the capital a Fair Trade City. At the launch he announced: "I've personally visited Garstang, the first Fair Trade Town in the world to learn how to make a Fair Trade Town successfully. We will do our best and we will encourage more people to be involved in the Fair Trade movement."

By invitation from the mayor, I visited Seoul for the Korean Fair Trade Week and World Fair Trade Day Festival in May 2013. MJ was my guide, who did a terrific job at making me feel most welcome, but then so did everyone I met. I only had two full days in Seoul, but they were unforgettable.

On Friday I was taken to the city hall to meet with Mr. Park, now the mayor. As I walked into his office, I could not believe the mass of TV cameras and microphones waiting to capture the moment of our meeting. It was surreal. Then Mr Park proudly gave me a guided tour of the city hall, including the Fairtrade shop and café 'Earth Village'. I was told that before Mr. Park became mayor that the city hall was not accessible to the public, but now there were children playing, adults reading and a beautiful Fair Trade shop and café that reminded me of the FIG Tree, only our Korean counterpart had the full support and backing from the mayor and local council.

Saturday was World Fair Trade Day and the celebrations were held in the city square in front of the ancient Gyeongbok Palace. A large map had been erected on a stage showing the city of Seoul, three countries that exported Fair Trade products to Korea, and the UK. I stood in front of the map with the mayor, Fair Trade producers and key representatives from the local community. We took it in turn to add coloured circles to the map identifying places supporting Fair Trade and Fair Trade products. The mayor added city hall to the Seoul map along with the temple added by a Buddhist monk and university, school and church added by the appropriate representatives. I was told the temple was the first Fair Trade Buddhist temple in the world. Circles identifying the Fair Trade products coffee, handicrafts and wine were then added to the three country maps by the corresponding producers and finally I was asked to add a bright orange circle with the name Garstang to the map of the UK, albeit being placed over London.

Fair Trade stalls filled the city square and extended along the central reservation of the Sejong-daero. I was most impressed with the Seoul city campaign, but it would be another five years before Seoul was to declare as a Fair Trade City.

The Seoul campaign supported by Mr. Park was run by the Korea Fair Trade Organization and sadly, as I'd seen many times before, there was a divide between them and others working to promote the FAIRTRADE mark as part of Fairtrade International. The latter believed that any 'Fair Trade Town' campaign in Korea should be primarily focused on promoting products carrying the FAIRTRADE mark as in the UK but opposed to the 'Big Tent' approach recommended in the International Fair Trade Towns Guidelines developed in 2013.

Bucheon is a city 20km west of Seoul located between the capital and Incheon International airport and they wanted to declare as a 'Fairtrade City' in 2016, making it the first Fair Trade Town in South Korea. Thankfully, as 2016 was the year I stood down from the International

Fair Trade Towns Steering Committee, I did not have to get involved in this diplomatic row. I offered to host a visit to Garstang by the Bucheon delegation, but they never came.

Bucheon became the first Fair Trade Town in South Korea in December 2016, with Seoul declaring in July 2018. With a population of just under ten million, Seoul would become the world's largest Fair Trade Town and I was invited back to Seoul to attend their declaration.

As before, I would arrive in Seoul on a Thursday and fly back the following Sunday, giving me only two full days in the capital. This time, however, I would be accompanied by my good friend Tadeusz, who would be there representing the International Fair Trade Towns Steering Committee.

A small stage had been set up in the city hall for the celebrations and decorations were hung from the ceiling above it. One of the many tips passed on to me by my 'presentation guru' Joe Human following my talk in Keswick in 2003 was to be aware of what was hanging above your head when speaking and how this may appear to the audience. I was never sure how it looked from the audience but avoiding the decorations while waiting for each line to be interpreted did result in a somewhat awkward, not to mention slightly longwinded, presentation.

That evening I enjoyed watching England beat Sweden 2-0 in the quarter finals of the World Cup with Tadeusz, MJ and Young-eun Lee, the project manager for the Korea Fair Trade Organization. It made a welcome change from two years earlier having to witness England being eliminated from the Euros by Iceland while drinking overpriced beer alone in a Beirut bar.

Tadeusz took an early flight the next day whereas I was to fly back overnight, giving me an extra day to spend in the capital. I visited one of the more than fifty Buddhist temples in Seoul and then decided to head for the city hall. I had taken a large amount of FIG Tree chocolate to sell during my visit and despite successfully selling much of it during the previous day's celebrations, I still had a lot remaining. It was heavy and not that easy to transport, and it occurred to me that because it was made in the world's first Fair Trade Town perhaps I could sell the remainder at wholesale price to the Fairtrade shop 'Earth Village' at city hall. It was a Sunday and city hall may not be open, let alone the shop and café, and then I had to find my way from the temple.

Having overcome the challenge of describing city hall in Korean when seeking directions, I finally made it. I half expected it to be closed and I could not get into the building until I remembered that the public access was down an escalator into the lower ground floor below. Relieved, I made my way to the shop and asked to speak to the manager, only to find she did not work on a Sunday. Thanks to the considerate and helpful security staff, however, I was able to call Nam Sook Lee on their phone and she agreed to take all my remaining stock. All I had to do now was return to the hotel to collect my luggage and the chocolate and make my way back to city hall before it closed.

FIG Tree bean-to-bar chocolate would be available to purchase in the city hall of Seoul, and the Fairtrade shop 'Earth Village' later became a member of the FIG Tree. I felt so proud of this and all our other international relationships and grateful to Mr. Won Soon Park for all he had done to help make Seoul the largest Fair Trade Town in the world.

Almost two years to the day from Seoul's historic declaration, I received the shocking news that Mr. Park had taken his own life following a political scandal. I could not believe it and my thoughts turned to his wife and daughter who had sat in my living room eight years before. Mr. Park was Seoul's longest serving mayor with an unprecedented three terms. However, I will always remember him as the man that brought Fair Trade Towns to Korea.

* * *

The 11th International Fair Trade Towns Conference was hosted by Saarbrücken in Germany in 2017 and was the second one held in the country following the conference in Bonn in 2010. I had made special edition almond milk and orange with cinnamon chocolate to sell at the conference. The Fair Trade Advocacy Office had also purchased 75 bars of custom labelled chocolate to use at the EU Fair Trade Breakfast in Brussels. I considered it both an irony and an honour that, despite Brexit, British FIG Tree chocolate was given to European Parliamentary delegates in the capital of chocolate. Once the new Brexit trade laws were passed, however, this would not be so easy.

Saarbrücken became Germany's first Fair Trade Town in 2009 and had a cross-border relation-

Bruce with Sergi from the Fair Trade Advocacy Office.

ship with four other Fair Trade Towns; Luxembourg, Metz in France and Trier, also in Germany. I visited Luxembourg for my first and only time as part of the conference and was fascinated to learn about their public procurement policy in using Fair Trade textiles when making uniforms for local authority workers. We were also treated to a stirring and heartrending presentation about cotton producers given by Anjali Schiavina from Pondicherry in India. Driven by Anjali and supported by my friend and Fair Trade Way walker Push, Pondicherry and Auroville became the first Fair Trade Towns in India in August 2017. There were now Fair Trade Towns in 31 countries across the globe.

Also in 2017, Graham and I developed and walked a new branch of the Fair Trade Way that went from Thomas Clarkson's former home at Eusemere Hill on the banks of Ullswater at Pooley Bridge, between the peaks of Helvellyn and Fairfield, to finish at Dove Cottage, the former home of William Wordsworth in Grasmere. This followed a route often taken by Clarkson and Wordsworth when visiting each other. It was while taking this journey in April 1802 that Wordsworth was inspired to write his famous poem *Daffodils* after seeing daffodils growing on the shores of Ullswater on his journey back to Grasmere.

Baskinta already had its own Literary Trail marked with 22 literary landmarks related to several acclaimed poets and novelists from the region including Mikhail Naimy, Amin Maalouf, Abdallah Ghanem, Suleiman Kettaneh, Rachid Ayoub and Georges Ghanem. I had taken some of the FIG Tree panels funded by our Heritage Lottery project to Baskinta to display during the Fair Trade Towns conference and one of them was on the Fair Trade Way. Inspired by this, Elie (the lawyer) wanted to find a way to link our walks and so we created the International Festival of Fair Trade Walks. We adopted a literary theme for the first festival in 2017, which was supported by the Scottish Fair Trade Forum and promoted on their website. As well as walking our new branch of the Fair Trade Way in connection with Wordsworth's famous poem, literary-themed walks also took place on the Literary Trail in Baskinta; in Pondicherry, organised and walked by Push; on the Bronte Walk at Haworth in Yorkshire; and in Scotland and Wales. Thanks to sponsorship from the Co-op we were again able to produce special edition FIG Tree chocolate to commemorate the event and to give to walkers taking part.

The Festival of Fair Trade Walks continued to be promoted by the Scottish Fair Trade Forum in 2018 and 2019. In 2018 we walked along the canal from Galgate to Lancaster, passing the sites where eight cotton mills once stood (the buildings were still standing for three of them) and guided by local historian Melinda Elder. In 2019 we again walked along the canal from Galgate, but in the opposite direction to Garstang in what was the 200th anniversary for the Preston to Lancaster canal. Some of the damaged or lost milestones along the route were replaced with new hand-carved ones. Jane was part of a stone carving group who were commissioned to make the milestones and she was solely responsible for the one placed at one mile north of Garstang.

CHAPTER 17

The Israelites

Following the flooding at St. Johns and the recommendations we received at our stakeholder's meeting, we set about seeking new premises for the FIG Tree in and around Lancaster. We were like the Israelites searching for our promised land. When Nicola was the Oxfam campaigns coordinator at the Manchester office, she once said that we should not think of the FIG Tree as a building, it was a concept far greater than that and it could be anything: "A bus, train or even a rickshaw." These words have been on my mind ever since and perhaps we were never meant to have a building? What would be, would be.

With or without premises, I was still able to continue to support Fair Trade Towns internationally when requested and we could still deliver our

chocolate workshops by going into schools and using other sites. After we left St. John's, Lancaster Quakers kindly let us use their meeting house free of charge until we found our feet again. But we needed to replace the income we were losing from no longer having the café or shop. Then it occurred to me: we were able to make chocolate and if I could find some retail outlets this would surely bring in the extra income required. In 2016 I made 59kg of bean-to-bar chocolate, an increase from just 17kg the previous year, with production peaking at over 121kg in 2017.

The cooperative Single Step Wholefoods were the first to buy our chocolate wholesale and they have been selling it ever since. Our standard 40g bars retail at £2.50 each and I offered them to Single Step for a wholesale price of £1.25, only to be told that the wholesale price should be 70% of the retail price and therefore we should either lower the retail price or charge them £1.80 for each bar wholesale. I was moved by their honesty and openness and felt these were the sort of people we need to do business with. I don't suppose I'll ever be faced with making this decision, but I vowed that our chocolate would never be sold in a supermarket, no matter how big we became.

The funding that came into the FIG Tree from my international work would cease when I came off the International Fair Trade Towns Steering Committee so my director's salary would also stop. I was still receiving a small amount as project manager for our Heritage Lottery Fund project, which also provided for Christine's salary as volunteer coordinator. Then we received a life saver.

The Rev. Chris Newlands asked if we could help with the running of the souvenir shop at Lancaster Priory. He had seen how Christine had run the shop at St. John's and believed the Priory shop could be improved if they were selling both our stock and theirs. They had previously run a café at the Priory, but Chris told us that they did not have a coffee machine or other facilities so when the café opened at the adjacent Lancaster Castle, they no longer felt able to compete and their café had to close. We, however, had everything needed to run a professional café including a coffee machine and other café equipment, and we also had the know-how but no premises. We saw the potential for a partnership, which gave rise to the FIG Tree @ The Priory.

Andrew Nicholson was one of the wardens at the Priory and he was more than familiar with our work, having been involved with our 'Go Global Go Ghana' project when he was a teacher at Garstang High School. I was looking forward to working with Andrew again and I had nothing but admiration for Chris. They clearly understood what the FIG Tree was about and made us feel welcome, but sadly not everybody at the Priory would feel the same way.

We started selling our bean-to-bar chocolate along with other stock in the Priory shop and at events, including the Christmas concerts where Chris allowed me to run a stall in the evening after I'd spent a busy day in St. Nic's arcade. In February 2017 I started to run a café in the Priory on Saturday's only, as a trial. It was obviously very quiet to begin with, but it confirmed my belief that there was potential to get something going that would be of benefit to both the FIG Tree and the Priory, but it would need a manager to run it.

Tom had now left home and although Ben and Anna were living in Lancaster, they were both full-time students. I held a meeting with Christine and Jane but understandably neither would take it up. Jane had done more than her share when we were in Garstang and was more than relieved to be out of it when we moved to St. John's. This was not something she would go back to. Christine was about to come off the pay role as the Heritage Lottery Funding came to an end and it would be great if she could then continue in a paid role as café manager. But she was already finding it difficult having to travel from Preston to Lancaster when we were at St. John's and she was not quite as convinced as I that things would work out at the Priory. She left us to set up her own chocolate business called Elliechoc chocolates that, for a while, bought some of our chocolate wholesale to sell online, albeit in very small quantities.

I had to tell Andrew and Chris that the FIG Tree could not provide a café manager. They seemed to think this was something that I could do, but I knew only too well what it involved, and it would only take me away from the main aspects of our work, thus substantially reducing our social impact and our raison d'être. I still felt I'd let them down, however.

Bruce at the Priory with Cat Smith MP, the Rev. Chris Newlands and Pauline.

Pauline had run the café at the Priory before and, to everyone's relief, now agreed to run it again in a voluntary capacity. The coffee machine was plumbed in, I trained several volunteer baristas, put Pauline in touch with our previous suppliers and Jane started making her excellent Tiffin again. We were up and running, open three days a week from Thursday to Saturday and from June 2017 the FIG Tree was paid 50% of the profits at the end of each month.

Initially, I was able to give a full day at the café on Thursdays and covered for Pauline when she needed days off over the summer. But when the conference season started in September I had to back off. Pauline decided only to open the café on Saturdays and slowly the café moved away from the FIG Tree ethos. Sales of FIG Tree chocolate declined from £692 over nine months in 2017 to just £91 over the eleven months the following year. What made the FIG Tree so special when in Garstang and at St. John's was everybody being behind the FIG Tree ethos and chocolate sales were totally dependent on it. Our partnership waned and we received our last share of the profits in November 2018. We let them keep all our equipment as a gesture of goodwill, except the coffee machine which they could use on an indefinite free loan. Soon after, they decided it was not fit for purpose and Graham and I retrieved it one evening. Our partnership was over, and we were left again without a base to work from.

There were no regrets, however, and both parties benefitted from the two years we were working together. Our partnership had provided us with an important lifeline when we needed it most. After the flood

everything we had was stored in the Dukes theatre warehouse and on the two balconies at St. John's, most of the furniture still dirty from the flood waters. We were able to clean up and move the items out of the Dukes warehouse when we had to in April 2016. But there was a lot more at St. John's and nowhere to put it.

In February 2017 we received a letter from the Churches Conservation Trust telling us we had to have everything out of St. John's by 1st April. Although we still had keys, we were no longer allowed unsupervised access to the church and the volunteer given the responsibility of supervising us was only able to do so on certain days and for very short periods at a time. We were able to sell the café tables and chairs along with some other items, but we still had the large Promethean Activboard and smaller Activtable, display cabinets, exhibition pieces and much more and it was going to take a long time to move it all. Simon again stepped forward with his fabulous moving skills and free use of his van. We were able to set up the exhibition, Activboard and Activtable for use at the Priory although this was not really appreciated. Eventually, the Activboard was sold and the exhibition and table stored at my home.

Another benefit from our Priory partnership was meeting Olu. Olu escaped a mob in Nigeria who were in the process of murdering him because of his sexuality. Remarkably, having suffered from unspeakable trauma, he fled to the UK in 2008. He was volunteering for the Red Cross in Bristol when he was picked up by the police. This was not unusual; he had been picked up twice before and released. However, this time he was taken to The Verne Detention and Removal Centre, which between 2014 and 2017 served as an Immigration Removal Centre. Its closure as a detention centre was welcomed by many human rights campaigners who said that the prison exposed vulnerable refugees and asylum seekers to inhumane conditions, indefinite confinement, and trauma.

Olu was being transported from The Verne to Harmondsworth and onto Heathrow to be deported when he called John, a life-long human rights activist Olu had met through the Lesbian and Gay Christian Movement. They had a brief conversation before Olu's phone was taken away from him. When he reached Heathrow and was told that he was going to be put on a plane back to Nigeria, Olu let out a scream and pleaded not to be sent back. Ten minutes before his flight he was informed that his place on the plane had been removed; the swift and decisive action taken by John and Olu's lawyer ensured that he did not board that plane.

After Olu was successfully prevented from being deported he was moved from London to Bristol, then from Bristol to Liverpool and finally Liverpool to Lancaster; ironically, historically Britain's four largest slave trade ports. When in Lancaster, Olu contacted Chris Newlands, who introduced him to me at the start of our partnership at the Priory.

Olu volunteered at the FIG Tree until June 2018 when he went back to Bristol to study law, wanting to help others in the same way he was aided. Olu was involved with all aspects of work at the FIG Tree: helping to run our chocolate workshops and demos, running stalls, volunteering in the Priory café and above all assisting with the making of bean-to-bar chocolate. His winnowing skills were legendary, and I often think of him when winnowing using 'Olu's technique' today.

After being awarded a six-month extension, our Heritage Lottery project would finish at the end of March 2017 and we needed to hold a closing event. The last possible weekend in March for us to hold the event was the 25th and 26th. This was the same year that would mark the 210th anniversary of the passing of the Abolition of the Slave Trade Act and, by an amazing coincidence, I discovered the act was passed on 25th March 1807. Our partnership at the Priory was in its earliest days and at its strongest and we had a visitor from Japan that weekend. Everything was coming together for the weekend of events we called '210 Abolition - Lancaster slave trade port to Fairtrade City'.

Our Fair Trade/slave trade exhibition was on display at the Storey building during the last four weeks of March. The weekend kicked off with two family chocolate workshops run by Christine at the Priory. Lancaster Quakers held a public Meeting for Worship in the afternoon followed by a debate, with the slave trade abolition and the FIG Tree central message as the motion: "It is simply immoral that people should be allowed to suffer in order to provide us with luxuries such as tea, coffee and sugar at a cheap price."

Two of our volunteers dressed as the period characters they played in our slave trade workshops in order to defend and oppose the motion. In defence of the motion was Mary Lawson - an 18th century young Quaker woman from Lancaster - who boycotted sugar like many of her female contemporaries and whose little-known diary survives in the Lancashire records office to this day. John Rawlinson was a prominent Lancaster Quaker merchant complicit in the 18th century West Indies trade who had inherited part of a slave plantation in Grenada from his father. John continued to argue for slavery until he died in 1799 and he was just the person to oppose the motion in our debate.

Although the characters were from the 18th Century, the debate was taking place in the 21st Century, thereby showcasing the views and opinions that fuelled arguments for or against the abolition of slavery while also presenting modern day thoughts and ideas of the Fair Trade movement. The discussion evoked many reflections on the links between current day injustices and the slave trade of the past.

As expected, Mary Lawson won the debate with ease having the support of the whole audience, which very much frowned upon the pro-slavery arguments made by John Rawlinson. Of course, things would have been very different in the 18th Century. As a young Quaker woman with abolitionist tendencies, everything would have been against Mary Lawson to the extent that she would not even be allowed into the debating chamber, never mind win the argument.

In the evening we held a celebratory Regency banquet and ball at the Borough pub and hotel on Dalton Square. The venue provided the perfect Georgian setting and they made every effort to provide a Georgian banquet within our budget that even included a pig's head. The music and dancing were also authentic, and our volunteers dressed in period costume, some even making their own ball gowns. Having played the part of Quaker slave trader Dodshon Foster for our workshops, I took the opportunity to dress as Thomas Clarkson for this final celebration.

Sunday was Mother's Day and Chris Newlands used the customary morning service at the Priory to deliver a sermon on our theme as part of our '210 Abolition' weekend. Chris knew the author and Church of England minister the Reverend Chigor Chike and managed to get him to give an evening lecture at the Priory entitled 'Looking Back, Looking Around and Looking Forward' to conclude our weekend of events.

Despite the flood and no longer having premises, our second Heritage Lottery project was successfully completed, which also meant the end of my salary as project manager. I had to reintroduce my director's salary in June 2017, but even with the income now coming in from the Priory café and chocolate sales, this was not sustainable. We became a cooperative in November 2017, which brought in a regular additional income from membership, and selling off some of our assets helped for a while, but it was clear that neither the FIG Tree nor Fair Trade in general could continue to provide me with an income.

There was no going back to vetting. I had been off the registrar for more than six years and I couldn't go back even if I wanted to, which I certainly didn't. But that was all I was trained for and other than that the only experience I had was in Fair Trade campaigning. Then Jane came across a job that she claimed had my "name written all over it". It was for a part time position as field interviewer with the Office for National Statistics (ONS).

The job entailed knocking on doors and persuading the residents to take part in an important study. I had to include in my job application an example demonstrating when I had led from the front and communicated with clarity, conviction and enthusiasm. The 'Garstang Story' was the obvious example to use. I was given a phone interview and offered the job soon after, to start work in April 2018.

But we were now in a Catch 22 situation; my new job and coming off the FIG Tree payroll made the FIG Tree more financially sustainable, but it also meant I had less free time to offer. After conversing with Graham, we both concluded that perhaps we had reached the point to call it a day and went into our AGM in June 2018 thinking it would be our last. We still owed a considerable debt to Rita, and I owed it to her to tell her our expected outcome before the meeting.

Seventeen members attended the AGM with eight apologies. We had a total membership of 62 and many more supporters across the globe. Graham introduced the meeting highlighting our problems in his chairperson's report. I added to our difficulties with the treasurer's report that followed and then we both did our best to answer the members' questions. Graham summed up our greatest need to have more people "with new ideas and new energy and time" and the members responded coming forward to fill the FIG Tree roles. We finished the meeting and the FIG Tree had not folded. Graham and I held an emergency board meeting soon after and we agreed to continue at least while we had enough members who wanted us to.

I purchased the FIG Tree chocolate-making equipment in order to pay for my final salaries and agreed to run the FIG Tree in a voluntary capacity while keeping the profits made from chocolate sales. I did this for two years until March 2020 when I was then able to give all the profits from chocolate sales and other services that I provided to the FIG Tree, thereby working in a fully voluntary capacity.

After the AGM, I visited Seoul for their historic declaration and then attended the 12th International Fair Trade Towns conference in Madrid in October. This was to be my last, as the year later the conference in Cardiff was held on my 60th birthday and I decided to spend the day at home with my family.

My 61st year was a significant one for me. In 1984 I shared a flat in Liverpool that was located a short walk from the International Garden Festival that took place that summer. I visited it often and on one occasion with my friend Mike, alias Gary, we played a fortune telling machine that rather bizarrely forecast the age of your death based on the answers we gave to several questions about our lifestyle. Although my lifestyle did not differ too much from Gary's, it told me I would die at the far younger age of 60. According to a computer 2020, would be my last year.

But things started to pick up. We were selling as much chocolate as I could make, and we had requests for as many school workshops as we could deliver. Tom had married Ruth in 2019 and their son, Jack was born in December. Ben, Anna and her boyfriend Matt were working towards their Masters. All was well, that was until Covid-19 struck and the first lockdown in March forced us to cancel the seven workshops we had 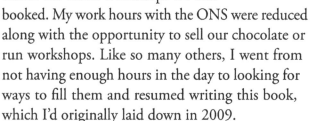 booked. My work hours with the ONS were reduced along with the opportunity to sell our chocolate or run workshops. Like so many others, I went from not having enough hours in the day to looking for ways to fill them and resumed writing this book, which I'd originally laid down in 2009.

Covid forced everybody to find new ways of working, most if not all of which proved to be better for the planet by reducing carbon emissions. Our AGM was held virtually, enabling nine members to attend compared to five the year before when we met at the Lancaster Friend's Meeting House. We had always wanted to be able to include members and supporters who were not local and especially those in other countries living in different time zones. Now we knew how to do so, this would be the way to continue for future AGMs.

On Monday 27th April I held another virtual meeting to celebrate 20 years to the day since the famous self-declaration that made Garstang the world's first Fair Trade Town. I was asked what I hoped to achieve by it, and I replied that on this occasion I didn't expect to achieve anything. Although I was still involved with some international work, I had missed seeing many of my campaign colleagues since I stood down as ambassador in 2016. I organised this as my own personal celebration to link up with the many activists that I had had the pleasure and privilege to call my friends over the last 20 years or more.

The link up started at 2.30pm and went on for four hours so people could join at a reasonable time from any Fair Trade Town in the world. Graham prepared a quiz with a prize of FIG Tree chocolate that went to Johanna from Fairtrade Sweden. Donations collected through taking part in the quiz were given to SALVE International, the charity run by Nicola to benefit street children in Uganda where, because of Covid, they had been imposed by a curfew they could not keep. A total of 37 people from 16 countries joined the link at one time or another; a very fitting celebration for a movement now made up of over 2,000 Fair Trade Towns across 34 countries.

Although we could not run our workshops, and chocolate production had been considerably reduced, I was still able to support the movement by recording films and or giving live interviews for campaign events in Bristol, Kumamoto, Japan and South Korea. Unfortunately, the 14th International Conference arranged to be held in Quito, Ecuador had to be cancelled due to Covid.

In May, George Floyd was murdered by police in the US city of Minneapolis, which led to the rise of the Black Lives Movement that swept across the world. Our work linking Fair Trade to the abolition of the slave trade and its legacy of racism was more appropriate than ever, but ironically our school workshops that could focus on this theme could not take place. I was, however, able to give a virtual presentation to members of the British Association of Fair Trade Shops (BAFTS) on the Black Lives Matter theme.

On Tuesday 4th August 2020 an explosion at the port of Beirut in Lebanon had destroyed much of the city, killing over 180 people. I was devasted when I heard the news and my thoughts turned instantly to the many people I knew there. Although some were badly shocked, I soon discovered that, thankfully, none were harmed.

The blast had accentuated the terrible situation already facing Lebanon: the Covid-19 pandemic, the economic collapse alongside the fluctuation of the Lebanese pound and the political turmoil facing the country. Over a quarter of a million people became homeless and many left the capital to seek refuge in the rural villages, including Baskinta where Elie (the lawyer) had launched their "Fair Citizen Initiative".

More than 40 volunteers in Baskinta responded to the Baskinta Baytouna Organization's (BBO) call for solidarity with Beiruti residents by providing food baskets, hygiene and medication kits, temporary accommodation and helping to rebuild homes and businesses in Beirut. Elie approached the International Fair Trade Towns Steering Committee to help raise the necessary funding and they turned to me and the FIG Tree. We launched the 'Fair Trade Towns – Beirut Bridge of Support' appeal. In the spirit of the 2016 conference theme, Building Bridges through Fair Trade, we hoped to build a bridge between the International Fair Trade Towns community and the Fair Trade Village of Baskinta to raise £30,000 towards providing much-needed relief for the Lebanese people.

There was a great response from Fair Trade Towns that we reached through the FIG Tree and from some national campaigns where Fair Trade Towns had been alerted to the appeal via national coordinators. But with over 400 Fair Trade Towns in the UK, no central message was circulated and only a handful of campaign groups that we had contacted directly through the FIG Tree were able to respond. As with the Bristol Declaration, we were unable to mobilise the global movement due, I believe, to some national campaigns setting their own targets and agendas for which this appeal did not fit in. Less than a tenth of our £30,000 target was reached.

Although there were some positives in 2020 it was a dreadful year, coming at the end of four years since Brexit was voted for in the UK and Trump elected as president in the US. From that point on, every year went from bad to worse, culminating in 2020 with the Coronavirus pandemic, the Black Lives Matter protests, the disaster in Beirut and a UK government that turned its back on the world's poorest. The Department for International Development (DfID) was replaced by the Foreign, Commonwealth & Development Office, making aid once again linked to trade and foreign policy. The aid budget was cut from the 0.7% GDP introduced by David Cameron as prime minister, and what campaigners had fought for since the Brandt Report was published in 1980. It was as if much of our campaigning had gone back by 30 or 40 years.

The global pandemic posed a real threat to the UN Sustainable Development Goal of ending poverty by 2030 because global poverty could increase for the first time since 1990 and, depending on the poverty line, such an increase could represent a reversal of approximately a decade of global progress in reducing poverty. In some regions the adverse impacts could result in poverty levels similar to those recorded 30 years before.

Progress had been made in that time, however. 2020 marked the 32nd anniversary of the Call to Action by Father Joseph Wresinski, which inspired recognition by the United Nations of October 17th as the International Day for the Eradication of Poverty. As the international community embarked on the Third Decade for the Eradication of Poverty, an estimated 783 million people lived on less than $1.90 a day in 2013, compared with 1.867 billion people in 1990.

We don't know what the future holds for Fair Trade, global poverty or climate change, but as I approach retirement age, I feel I deserve to retire from my voluntary work and just focus on my paid job. I have to some extent 'done my bit' and it is now time for me to pass the baton onto the younger generation for them to decide what challenges we face and what actions to take. But of course, if there is anything I can do to help or inspire them then I'll happily do so.

I remain optimistic, however. In my earliest campaigning days when Oxfam was accused by the Charity Commission of taking a political stance by calling for the boycott of South African products, I was certain that one day we would see an end to Apartheid in South Africa. But I did not believe it would happen in my lifetime. Even if we do not reach the UN target of ending world poverty by 2030, I am just as certain today that, like Apartheid, it will eventually come to an end, albeit perhaps not in my lifetime.

We Are What We Are

Ubuntu was the name for the first Fairtrade cola in the UK that we were proud to promote and sell at the FIG Tree. It takes its name from an African philosophy that places emphasis on 'being self through others'. It is a form of humanism that can be expressed in the phrases 'I am because of who we all are', expressing our need for others.

In contrast, the Western philosophy conceived by the 17th Century French philosopher, René Descartes, "I think; therefore I am", was a corollary of his isolation. Descartes shut himself in a room with an "oven" (probably a cocklestove) to escape the cold. While within, he had three dreams and believed that a divine spirit revealed to him this new philosophy. He found that he could not doubt that he himself existed, as he was the one doing the doubting in the first place.

Perhaps the two philosophies are not in conflict, but due to Western dominance, Descartes's viewpoint is the better known. To some extent there has been a rejection of our reliance and dependability on others, giving rise to a focus on the individual and, as Margaret Thatcher once decreed, putting an end to any such thing as 'society'. Fair Trade, however, accentuates our dependability on others and promotes the belief that we all benefit by helping each other.

In writing this book I have not been afraid to reveal who I am, including my faults such as my immaturity and naivety. People have often asked why I put myself down, but as well as accepting my bad points I am also aware of my good points. We are what we are and by acknowledging both the good and the bad within ourselves we are better able to play to our strengths and, when possible, avoid our weaknesses.

All my life people have called me a dreamer, an idealist, and I've been persistently told that one day I would grow up. I have always believed that by aiming high you may not reach your goal, but you would accomplish many things in striving to do so. But even my idealistic expectations have often been surpassed, with my dreams being fully met.

Cynics tell me that people cannot change the world, but if one looks back at our history it's easy to see the opposite is true. It is rarely governments or people in power that change the world, but nearly always the collective actions of ordinary people.

This book has helped me to reflect on my life, not just my achievements but also the hardships and low points. I remind myself that no matter how hard it has been, no matter how painful, it has all been worthwhile in the end. If you bang your head against a brick wall for long enough it will eventually fall, but you will be left with one heck of a headache.

We can and will achieve our dreams.

It is important to know who you are: both the good and the bad, the strengths and the weaknesses, and then to stick to your principles. In the end, always do what you know to be the right thing. Be truthful to yourself or, as I would say, true to your 'God'.

The Exchange Poems

A selection of poems from *The New Koforiduan* by Robin Graham written during our exchange visit between Garstang and New Koforidua in August 2004.

WEDNESDAY

DID ANYONE SLEEP?

Did anyone sleep?
Did anyone sleep?
The anticipation,
The planning,
Everything has to fit together like a jigsaw puzzle
In Europe and Africa.
Coming together;
Together;
Together.
Did anyone sleep?
As they come
To the airport
In England
To wait
For the plane…
And as we lay in bed
In Ghana
For the same…
Did anyone sleep?

We waited in Accra
At the airport,
Outside,
For the announcement:
The flight has arrived…!
End of the waiting.
Now just waiting
For meeting.
Now just meet
For greeting.
Now just greet
For travelling
Together,
Together.
Did anyone sleep?

Together we come
With Kofi our driver
Closer and closer
To New Koforidua,
Past canopies
Of canopies
Of lives.
Did anyone sleep?

They greet us
In darkness
At Kuapa Kokoo
Kumasi,
We see
Why this exchange programme began.
We greet as one.
Then are fed
Fine hospitality,
Pepper sauce,
Jollof rice,
Red Red,
And lots of green green salad.
Did anyone sleep?
We drive to go on
And back
To New Koforidua.

We are greeted
And greet:
An all-welcoming Akwaaba.
Then warmly with our hosts
We find our new homes
And everyone sleeps.

THURSDAY

SWEET DREAMS

Sweet dreams,
Made from today
And all todays.

Sweet dreams made real
In cocoa forests,
Like nectar around cocoa beans.

Sweet dreams to treasure
Bathed in Ideal milk,
In palaces
And housed by friends.

Sweet dreams of futures,
Of friendships new and old
And now renewed.

Sweet dreams of understanding,
To take beyond our dreams
And to make reality.

Sweet dreams in playgrounds,
And play areas begun today,
And honest negotiation,
And patient understanding.

Sweet dreams in shared tradition,
Shared with us this night,
As your guests.

Sweet dreams
When all is gone
And darkness beckons,
Such dreams remain
Tonight
And all tonights
With us,
Always.

Sweet dreams.

FRIDAY

THE DURBAR DAY

One minute awakened by morning murmurings,
The next, waiting for the Asante King.
A minute more, buy Cadbury's in a shopping mall…
Invited! We are invited!
And slip seamlessly from world to world,
Re-tuned like the dial on the radio.

Now our hosts, do they take care of us so well,
That the very next minute
We are paraded before kings,
Given gifts by them in Kente woven names;
In another world from world
We dance for strangers who aren't strangers
But friends in this moment.
We slip seamlessly from world to world,
Re-tuned like the dial on the radio.

And like radio stations programmes change,
We end the day at night with stars,
Taking Star Beer at a spot --
A Ghanaian pub!
Then to bed, to sleep.
Today has been just one world, of such diversity,
Re-tuned like the dial on the radio.

But as we hear the music, we listen to the news.
Not a day to take lightly.
Not a day to forget.
Not a day to easily understand.
This is a day with questions and commitment
And solemnity in joy.

SATURDAY

THE ENSTOOLING

Life as a struggle
We fight and fight
To make right
The wrongs
And injustices
In this one world.

The recognition
That they bestow
Upon our leader, Bruce,
Nana Kwadwo Osafo 1st,
Is not just
The recognition
He deserves
But unjustly
What our own people
Struggle to recognise.

We engage
With the fight
Despite
The setbacks
And
One by one,
The influence
Of Individuals
Challenges the path
Of those who cannot care.
We fight
On and on.

SUNDAY

THE NEW KOFORIDUAN

I am a New Koforiduan!
I'm learning the ways of the town.
I can use a "hole in the ground" toilet,
And I'm finding my way around.
I acknowledge when they call out "Obruni!"
Respond "Hoye" to "Etisen".
I'm just starting to settle in here,
With Nana Bruce and the Garstang friends.

I know where to buy first class groundnut,
Get oranges straight from the farm,
I'm steady on my feet now around here
With ten children clinging on to each arm.
I've started to observe bits of action,
Instead of watching the uneven ground,
And with my teeth I tear open water sachets
And spill no more than half all around.

I am a New Koforiduan!
But today we say a farewell.
Maybe we'll never come back here,
And just have these stories to tell.
I'll miss all the waving small children
Whose constant saying "bye bye"
Has prepared me a little for my journey.
And I smile so they don't see me cry…

As we leave, we pass the play area,
Built by Richard and James.
The girls are sorry they're leaving.
The children get on with their games.
And our flags now fly by the roadside
For all passers by to enquire
About the linking of New Koforidua
With Garstang in the Borough of Wyre.

MONDAY

THE CASTLE AT CAPE COAST

Glorious,
Vast,
Open, but dishonest
Is the slave trade castle.
For weeks in darkness dungeons
They would keep human beings,
Wear down their minds and hearts,
Break them down
So that they couldn't fight back,
Then take them to their ships.
Some died,
But always there were more,
Sold on by tribes who've gone to war
Just to capture slaves.
I can't let myself feel the pain
Of those beautiful men and women.
As I walk around
I'm aware of my fear;
Fear of falling down the stone steps,
Fear of looking stupid,
Fear that I am going to join those people
Who watch life
Through closed curtains.

EVER AFTER

AND FRIENDSHIP TODAY

Each day may start cloudy,
With a breeze teasing the branches of the trees.
Rain may fall, like tears of mixed emotion,
Yet leave no trace once clouds reveal the sun.
Even when the day moves into night,
Skies reveal the clarity of stars hidden by the day.
I know tomorrow doesn't yet exist,
Only today, and then tomorrow's today.

Each friendship may start cloudy,
With a breeze teasing the branches of the trees.
Rain may fall, like tears of mixed emotion,
Yet leave no trace once clouds reveal the sun.
Even when the friendship moves to night,
Skies reveal the clarity of stars hidden by the day.
I know tomorrow doesn't yet exist,
Only today, and then tomorrow's today.

THE FAIR TRADE POEM

100 FAIRTRADE TOWNS

While the Romans set up villa in Mamuciam
    (that's Manchester),
Expansion built with cruelty and slaves,
They made Britain the "Granary of Europe":
Good for trade, but not how decent chaps behave.
Then when Norsemen came and plundered
Northern England,
And Danes almost destroyed us in a raid,
They pillaged! They didn't pay a penny!
Was that fair trade? I say, "Was that fair trade?"

When William the Conqueror invaded,
He gave Salford to Roger de Poitou.
But don't be thinking you can go and ask Her Majesty
To make a special gift of it to you,
For it's grown beyond the right to have a market.
It grew buildings where trees and grass once lay.
Industrialised, unhealthy and polluted.
Was that fair trade? I say, "Was that fair trade?"

So as Lancashire was growing rich on cotton mills,
Prosperity lay in the hands of a few.
There was dangerous, unsanitary working,
With social change and justice overdue.
Though canals and railways were marvellous,
And Man Utd won the League in 1908,
A working man's life expectancy was low.
Was this fair trade? I ask you all, "Was this fair trade?"

246

Salford and Manchester are now fine cities,
Where Take That, John Cooper Clarke, Oasis,
Elkie Brooks, Hermans Hermits, Lisa Stansfield,
          The Smiths, Thin Lizzie and Vimto
          - to name but a few - were made,
Infrastructure, health and education
Visibly improve with each decade.
But the farmers around the world who are supplying us
With goods which add a sweetener to our lives,
Are suffering from Western exploitation.
Can you imagine how a family there survives?

Now it takes a certain kind of individual,
Even though we all breathe the same air,
To stand up to be counted, make a difference,
Fight for the right for prices to be fair.
Fight for self help and self-empowering,
Fight for hospitals and sanitation.
Fight for stability through sound financing,
Fight for training and for proper education.

But individuals can bring change to the world!
Breathe life into a concept like Fairtrade.
Individuals build up to make communities,
And with wisdom, good partnerships are made.
So let's demonstrate the power of the individual,
When family and friends we can persuade:
Get a positive reply when we enquire:
"How about it? I say, "Let's buy Fairtrade!"

Then all we have to do is eat more mangoes,
Drink fruit juice, tea and coffee, beers and wine,
Sweeten chopped bananas with pure honey,
Remind ourselves that chocolate is divine!
Kick footballs, and give lovers perfumed roses,
All products that can be Fairtrade through and through,
Check they have the Mark, the Fairtrade Mark,
Because then we can be sure that it is true

That in Malawi, Ethiopia and Ghana,
Ecuador, The Windward Islands and Peru,
And all the 49 Fairtrade producing countries
A farmer and his family thank you.
And though we're getting fatter and have migraines,
The choice is there and really must be made:
They shouldn't suffer through our greed and selfishness
When there exists the option to buy Fairtrade.

So we bade welcome to our visiting food producers,
And those from other towns who'd paved the way,
Converging here on Salford and Manchester,
Humbly, joyfully invited for the day
To celebrate the passing of a moment
That saw the Fairtrade Town parade expand,
100 Towns that day, and now tomorrow
We'll munch Fairtrade chocolate right across the land,
And fresh bananas.
Yes, we'll munch on Fairtrade mangoes through the land,
And kick their footballs.
We'll warm up with Fairtrade hot drinks through the land!

Glossary of terms and organisations

BUILD – Building Understanding through International Links for Development, BUILD is a North – South coalition of agencies committed to promoting the development of new links for peace, prosperity and justice. Formed in 2002 with UKOWLA as the lead agency, they work together to promote international partnerships for development and learning between communities (local authorities, schools, faith groups, hospitals, etc.) in the UK with counterparts in Africa, Asia, South America and the Caribbean.

Fair Trade – Fair trade, written as two words, means that something has been fairly traded. Fair trade exists between companies in developed countries and producers in developing countries to help those producers achieve sustainable and equitable trade relationships.

Fairtrade – Fairtrade, written as one word, is an international standards and certification system in which producers and buyers agree to uphold certain minimum standards and payments and, in return, their product can be labelled with the FAIRTRADE mark.

FAIRTRADE – FAIRTRADE, written as one word in upper case, refers specifically to the FAIRTRADE mark licensed in over 20 countries by the Fairtrade labelling initiatives, which are members of Fairtrade International.

Fairtrade Foundation - The Foundation was established in 1992 as the UK member of Fairtrade International. The Fairtrade Foundation is an independent, non-profit organisation that focuses on four key areas of work in the UK:

- Licensing the use of the FAIRTRADE mark in the UK.
- Helping to grow demand for Fairtrade products and empower producers to sell to traders and retailers.
- Finding new ways of working with partners to support producer organisations and their networks.
- Raising public awareness of the need for Fairtrade and the significant role of Fairtrade in making trade fair.

Fairtrade International – Formerly known as FLO (Fairtrade Labelling Organisation), it unites over 20 labelling initiatives across Europe, Japan, North America, Mexico and Australia and New Zealand, as well as networks of producer organisations from Asia, Africa, Latin America and the Caribbean.

Fair Trade USA – Formerly known as "Transfair USA", it was the Fairtrade Labelling Initiative for the USA until it broke away from Fairtrade International in 2011. It sets standards and certifies and labels products that promote sustainable livelihoods for farmers and workers and that protect the environment.

The FIG Tree (Garstang) CIC – The FIG Tree was set up in Garstang as a Fair Trade visitor centre, café and museum in November 2011, primarily to support the International Fair Trade Towns movement and provide Fair Trade workshops for schools. It moved to Lancaster in 2015 but, due to flooding in December that year, now operates without premises. FIG stands for 'Fairtrade In Garstang'. The FIG Tree is a Community Interest Company (CIC) that became a members cooperative in 2017. Further information on The FIG Tree is available on the website at: www.fairtradecentre.org

The Lorna Young Foundation - The Lorna Young Foundation is a UK registered charity that works towards the eradication of poverty by helping disadvantaged groups through the medium of ethical trading. It works across various African countries as well as in the UK, supporting disadvantaged people to become ethical entrepreneurs.

UKOWLA - The UK One World Linking Association was founded in 1985. It provides training, information, advice and assistance to international exchange programmes between the UK and the developing world and raises public awareness of education, health and cultural issues of the developing world in schools and communities in the UK.

WFTO - The World Fair Trade Organization is a global association of 401 organisations that are committed to improving the livelihoods of economically marginalised producers. The WFTO has members in 76 countries. Members are primarily fair trade enterprises whose business model is verified by independent audits and peer reviews.

Timeline

1973
- Won Magpie competition to go on safari in Kenya.

1979
- September - Started at Liverpool University Veterinary Faculty.

1980
- 8th December - John Lennon murdered in New York.

1981
- Summer - Hitched across Europe for eight weeks and visited eleven countries.

1984
- Summer – Liverpool International Garden Festival.
- December – Band Aid's 'Do they know it's Christmas?' tops the charts in the UK.

1985
- July - Qualified as a vet.
- 13th July - Live Aid.
- August - Moved to Dungannon, Northern Ireland, to work for MAFF and formed the Dungannon Oxfam Group.

1986
- January – Started work at vets in Handsworth Wood, Birmingham.
- August – Started work at vets in Allerton, Liverpool.

1987

18th October – Start of my first period of depression in Liverpool and my 'lost weekend'.

1989

- 9th January to 29th March - Central America trip.

1992

- 23rd April - First meeting of the Garstang Oxfam Group.
- 30th May – Married Jane.
- July to October – Garstang Oxfam Group survey that showed that 82% of people would buy products that were identified as giving a better deal to Third World producers, compared to 81% in the national survey.

1993

- 16th December – Ben's birth.

1994

- March – FAIRTRADE mark introduced into the UK.

1995

- 15th August – Anna's birth.

1999

- December - Garstang Victorian Festival, and shaved beard for the 'Give it up for Ghana' Oxfam Fast.

2000

- 7th March - Fairtrade Fortnight meal at the Jacobite restaurant.
- 27th April - Public declaration of Garstang as the world's first Fair Trade Town.
- September – First Fairtrade/slave trade project launched.

2001

- March - Fair Trade Town road signs erected in Garstang.
- 14th July to 5th August – Go Global Go Ghana. First visit to Ghana.
- September – First Fairtrade Towns Actions Guide published by the Fairtrade Foundation.
- 22nd November – Garstang officially awarded Fairtrade Towns status at a ceremony attended by Harriet Lamb and Tony Robinson.

2002

- January - Garstang Fairtrade Steering Group formed.
- 13th January – Chester declared the world's first Fairtrade City.
- 4th July - Ammanford declared the first Fairtrade Town in Wales.
- 22nd November – Haworth declared the world's first Fairtrade Village.
- 27th November - Strathaven and Aberfeldy declared jointly as Scotland's first Fairtrade Towns.

2003

- 1st July - Started work with Fairtrade Foundation.
- 22nd September – Clonakilty declared as first Fairtrade Town in Ireland.
- 25th September – Day of mum's passing.

2004

- 5th March – 10 Cities declaration in the UK.
- 12th March – Cyclists arrived in Garstang to mark the 10th anniversary of the FAIRTRADE mark.
- 14th March – Traveled to Peru for Oxfam Overseas Challenge and visited the coffee farmers at COCLA.
- 15th to 25th August – Garstang and New Koforidua exchange. Second visit to Ghana.

2005

- 3rd February - Nelson Mandela launched 'Make Poverty History' campaign in Trafalgar Square.
- 7th March - Manchester and Salford declared jointly as the 100th Fairtrade Towns.
- 1st July - Ghent declared the first Fair Trade Gemeenten in Belgium.
- July – Awarded Beacon Prize for Creative Giving at the Foreign and Commonwealth Office.
- 1st & 2nd October - US Fair Trade Conference, Chicago.
- 3rd October – Day of Graham's passing.

2006

- March – Ideas Bank Fair Trade Towns Conference in Oslo, Norway.
- 8th July – Media declared as the first Fair Trade Town on the American continents.
- 17th May - Malmo declared as the first Fair Trade City in Sweden.
- 23rd August – Sauda declared as the first Fairtrade-Kommune in Norway.
- 25th August to 6th September - Third visit to Ghana
- 20th & 21st November - First International Fair Trade Towns Conference in London, UK.
- 8th December – Start writing this book.

2007

- 3rd June - Garstang and New Koforidua partnership agreement signed in both communities by the members of GANKLA and NKGALA.
- 24th July – Launch of Prime Minister Gordon Brown's book 'Britain's Everyday Heroes' at the Methodist Central Hall in Westminster.

2008

- 25th & 26th January - 2nd International Fair Trade Towns Conference in Brussels, Belgium.
- 15th August – Copenhagen declared as the first Fair Trade City in Denmark.
- 16th – 30th June - Fourth visit to Ghana.
- 27th to 31st August - National Fair Trade Towns Conference in Sauda, Norway.

2009

- 6th & 7th February - 3rd International Fair Trade Towns Conference in Lyon, France.
- 18th February - Awarded MBE for services in support of Oxfam and Fairtrade at Buckingham Palace.
- 2nd April - Saarbrücken declares as the first Kampagne Fairtrade Town in Germany.
- 5th August – Tampere declares as first Reilun kaupan kaupunki in Finland.
- 25th to 30th October – First walk of Fair Trade Way from Garstang to Keswick.

2010

- 25th February to 5th March – Visited Japan to support Fair Trade Towns.
- 28th September to 1st October – Sauda Fair Trade Conference, Norway.
- 1st November - 500 Fairtrade Towns Bike Ride; cyclists rode into Cardiff on the day Bicester declared as the 500th Fairtrade Town.
- 5th & 6th November - 4th International Fair Trade Towns Conference in Bonn, Germany.

2011

- 22nd February - The FIG Tree incorporated as a Community Interest Company.
- 5th to 19th April - Fifth visit to Ghana.
- 4th June – New Koforidua declared as the first Fair Trade Town in Africa and Kumamoto as first Fair Trade Town in Asia as joint 1000th Fair Trade Towns worldwide.
- 9th – 11th September - Fair Trade Towns USA and Fair Trade Universities Conference in Philadelphia.
- 19th & 20th November - 5th International Fair Trade Towns Conference in Malmo, Sweden.
- 21st November - The FIG Tree visitor centre opens in Garstang.

2012

- 1st July – Fair Trade /slave trade Heritage Lottery Fund project starts.
- 1st September – Finished work at Fairtrade Foundation, but extended for three months and taken mainly as sick leave.
- 10th & 11th November - 6th International Fair Trade Towns Conference in Poznan, Poland, and Poznan declares as first Miasto Przyjazne dla Sprawiedliwego Handlu.

2013

- 27th April – Author and patron Joanne Harris visits The FIG Tree in Garstang.
- 9th May - Menjez declared as the first Fair Trade Town in Lebanon.
- 8th to 12th May – Visited Seoul for the Korean Fair Trade Week and World Fair Trade Day Festival.
- 30th June – Fair Trade/slave trade Heritage Lottery Fund project finishes.
- 28th & 29th September - 7th International Fair Trade Towns Conference in Oslo, Norway.

2014

- June – First of 20 weekly sessions at the Tuke Centre, York.
- 9th to 14th October - Benoit and Lory visited Garstang to explore Fair Trade Towns in Lebanon.
- 10th November – The FIG Tree closes in Garstang.
- 29th & 30th March - 8th International Fair Trade Towns Conference in Kumamoto, Japan.

2015

- 7th March – The FIG Tree opened at St. John's church in Lancaster.
- April - Last of 20 weekly sessions at the Tuke Centre, York.
- 1st April - 'The FIG Tree relocating to St John's Lancaster' Heritage Lottery Fund project starts.
- 6th to 15th June - Visited Lebanon to see the launch of nine Fair Trade Villages.
- 4th & 5th July - 9th International Fair Trade Towns Conference in Bristol, UK.
- 18th July - Fair Trade Live event at St. John's and in six other countries across the globe.
- 10th to 26th November – Sixth visit to Ghana.
- 5th December - Sustainable Development Goals @ The FIG Tree and day of the flood.

2016

- 16th June - Murder of Jo Cox, MP for Batley and Spen in Birstall, UK.
- 23rd June – UK referendum votes for Brexit and leaving the EU.
- 29th June to 3rd July - 10th International Fair Trade Towns Conference in Baskinta, Lebanon.

2017

- February - Café opened at the Priory in Lancaster.
- 25th & 26th March - '210 Abolition - Lancaster slave trade port to Fairtrade City' weekend of events.
- 31st March – 'The FIG Tree relocating to St John's Lancaster' Heritage Lottery Fund project finishes.
- August - Pondicherry and Auroville declared as the first Fair Trade Towns in India.
- 14th to 17th September - 11th International Fair Trade Towns Conference in Saarbrücken, Germany.
- November – The FIG Tree becomes a members cooperative.

2018

- 19th March - Started work as a field interviewer for the Office for National Statistics.
- 18 June – AGM where it was debated whether The FIG Tree should close.
- 19th to 21st October - 12th International Fair Trade Towns Conference in Madrid, Spain.
- 1st November – End of partnership with the Priory in Lancaster.

2019

- 28th July to 5th August – Seventh visit to Ghana.
- 19th October – 13th International Fair Trade Towns Conference in Cardiff, Wales.

2020

- 16th March – First Covid-19 lockdown in UK, and resumption of the writing of this book.
- 27th April – Virtual meeting to celebrate 20 years since Garstang became the world's first Fair Trade Town.
- 25th May - Murder of George Floyd by Minneapolis police in the USA giving rise to the Black Lives Matter movement.
- 4th August – Explosion at the port of Beirut destroying most of the city.
- October - 14th International Fair Trade Towns Conference in Quito, Ecuador cancelled because of Covid-19.

Lightning Source UK Ltd.
Milton Keynes UK
UKHW020753311021
393094UK00006B/108